Serious Flyfishing

Serious Flyfishing

By John Waite

Published by
The Serious Fisherman
P.O. Box 14225
Spokane, Washington 99214-0225
(509) 922-5832

First Edition, 1997
Printed in the U.S.A.
10 9 8 7 6 5 4 3 2 1

Waite, John.
Serious flyfishing.

Includes bibliographic references and index.

1. Fly fishing. 2. Fly tying. 3. Flies, Artificial.
4. Fly casting. 5. Fishing survey. I. Title
799.1'24—dc21

International Standard Book Number: Hardbound, 0-96580-050-4
International Standard Book Number: Limited Edition, 0-96580-051-2

Library of Congress Catalog Card Number: 97-92208

Table of Contents

Note

This book is meant to provide useful information regarding the subject covered and to entertain. Information extension includes comment on others' thoughts and writing requiring brief examples of or references to such, and is meant to inform using scholarship's methods yielding research aimed at investigation, questioning and practical application of theories.

It is not the purpose of this book to use all the information available but that viewed as pertinent to meeting the objectives first stated above. Repeated effort has been expended to make this book useful and accurate. There may, however, be mistakes both typographical and of content.

The author and publisher shall have neither responsibility or liability to any person or entity for loss or damage caused, directly or indirectly by the information contained in or excluded from this book.

If you do not wish to be bound by these statements, single copies may be returned for a refund of the price paid the publisher.

Acknowledgements

Cover and Chapter Heading Art: Gene E. Lorenson

Cover Design: Author

Text Illustrations: Stream scenes and fish sketches, Gene E. Lorenson; other illustrations, by author

Front Inside Cover Photo: James D. Whitehead (Clearwater River, Idaho)

Color Fly Plate Photography: Grophoto, George R. Olson

Flies for Color Plates: Tied by author

Copy and Proofreading: Michele Opsal

Book Design and Assembly: River Graphics, Portland, OR

Research Library: Vern and Joan Gallup, owners

Flyfishing Survey Name Providers: Listed at end of Chapter 13

Flyfishing Survey Pollees: Listed at end of Chapter 13

Unceasing Support and Help, Kathy Waite, spouse

For Advice, Test Reading, Criticism and Encouragement: Mike Bilyew, Alice Deaver, Roy Harrop, William Jones, Tom Pappas, Joyce Sherman, Mark Stimpfle, Patrick Waite, Troy Waite and James Whitehead

And, Most Importantly:

> Trust in the LORD with all your heart
> and lean not on your own understanding;
> in all your ways acknowledge him,
> and he will make your paths straight.
>
> *Proverbs 3:5,6*

Chapter One: Groundwork

This book is different and distinct. Distinctiveness arises with benefit attainable by viewing flyfishing, its tackle, practices, practitioners and industries in ways that expose fallacies and dangers destructive to flyfishing, its enjoyment and success. Different perspectives call for unconventional procedures.

In-depth examination of cardinal but, nevertheless, widely misunderstood, ignored, abused and little known flyfishing subjects is undertaken. Given the extensive number of flyfishing books such promise of information unknown might be thought strange. Yes and no, ideal and normally simplest flyfishing practice we'll be probing frequently differs from the familiar, common, recommended or "correct." In consequence, flyfishers with thicker hides and a genuine yen to improve their flyfishing may benefit most.

I've written for people earnest about understanding flyfishing, improving or learning. There is little nonchalant or for persons of shallow motivation or fleeting enchantment with flyfishing's romance or popular image. To the extent they improve or protect flyfishing's traditions and future, history and economics are incorporated and relied upon—or questioned. Restrictive parameters are used.

Experience and research considered, supported or proven legitimate by nature's laws, historical fact or plain horse sense are the criteria used as the basis for findings or conclusions. Few flyfishing stones, even sacred ones, are left unturned. Such methodology may irritate the flyfishing sensibilities of some. I see my job as accurately and, to the extent I'm capable, fully informing and aiding anyone needing or wanting flyfishing help.

New idea adoption usually requires recognition and acceptance of better ways and abandonment of old and comfortable but, nonetheless, unsound ideas. That's difficult for some; flyfishing is habit controlled and engenders too much foolish ego entanglement. As problematical, most have just heard too much bunk from flyfishing "experts," falling for "truth" in the past. They're justifiably leery. Until I earn your trust in what I say, by what I prove or support and as judged correct by your good sense, all I ask is that you read with an open mind.

Experienced and emerging flyfishers should benefit from better flyfishing understanding. Even advanced flyfishers, open to better ways, might profit from proven or common-sense supported methods and thinking. People seriously contemplating learning to flyfish will learn how to start correctly and avoid pitfalls. Flyfishers suffering confusion-caused, waning interest could be rejuvenated and those with degenerating interest for other reasons may be revitalized as well.

To accomplish book purpose and to avoid further flyfishing confusion, writing is occasionally detailed as some ideas thought to be *true* just aren't. Such periodic, thorough examination is meant to serve true understanding. Too much modern flyfishing discourse hits only perceived high points or serves popularity yielding shallow understanding and generating mistakes that are easily avoidable. But you are encouraged to make needless mistakes by many within flyfishing—consider writing-caused encouragement.

There is huge difference in the meanings of the words "may" or "might" compared to "will." Writers, including those addressing flyfishing, are conditioned to write *strongly* and *positively,* and that's what we see. They say things as, "my new mayfly pattern *will* catch more fish" or "this new graphite *will* make you a better flyfisher." Such implications or statements are patently false for a host of reasons; but the statements are strong. While many readers might not believe bogus statements, why should anyone have to put up with them and be required to automatically disbelieve a portion of flyfishing writing they read? The manuals writers have read and coaching they have received encourage *strong* writing. Quest for strong writing can cause partially true, even false, information to be stated or implied as fact. Some authors are ignorant or uncaring of damage done by "authoritative" self-indulgence.

I don't at all care to use soft words that appear to hedge or "weasel." It's sometimes *necessary,* however. Respect for ever-present exceptions, things yet to be fully understood and awareness my research and experience are less than perfect must be maintained. *Conversely,* when your eyes witness words goring flyfishing's sacred oxen, pointing out *provable* fallacies of conventional thought, I will be most positive and *expect* to be believed. What I'll say is rooted in fact and natural law and with always fought-for, minimal damage to *honest* flyfishing and flyfishers.

Flyfishing is understandably and correctly different things to different persons. Differing flyfishing is more convoluted than obviousness of water type, fish species or geography. Differences can involve living romantic fantasies, looking correct or using only the latest or "best" tackle. Fishing to gullible or too vulnerable fish and reliance on technology over skill seem important and the ways of growing numbers of "flyfishers." Getting away from something, not to, flyfishing appears a major stimulus for many. I have negligible understanding of modern, weak or tradition lacking motivations to flyfish or continue flyfishing hobbled. I haven't addressed them and couldn't if I wanted. There are more important things to consider.

I'll elevate traditional and ethical flyfishing practices and tools to derive effectiveness and enjoyment. That involves ongoing but enjoyable learning providing continual mental and physical stimulation. Don't be fooled. Within such discussion, practice, learning and stimulation, always dominating, lies acquiring ability to catch fish—if, how and when you want to catch them. In large part that requires simplicity and efficiency of tackle.

Correct tackle selection is obtainable only by comprehensive understanding of fly tackle and its correct use—also its limitations. A flyfisher needs know *why* certain tackle is used in certain ways. Understanding the how and when of using it then becomes easier and allows concentration on more important things: fish habit and behavior, watermanship, developing confidence and having fun. Doing things fundamentally right in tackle selection and use, speeding proficiency and enjoyment, fosters self reliance and confidence.

Flyfishers aren't all intrepid or dedicated self-starters. That's natural enough, but many consider, or are lead to believe, flyfishing to be more difficult than it is. Tentative or misdirected flyfishers find it easy to follow others (perhaps unworthy) rather than thinking and acting for themselves. Failure to reason for oneself, to act with gumption and ambition and to practice a little expose flyfishers to multiple problems and guarantee sub-par results. We'll examine such problems. A few people legitimately lack time to learn or practice flyfishing skills. Lack of time, however, is one of the all-time lamest of excuses. People usually find time for what they *sincerely want* to do. Yet even honest sincerity can be undone.

Deriving maximum enjoyment from flyfishing and achieving greatest success thrives on simplicity and efficiency. It's common to see flyfishers fighting shortcomings of or inability to use tackle as they go about fishing incorrect places, at wrong times or in wrong ways. A good many flyfishers fail to appreciate how time wasting, dysfunctional and inefficient tackle sold by an overly profit motivated, largely uncaring and unlearned industry can be. It's made clear herein. Flyfishing's sell-side causes many problems.

The recent growth and the type of people involved in flyfishing writing, manufacturing and sales has outpaced the time required for many, who advise flyfishers, to gain *meaningful* experience or understanding of flyfishing. Lack of astuteness, escorted by intense profit motivation, doesn't keep unqualified sell-siders from professing accurate knowledge, even wisdom. They add mightily to flyfisher dismay. In fact, confusion in the minds of flyfishers helps the industry achieve its selfish goals.

Maybe flyfishers don't understand how some in the fly-fishing industry view business dealings. The following could easily come from a "guide-book" for conducting flyfishing business. The first three words found would be: "Get the money"; followed by "No one ever went broke underestimating the stupidity of flyfishing's buying public"; and then "It's better to be wrong and respected than right and considered part of the lunatic fringe." I would prefer the loony label to remain correct of recommendations to you. The respect of industry people, undeserving of respect, is of small importance to me. Lots of truth is unknown or withheld and problems caused you by those seeking peer respect—or profit. Even fellow flyfishers assemble stumbling blocks in your path.

People often claim serious flyfisher status or flyfishing knowledge without ability to substantiate such notions through performance, valid experience or caring action. It's fine not to be overly serious about, or effective at, flyfishing if that gives a person joy. Trouble is, people lacking wisdom or ability customarily expound authoritatively. If they've fooled themselves, don't let them fool you. We'll examine and learn to recognize the effluvium of those subscribing to too much that's unsupported by correctly stated natural law, conclusive research or at least common sense. Flyfishing fools aren't suffered or catered to herein, and you do not have your hands on another "mood," superiority or "nobility" of flyfishing mumbo-jumbo book. We *won't* be searching for psychological justification, the "true meaning of" or some mystic spirit of flyfishing. We *will* stick with flyfishing's substantive and real purposes: catching fish effectively, having fun and protecting flyfishing's future as we may.

Flyfishers are bombarded with information from many sources—much seen or sensed to be awash with inaccuracy and hyperbole. To protect ourselves we tend to ignore most and embrace only that easy to believe or perhaps flattering. But that type information could be, and often is, incorrect. And what of correct and useful information thus caused to be matter-of-factly ignored?

Advice, particularly "how-to" and despite documented proof, strong support or basis in common sense, is ignored by most needing such advice. Possibly because it's too general or contrary "accepted" thinking—more likely because it requires reader change, thought or practice. I'm going to tell you things you won't want to believe, that contradict "correct" thinking and that you've probably never heard before. Anyone reading this book for warm and fuzzy "feel good" reasons or believing they may learn by osmosis rather than thought and some effort might be disappointed.

It's said, "all writing is an act of ego." I admit to that and also to having biases. My biases are supported by the methods I've stated and will state once more: fact, reason, natural law, common sense and what I reckon decent and valid experience. You judge legitimacy. I've mulled and re-mulled material in this book around my head for over 35 years of flyfishing, most intense. Why was what I learned, was correctly taught or observed often contrary to prevailing and gratuitously extolled flyfishing thought and practice?

Do writers, as they are told, owe allegiance only to themselves? Not always. I feel strong allegiance to readers *if* they are open-minded, striving flyfishers honestly concerned with flyfishing's welfare. I don't want to lead brother flyfishers astray. I don't fear, nor is my writing controlled by, the flyfishing industry including its publishing or editing arms. Sadly, most authors are controlled, even though they may *swear* they aren't. Some undoubtedly know about flyfishing's unseemly sides but fear writing about them, wouldn't see work published if they did, or would lose face and future income from the cliquish industry if such writing were published. That's *control,* and it's most prevalent.

Flyfishing writing I read is recurrently obscure or coy concerning things needing full airing and understanding. Writing shouldn't be obscure or ignore vital topics. You won't need to read between the lines herein as little attempt is made to be subtle despite its supposed effectiveness as a writing tool. Subtlety allows, even generates, misunderstanding unless you are a more skilled writer than I, maybe even then. What's written is blunt and either largely correct or not. Popularity or acceptance of findings by typical industry types, *or* their flyfisher sympathizers, isn't considered. Time and the experiences of the only important people in flyfishing—down-to-earth, competent or seriously aspiring flyfishers—will fairly judge what is written based on truth, logic and help received.

We'll examine the flyfishing industry's pervasive but perhaps changeable influence on your flyfishing. Flyfishers are forced to participate with the industry, but *level* of participation is up to you. It's not only your time, money and enjoyment at stake, but also the welfare of everyone's flyfishing. You'll soon see why. For now, trust that flyfishing's sucking bog of incorrect information and products can be safely negotiated if you keep your feet on solid ground, your head out of the clouds and follow common sense. I endeavor to make flyfishing easier, less expensive, more enjoyable, effective and maybe of permanence for you and you in turn for others.

So far I've outlined the content and philosophy of the following chapters in very general terms. Each chapter examines a pertinent flyfishing subject with considerations seldom seen or used. What follows just now is a little flyfishing history that helps set the stage for the upcoming chapters. If you're considering zipping ahead to the meat of the book and skipping this section, know it contains keys to fully understanding the rest.

Datus Proper, a decent and perhaps wise writer, said flyfishing books come too fast and have little of real, new, useful information and are only unclear rehashes of ideas discovered and discussed years ago. He could have included magazine articles and videos. Mr. Proper also noted many authors claim old ideas as new, or worse, new *and* their own. Such actions are common and signify lack of potent and adequate experience, research or ethics. I've tried to avoid stymieing you by such writing faults and cleaving to true knowledge accurately construed but won't be so brash as to say I've been completely successful.

Ray Bergman, a fine fishing writer of old, said fishing is always some part conjecture and theory and to remove it would damage the sport. He's certainly right. Conjecture and theory, however, should always be pursued from a solid base of rational thought, fundamental truth and cogent experience if successful flyfishing is the goal. Hare-brained flyfishing theories abound. We'll discuss lots of theories, always trying to keep one foot solidly anchored in the indisputable.

It's said there are twelve pinnacles of flyfishing knowledge. They're chronologically represented by the writings of Berners, Walton, Cotton, Ronalds, Stewart, Norris, Halford, Gordon, Skues, Mottram, Hewitt and Jennings. Flyfishers all stand on the shoulders of these men. Time span of their writings is from the near Dark Ages to modern times. Most recent (post 1950) writing adds only *tidbits* to that discovered or at least expounded years and years ago. People "discovering" or advancing "new" ideas today are either overwhelmingly under-researched or seeking to sell you something. Can they then be trusted to give accurate advice? Understanding the largely fixed boundaries and the genesis of flyfishing knowledge is more than comforting—it's protective.

Flyfishers, and writers, would profit by always remembering there is very little new under the sun. That avoids getting lost in supposed new information. T. S. Eliot: "Where is the wisdom we have lost in knowledge? Where is the knowledge we have lost in information?" I take Eliot's words to heart and endeavor to extract wisdom from knowledge and information. Wisdom is found in trifling quantity in too much contemporary flyfishing practice, thought and writing—despite its *selling* well. Accurate knowledge, combined with true understanding—equaling wisdom—will protect us from the perversions of the sell-siders or self-destructive tendencies. There are other reasons to seek wisdom.

The world's knowledge is contained in libraries; also found are endless incorrect words and ideas. Literate and qualified flyfishing minds say much found in flyfishing's library is wrong from inception, overly biased or poorly researched. That's partially explained because modern flyfishing authors work in highly competitive environments *limited* by a near *finite* pool of knowledge. There are yet more reasons to be careful.

Traps exist that many writers fall into and *you* suffer for. It's impossible to convey real knowledge, originality or authority that isn't owned. Moreover, true originality of ideas is very, very rare. *Many old and true ideas, however, are much misunderstood.*

We've seen writers often infer or state opinion or hearsay to be fact; a good many envision their readers and write to them. Such writers say what they think readers want to hear, what won't make waves or what will sell. Who hasn't been led astray by illegitimate types spouting erroneous information devoid of wisdom or twaddle dominated by crony acceptance and financial gain. It's the way things are commonly done. I've tried hard to avoid that commonality.

Researching recently caused me to read or reread a good many flyfishing books as I searched for the documented basic truths of flyfishing. Along the way, I encountered Howard Blaisdell's, *The Philosophical Fisherman.* It's a great book, perhaps the best on fishing or flyfishing I've ever read. It's apparently little known or at least seldom quoted by modern writers. Despite the book's wisdom and utility, it's iconoclastic, almost requiring readers do some soul searching. That might explain its failed acceptance by "sophisticated" flyfishing writers and the "elite" industry. Speaking of the *sophisticated,* Roderick Haig-Brown (perhaps flyfishing's most loved and respected author) understood sophisticates when he disclosed: *"The naïveté of the sophisticated."* His diagnosis is uncannily valid. Whenever you see the words *sophisticated, sophisticate* or *sophisticates* <u>*anywhere*</u> in this book, mentally replace them with *"Naive."*

Getting back to the fine old book, *The Philosophical Fisherman* and its modern day obscurity, I was surprised to see it referenced in a recent issue of *Field and Stream.* In a reprint of an old, but classic article by H. G. "Tap" Tapply (of "Tap's Tips" magazine column fame) was the statement that Blaisdell's, *The Philosophical Fisherman,* was the only fishing book Tap ever read more than twice. Mr. Tapply was widely known, read and respected. He earned that respect, and several generations of fishermen learned from his writings. Tap was an accomplished fisherman, had a fine sense of humor and was down to earth. His most favorable and learned opinion of Blaisdell's iconoclastic and useful, albeit largely ignored, book gave me extra encouragement to attempt helping flyfishers by writing.

A later chapter contains detailed coverage of the largest survey of *experienced* flyfishers I'm aware of ever being conducted. The survey was eight pages in length requiring 175 responses from each of its 264 respondents. It covered all flyfishing types, topics and divulges many thousands of years of experience. Poll results represent the combined and in noted cases, individual opinions of many knowledgeable flyfishers. To avoid a book with too many voices, survey data is reserved until a later chapter, mostly. I suggest you read the chapters in numerical order to gain advantage of building perspective.

Entry of more women serious about flyfishing, into flyfishing, is welcomed and past due. To accommodate word flow, masculine terms are usually used as they circumvent stumbling reading by minimizing unneeded words or non-sex pronouns. Use of masculine terms only is long common in English. Any such terms *always* graciously include the feminine.

Flyfishing is an old and great sport. You usually see it spelled fly fishing or fly-fishing and occasionally flyfishing according to its etymology. I elect the latter for it and related words. Flyfishing has been around long enough to warrant, and is absolutely worthy, a one-word name. It's older than baseball or is it base-ball? Base ball?

I hope you enjoy the book and find it useful.

Chapter Two:
The Flyfishing Economy

"A superior man knows what is right;
an inferior man knows what sells."
Confucius

Fly tackle, casting and flyfishing are discussed in detail in later chapters. This one examines other problems we face. Forewarned is forearmed and spending a few minutes now will pay dividends later.

There are at least two sides to any flyfishing business question, and I'm not naive concerning business. How business "gets merged" with something as treasured as flyfishing causes me anxiety. I know it's both wrong and futile to expect everyone to live by my rules of flyfishing business engagement. But should I live to 100, I'll never understand how and why people invent and produce some of the stuff they do. Can money be that important? Nor will I understand flyfishing consumers allowing themselves to be so easily duped or caring so little of flyfishing's heritage and future. I suspect many live in "a mellow apathy." See what you think.

The Players

A flyfishing industry is composed of all people and firms that produce, market, sell goods or services, write, lecture, publish or in any way generate income from flyfishing. The industry's purpose is to make profit by encouraging or influencing consumers to buy as much as it can, however it can. Your function as a consumer is to remain educated and buy flyfishing necessities, needs and wants—in that order—as economically as possible. The only sensible exceptions to consumer function are unlimited funds or no other uses for money. We are all fooled or act stupidly at times but should strive to prevent reoccurrence.

Flyfishing Consumers

There are different types of flyfishing consumers, and their motivations might be difficult to understand. Marketing specialists identify so-called prestige, value and price buying flyfishers. Understanding the motivations of prestige and price buyers perhaps isn't difficult; the ambiguous term "value buyer" gives me problems. Webster doesn't help much. Value isn't necessarily worth, price or utility but some slippery, indefinable and variable combination. Anyway, and for many markets, it's believed value buyers form by far the largest segment. Price buyers are said to be much less common and prestige types only about ten percent of the total. I suggest prestige-buying flyfishers, or at least the share of total flyfishing dollars they spend, make up a larger than normal portion. If not, why is so much flyfishing product and advertising aimed at prestigious ideas and misconceptions?

Prestige-motivated flyfishers buy tackle to brag-of, show-off, feel smug about or to demonstrate what they suppose to be correctness—whether they care to admit such motivations or not. Such buyers often have little real understanding or caring of utility, sensibility, true quality, balance or cost of tackle. Some purchase tackle thinking they know something about tackle. Mostly they equate high price, eye appeal or "expert" opinion to quality and utility. If a person desires and can afford something, what's the problem? Despite the urge to quickly say "nothing," there are negative ramifications for us all.

Economic history has shown that if too many buyers refuting common sense are tolerated, economic order is compromised. Consumers have crucial function in the flyfishing or any market. Their function is to keep producers honest and ensure proper allocation of resources, competitive prices and a flow of *decent* products. We can't, as a total consumer base, ignore our responsibility. Too many naive or prestige buyers damage remaining consumers' ability to do their job honoring market responsibilities of keeping producers and sellers focused and virtuous.

The flyfishing industry cultivates prestige buyers. It's done with images of flyfishing romance, nature adoration, correctness and sophistication. Their efforts are ignorantly aided from outside the industry. (Insurance, travel and vehicle advertisements featuring posh flyfishing themes.) The recent movie, *A River Runs Through It,* accelerated the "yuppifying" of flyfishing.

Industry-painted mind images prove most alluring to the too urbanized, too gullible and too long off the farm. Flyfishing is matured and despite refinement has survivalist, semi-primitive foundations and undertones of purpose—as trapping or hunting. It's always been best understood and practiced by persons with direct understanding of such basic motivations. Not surprisingly, most of them will have rural upbringing, yet most new flyfishers have never seen a turnip truck. It's ironic. The ethos of many modern flyfishers ignores flyfishing roots—roots likely seen as unseemly, even contemptible but nonetheless, fundamentally true. How does a neo-flyfisher who is pro-flyfishing, but anti-fur, anti-hunting and anti-gun rationalize such contradictions? If they are rationalized, will that person ever really understand flyfishing? Flyfishing is now portrayed and maintained as upscale, correct, prestigious and expensive. It befits a new movie title, perhaps: *A River, Of Sophisticated Money And Thinking, Runs Through It.*

Another type of consumer, the price buyers, might be seen as foolish. They pay good money now for stuff that won't last or do the job rather than digging deeply or saving until decent tackle can be purchased. Perhaps they are fooled by the prevalence of misinformation concerning tackle. Maybe they're only ignorant or habitually short of funds. Such reasons aren't criminal, and all are changeable. Some consumers always know how to shop wisely, and there are good buys in decent tackle for anglers knowing where to look.

Value buyers, however, keep the economic ship of flyfishing somewhat afloat. It's admirably done despite constant harassment from sellers trying to trick them into acting like prestige buyers and also into thinking products have value (real, reasonably priced worth) when they do not. Product value failings are usually defined by trifling real and dependable utility or too high price for that possessed. We'll get into a lot of the particulars in due course.

Free market economic theory tells us, in part, that poor or improperly priced products and inefficient firms will be eliminated from the market place. It works, too, eventually. "Eventually" runs into years while flyfishing consumers face fruitless and overpriced products from a sorry industry. Markets aren't static, but always imminent. Questionable products, firms to produce and dealers to sell them, not to mention flyfishers to buy them, seem never ending.

Newer flyfishers seldom have knowledge of historical prices of quality flyfishing items. There have come lately, many new flyfishers. They can assume recent prices, some several multiples of recent years, are normal. Too many, willingly paying too much, cause unreasonable prices to stick. Beginning flyfishers, and many who aren't new, fail to understand what defines quality. Similar to prestige buyers, newcomers erroneously think higher price, or a shiny exterior assures better quality, functionality and durability.

Production, Pricing and Promotions

Manufacturers and other sell-siders say they produce or stock new products based on customer request, need and market surveys. But producers' and sellers' ears are too sympathetic to requests of their elitist and sophisticated cronies. We're told products are introduced only after extensive research and testing. A manufacturer's "extensive" testing can be biased, rushed or otherwise flawed. A common reason is to introduce something "new" or upstage the competition. More important than flyfisher requests (based on wisdom or not), survey results or need are producers' judgments of what the suckers might buy and how high a price they will pay. Short run thinking dominates.

Producers' advisers, magazine product reviewers or writers covering and accelerating producers' new products, may simply be industry's stooges. Magazine publishers are well paid for lots of advertising. They and editors could be "paid for." They don't speak the whole truth—maybe don't know the truth—about products. Many flyfishers tend to be gullible; they believe product reviews, articles, advertising and promotion. There is encouraging action from outside flyfishing. Procter & Gamble, after realizing they were confusing and overwhelming their customers (that's being kind) in the quest of increasing sales, recently reduced its product line by 33%. Consumers appreciate that type of action and profits are up. Flyfishing moguls should take note.

Buying right, every time, requires flyfishers maintain perfect product knowledge. Who owns such insight? There is just too much to understand. Tackle sellers keep things intentionally confounding and overstated to fool and influence our decisions. Product *differentiation* implies benefit that's largely theoretical, false or caused to be imagined. Differentiation is a primary selling tool of the hucksters. Hypothetical product differentiation combined with glitzy or dreamy promotion slay most flyfishing consumers. It's hard to avoid. Sellers know few buyers *really* understand flyfishing or fly tackle and certainly not as well as they think they understand. A market atmosphere acutely favoring sellers exists. It's accentuated by buyer sloth, prestige seeking and consumer unawareness. Lots of innocent consumers are taken advantage of: lots also get what they deserve.

Most advertising, promotion, created images and "mind" fishing only titillates. Such phoniness does not inform. Advertising and promotion *always* add to product costs. Why should serious and informed flyfishers be asked to pay the costs of applesauce promotion and asinine advertising? They sure are and, regrettably, do.

Fly tackle and service buyers are lambs among wolves for the most part. Unless you care to waste money, experience frustration or be laughed at behind your back, it behooves you to learn about and understand industry's tricks or ignorances—certainly those concerning basic, important and expensive items of tackle and services and also certainly casting and flyfishing technique. Those topics and more are covered in upcoming chapters. Let's examine the industry further so you will know more of whom and what you are dealing.

Two Industries

There are actually two flyfishing industries I'll attempt to define. One, the "Elite" industry, is composed of manufacturers, or special divisions, and retailers (some with catalog operations) that usually sell or address only flyfishing products. "Top end" products are accentuated. Fly shops belong here. Larger flyfishing manufacturers and magazines tend to fit the Elite industry. Despite widely varying, narrow business specializations and citified human shortcomings, members of the Elite somehow radiate an all-knowing aura concerning flyfishing. Some may be quite knowing. Others are just too sophisticated.

The "Other" industry has some producers but more retailers. Retailers might operate chain stores or catalog operations and usually sell products other than those for flyfishing. The various "Mart" type stores belong in the Other industry to the extent they sell fly tackle. Future references will be to the flyfishing "industries" rather than "a" flyfishing industry.

The Elite wages war on the Other via print and speech spreading innuendoes and falsehoods. The Other industry largely ignores the Elite and keeps on doing what it does well. I know fine and caring flyfishers working in the Other industry with feelings hurt by the Elite's attitudes and actions. Affronts occur in many ways by people supposedly representing both industries that tend to ignore the Other. One day the Elite may well regret insulting the Other.

Actually the Elite fears the Other. When potential profits are entwined with fear of competition—see it as one side of a coin—you will find the opposite side of that Fear coin to be Greed. American retailing is always changing. It continues to move to larger, carry and do-it-all stores with or without catalog operations and longer term thinking. Elite industry retailers are heard to whine, saying the Other industry ruins the flyfishing market by selling at prices too low to maintain reasonable profits. Elite retailers believe the Other does so partially through ability to buy products more cheaply than the Elite. That might be true; however, it *is* true that the Other industry's retailers are often more efficient. And what is "reasonable" profit anyway? Major Elite manufacturers have two faces. They sell to their Elite kinsmen and the Other's retailers. Money must sooth conflict of interest.

Elite manufacturers fear the Other may one day become too powerful, dictate prices to be paid for resale goods and steal power. But fearful Elite producers are the same ones that in the past have and may again agree to, or in greed offer, lower prices to the Other's retailers. They could just say "no." There are few flyfishing "wholesalers" anymore. Sales are commonly direct to retailer from manufacturer.

You find representatives, usually top officers, of the largest Elite producers or publishers dominating the boards of directors and advisory panels of flyfishing's few organizations. In consequence, a few Elite members tend to generate or overly influence the positions and directions flyfishing takes and maintains. They have Power. You know about power. It corrupts.

Pro-Shop Programs and Products

Powerful Elite producers, to keep fly shops placated about selling or selling at lower prices to the Other industry *and* to make more money than they otherwise could, have instituted special "pro-shop" programs—programs designed to place "top-of-the-line," products only in flyfishing specialty shops. To qualify, shops must meet eligibility requirements. That can include minimum orders, stocking of certain products, teaching flyfishing classes, selling only at "sacred" prices and maintaining a bona fide store-front. In return, and among other things, shops receive supposed protected territories. Many modern day shops lean heavily on such manufacturer-controlled programs. Their managements abdicate power believing pro-shop programs give them advantage over the Other, even their Elite sister shops. Advantage probably is gained with new, prestige and fooled value buyers.

Special pro-shop products have few, if any, performance characteristics superior to lower priced products sold by the Other's catalogers or retailers. The belief that they do is testimony to the effectiveness of the Elite's overstated promotion and lack of flyfisher and retailer knowledge and understanding. Many in the Other could care less. The largest of near pure, Other-type catalogers also sell the Elite's pro-shop-only products. "How so?" you might ask. A Cabela's buyer confided that

Scientific Anglers 3M (SA) allowed Cabela's to concoct a couple of flyfishing classes to qualify as a "pro-shop" and justify Cabela's selling SA pro-shop products, even through its catalogs, without "real" fly shops raising a stink.

It's reasonable to speculate SA and other manufacturers would further turn their heads and maybe abandon pro-shop programs before losing Cabela's, other large cataloger's, and chain store's extra and large sales. How are fly shop territories protected from chain stores or catalogs featuring "pro-shop" products sent everywhere to nearly all flyfishers? Perhaps the power-abdicating fly shops don't worry too much—yet. So far, businesses selling pro-shop tackle are all charging the same prices. Chain stores and catalogers are usually known for selling exemplary tackle reasonably to common flyfisher benefit. I haven't seen the $50-plus "top" SA lines or much special pro-shop tackle of other producers discounted below their sacred pro-shop prices—again, yet. I have seen Sage rods on sale at "bargain" prices.

Big Business

Flyfishing tackle manufacturer (particularly of lines) Scientific Anglers 3M (SA) is a division of Minnesota Mining and Manufacturing, one of the largest Corporations in the Americas and one of the Dow-Jones 30 Industrial stocks. The *management* of such large corporations survive on and demand ever increasing revenues. It's required so profits may rise, so stockholder value and dividends can increase and so stockholders won't revolt demanding that selfsame management be fired. How many corporate big-shots, or directed underlings, care (or will take action) if fly tackle he sells is unneeded, fails to markedly benefit users or that company marketing plans are unfair when his butt might be canned for failure to sell?

I was told—by someone I have no reason to doubt and in position to know—that Scientific Anglers gave serious consideration to severely reducing their flyfishing presence not many years ago due lack of required profitability. Hordes of credulous new flyfishers, buying huge amounts of tackle through many new shops and at elevated pro-shop program prices, apparently reestablished high profitability. SA also makes fly lines for many of their competitors (Teeny, Wulff, Orvis). Those competitor-customers sell many more fly lines to SA's benefit. I like and use older SA lines and would not like to see SA gone. But there has to be an acceptable middle ground that doesn't require $30 to $60 be paid for a cheap to produce, "top" fly line. On second thought, and maybe if SA were gone, decent, reasonably priced lines could emerge. I've used some fine lines from England.

Flyfishing businesses probably find their actions easy to excuse because so many flyfishers literally invite exploiting treatment and prices via ignorance or apathy. Maybe flyfishers who don't, or don't care to, understand basic economic flyfishing rationale are the ones with unlimited income or no better use for money than foolish, unneeded or overpriced fly tackle.

Recent times have been easy for flyfishing sellers. Streets have been paved with the gold of the new, unenlightened, prestige seeking and fooled. All the industries' members have had to do is hyperbolize, advertise and gather the gold. When times turn against flyfishing sellers—as they will sooner or later—such programs will likely fail, as they should. That happened to an arrogant ski industry's pro-shop, price-fixing programs some years ago. Heard of any shortages of decent ski equipment lately? The pro-shop programs of SA, Cortland, Sage, Loomis, Orvis or any other flyfishing seller result in fixed prices. If the flyfishing industries were larger, we might see the government anti-trust folks sniffing about. Waiting for the long run, natural, collapse of price-fixing schemes causes too many to pay too much for overrated products.

Arrogance Exposed

The Elite industry, of course, believes (or deludes itself) that pro-shop programs are most beneficial to flyfishers, further justifying high prices. *Fly Tackle Dealer (FTD)* magazine is the dominant voice of the Elite. The Other doesn't have a voice I'm aware. *FTD* often features press on the need for and supreme importance of many, small flyfishing specialty shops to sell pro-shop goods. A recent and typical *FTD* article says: *"Only fly shops can promote and teach fly fishing properly and insure a continuing flow of new flyfishers."*

What do you think of that? It's false as well as arrogant, and I'll prove it. First, just what is teaching flyfishing "properly"? If the Elite thinks it can teach flyfishing "properly," it can't. It's understandable, but inexcusable, that *FTD* would say something so fraudulent and self-serving: *FTD* is aimed at Elite retailers that buy from *FTD's* advertisers, the Elite manufacturers. Oh yes, flyfishing does have a good-old-boys club.

We'll consider reputed ability of Elite fly shops to uniquely facilitate a continuous flow of new flyfishers later. For now, let's look further into the Elite's ability to ". . . *promote and teach fly fishing properly*. . . ." As previously mentioned, later in this book are results of a survey of experienced and knowledgeable flyfishers from across the USA and Canada. Its purpose was to discover what garden-variety *but* learned and knowledgeable flyfishers think about all aspects of flyfishing. One of the questions begs examination now.

In question No. 66 I asked the pollees: "What do you like or dislike about fly shops?" About 300 comments resulted; 71 percent had a similar tone, as follows:

> "Too high priced, snooty, snobbish, elitist, cliquish, bad advice, lack knowledge, poor attitude, inbred, full of bull-shit, useless inventory, pushy clerks, poor quality, hard sell, degrade certain brands, poorly stocked, push only high-priced brands, arrogant know-it-alls, all the same, make me feel inadequate, treat women poorly, treat beginners poorly, only go to the good ones, and don't use them."

The 29 percent "positive" answers *almost always* had the qualifiers "sometimes," "generally," "usually" and "mostly" appended, largely diminishing positive connotations.

Common, but proficient, flyfishers do not support the Elite's opinion of itself as be-all, end-all, flyfishing experts and teachers. The results show fly shops radiate much harmful to flyfishers and flyfishing. The Elite, as evidenced by repeated self-serving comment in *FTD* and elsewhere, continues to think that it offers exalted service through its shops. Is it the kind of service we need, or want? Are industries' members overwhelmingly out of touch with genuine flyfishers, uncaring and greed dominated? Could the large number of polled flyfishers (264) be wrong in such a lopsided opinion of fly shops? Perhaps the Elite has taken a page from the politicians' handbook: Tell a lie often enough and you can make uninformed people, including themselves, believe most anything.

Fly tackle producers, also sellers, would have you believe higher priced pro-shop goods are yet further justified. They say such prices allow lots of money to be spent on research and development to bring you ever better products—bunk. Tremendous chunks of producer budgets have to go to pay for distorted, illusory advertising and promotion. Continuing slick color ads in bunches of magazines, splashy attendance at numerous sport shows and flamboyant promotion do not come cheaply. Producers are "buying the market" by capitalizing on flyfisher ignorance, creating sophisticates and painting mind pictures. It isn't cheap to do or maintain. But $300 waders and reels, $250 plus rods and lots and lots of $50 fly lines have paid for gobs of advertising. Can it be sustained? Do adequate numbers of gullible anglers exist or has the Elite shot themselves in their collective foot?

Industries' "rip-'em-off disease" is ferociously communicable, particularly since industries' members sleep in a more or less common bed. When one producer markets a higher priced rod, reel, line or whatever, competitors are free to raise their prices to similar levels. It's done following aggrandizement of usually "new" products by shameless marketing of minute peculiarities, either imagined or specially created. Are such products needed?

It's no wonder we won't see truthful articles printed in the flyfishing rags concerning industries' marketing practices, pricing or products. Magazine publishers depend on advertising revenues, not magazine sales. If revenues are stimulated by competition and lots of new products, so much the better. Only a fool (or a rare truthful, honorable and knowledgeable editor or publisher) would spurn hands feeding them with advertising dollars. It's a win-win situation for all inside the industries. Who cares about the customer-suckers—or the fish? But remember, the customers of manufacturers are the retailing fly shops, catalogers and discounters. (Some, none to bright per Question No. 66.) Retailers, however, have little to fear for "Bigger Sucker Theory" works to protect them from deservedly eating half-witted purchases. To whom do end-using flyfishers sell their purchase mistakes? *Bon appétite*—enjoy.

Pro-shop retailers naturally support producer guile and pro-shop programs; they're given thick slices of profit-pie. Shops believe they make more money in two ways.

Manufacturers of pro-shop goods may provide lower than normal dealer prices. If not, they have high *dictated* retail prices that so far haven't been seriously violated. Low cost, high protected selling prices or both create fat margins for dealers. Shops also enjoy wide-spread, producer paid, overstated advertising to fool flyfishers, support and increase sales. Additionally, producers of pro-shop products may subsidize advertising retailers independently undertake, tend to stroke their retailers heavily and dole out lots of free goodies. Do you have any doubt why fly shops push the big name, high priced stuff at you? It has little to do with better fishability.

The Elite still cites "failure" of the ski and general fishing industry's small, pro-type shops. Their chorus says failures were due to excess "outside" discounting that destroyed shops' abilities to maintain high profit margins. You and I can, however, still buy *any* general fishing tackle item, piece of ski equipment or service we need or desire, *and it will likely cost less* than it would have cost at a specialty shop. Are there fewer ski hills or less fishing because shops failed? Do we need, should we suffer or support flyfishing pro-shop programs with primary function of increasing prices? What about shops having outstanding effect of misinforming and offending flyfishers? Shops and programs often undermine the "good" in and of flyfishing. (See results of question No. 66 again if you doubt.)

I researched the demise of the small ski shops and found it directly the result of customer-alienating arrogance on the part of shops and manufacturers. Equally at fault were inflating price programs having no sound basis in free-market economics, thus, no chance of long-run success. Several low snow years could have been the catalyst (water conditions, fish numbers?). Sound familiar?

The Unsung

You will remember the Elite industry says—per its *FTD* mouthpiece's article—that, "*Only fly shops can . . . insure a continuing flow of new flyfishers.*" That statement blatantly ignores the great many nonindustries' mentors who teach friends or family and otherwise tremendously facilitate flyfishing. It's exceedingly arrogant belittling the work and efforts of the Federation of Fly Fishers (FFF), Trout Unlimited (TU), Izaak Walton League and many other local clubs—clubs capable not only of increasing the flow of newcomers, but also nurturing them in the spirit and ethics of flyfishing. They do that while also completing civic-minded works enhancing and ensuring the welfare of everyone's flyfishing. Can the industries match such fine work? Do they care as much about ethics, flyfishing spirit or fishery health? The industries' self-centeredness doesn't support or sustain what's truly important about flyfishing. There are industries connected individuals, shop owners and shop workers who do support honorable and ethical flyfishing, but as a whole the industries' efforts stink.

Clubs are not in the Elite or Other industries. They are largely non-profit, do yeoman's work and function with dedicated volunteer labor and donations. You might consider joining one or donating some of the money this book will save you to local club causes. Clubs are found nearly everywhere.

But TU and the FFF have large national structures. Their policy-making boards of directors always seem damnably loaded with the Elite's personalities. That's why I recommend you do your business with the *local* clubs, even with sportsman's clubs or associations of local nature without national or regional structure. The best works are always done locally by people who get their hands dirty. The most important work isn't accomplished by lip service from big shots. They, too often, operate thinly veiled to first benefit self and business interests. Industries' counterproductive, flyfishing damaging, big shots pervade flyfishing.

Industries' Goals

Examine the American Sportfishing Association's (ASA)—the united trade organization of general sport fishing—published goals:

1) To ensure a viable fishery resource in terms of clean water and availability of game fish.
2) Increase participation in the sport of fishing.
3) To increase the profitability of the industry.

Here's what Tom Bedell, President Outdoor Technologies Group (Fenwick, Berkley, Abu Garcia), says: "Each of us needs to accept responsibility for the future of fishing." He states the following ways:

a) Protect and improve our water resources;
b) Improve fishing so people catch more fish;

c) Increase accessibility and awareness of places to fish;
d) Educate people on how to fish;
e) Motivate people to go fishing;
f) Offer fishing tackle products and accessories that help people have fun—lots of fun—while they are fishing!

Having read those statements, now look at the mission statement of the North American Fly-Tackle Trade Association (NAFTA). NAFTA is the flyfishing industries' single encompassing trade organization.

> "The purpose of the North American Fly-Tackle Trade Association is to enhance and represent the fly fishing industry through education, promotion and research."

That's a bland, obscure, cliché and triviality-filled utterance compared to "do something positive" general fishing industry statements. You notice it doesn't have one lousy word about protecting or furthering fish and fisheries or helping flyfishers, only ". . . enhance and represent the fly fishing industry. . . ." I read trade publications routinely. It's most unusual to see anything from *FTD* or NAFTA concerning the betterment of everyone's flyfishing or the future well being of water and fish—just gossip or babble about how to sell you more, make more profit and defeat the Other.

I was recently told by a NAFTA official that great care is taken procuring a meeting room for the 15-member NAFTA board of directors: "It has to be very large to accommodate all their egos." NAFTA could be a most useful organization—but isn't. What do the sellers NAFTA represents expect customer-flyfishers to catch with the tackle and services they plan to sell them? Apparently it isn't considered. If unconsidered and not addressed where it should be—prominently, as other fishing organizations do—then logic says it's deemed unimportant. The Elite doesn't care about your flyfishing. Elite industry members have your money and their connections to fly away to exotic or so far unspoiled places to fish. Any of them asked you to go along lately?

Neither NAFTA nor the industries realize a major function must be protecting and enhancing your fishing. It only makes good sense, for them, that they should. Granted, exhibiting good sense isn't their forte. Ignoring and offending flyfishers and those things critical to flyfishing's best welfare is business absurdity. Broach resource-ignoring, money-grubbing attitude of the industries to any of its manufacturing members and you will likely be treated to an inaccurate explanation extolling the massive, fishery bound, excise taxes (10% of wholesale after deductions) producers pay. Explanations I've heard assume I'm stupid—either that, or the "explainer" is. I've filed an excise tax return each quarter for the last 20 years or more. Excise taxes, like most taxes, are passed on to final purchasers—you pay excise taxes.

Further consider the flyfishing industries' taxation: corporate income tax rates vary but for sake of near accurate example can be said to approximate 35% of profits, at this writing. Many of industries' firms have corporate structure. Now corporations, as well as differently structured businesses, perform stunning accounting contortions to minimize taxable profit. That includes taking advantage of legitimate deductions, salary bonuses, reserves, depreciation, product development dodges, gimmicks and loopholes of many sorts. Dollars are thus pulled from profit, and each one eliminates 35 cents of tax. Or one pre-tax dollar contributed to charitable fish or habitat improvement costs its donator only 65 cents since 35 cents would be paid in taxes anyway.

Many caring *nonflyfishing* businesses donate heavily to business-connected worthy causes rather than pay taxes. It's good business; customers are impressed. If the flyfishing industries cared and didn't waste so much money on hyperbole and promotion, they might have funds to do many times the good of *any* cost to themselves—*many times* the good, because industries' wasted dollars could be magnified by volunteer labor and often materials facilitating projects of many kinds benefiting flyfishing. Industries' total sales and likely their profits would grow, certainly be reapportioned. Consumers and flyfishers are more alert than industries' leadership realize; they would gladly spend more with those firms seen to do flyfishing measurable good. More firms would then contribute to fishery improvement, and their sales and profits would grow at the expense of non supporters.

Enigma

I have mixed feelings about the industries. I owned a fly shop, guided many years, tied flies and sold materials for many more. Decent people do work in the industries—more than I might give impression—but it's difficult excusing misdeeds even "decent" people do or allow. Sales people need to sell but often have fear and greed dominated thinking or principles. Many will sell (or are told to sell) something every chance given. If sellers have excess debt to service and justify rapacious selling for that reason, it's more testimony to poor business ability.

Flyfishers endure wrong equipment or follow bad advice because fly shop staffs may be half-learned, scared or less than virtuous. Rather than admit a lack of knowledge or decline inappropriate selling—excusable and appreciated virtues—shop workers can claim understanding, erroneously think they have it or sell anything they can. We know fly shop owners have to buy before selling, and many lack indispensable flyfishing understanding and wisdom themselves as Question No. 66 reveals.

Shops' buyers can't avoid exposing a lack of flyfishing or business acumen to slick manufacturers or their sales representatives. Shops can be taken severe advantage of by producers. That helps account for the irrational stuff found in fly shops and pawned off on timid flyfishers. Other shops buy anything they think they can sell, regardless of product reasonableness and particularly if it's "new," verifying ". . .an inferior man knows what sells" as fully quoted in this chapter's preamble.

Most of us don't expect merchants to know everything, therefore, no disgrace, loss of face or professionalism arises if they do not. But it takes backbone and intelligence to recognize and admit topical flyfishing ignorance and particularly to decline ravenous, but easy, selling. Flyfishers, like all humans, appreciate honesty and integrity. They want to trust flyfishing merchants but constantly court misery due the charlatans—*Caveat emptor*.

Producers and sellers are needed not, however, in form or with the attitude of many in the Elite and some in the Other industry. The industries harm themselves in so many ways, some, likely unknown. A fellow who supervises the tying of lots of flies in the Orient recently told me his Japanese contacts have been mistreated by American fly tackle producers and suppliers so frequently they will shop anywhere in the world rather than coming here. If given legitimate chances to sell overseas and bring dollars home, we should do so. I'd guess the Japanese, and others, would cooperate to higher degree if the Elite were not so contemptible. I sell to the Japanese and have learned they can be quite gullible and "prestige buyer" like. I don't see that as reason to take advantage of them.

Responsibilities

Both flyfishing industries are largely out of touch with what's important to genuine flyfishers. But some people, calling themselves flyfishers, have no idea of what's undeniably important about flyfishing either. The bulk of the American consumers, including flyfishers, tend to be overly concerned with *superficiality.* Flyfishers worthy the name, however, are concerned, overwhelmingly, with the welfare of fish and fisheries, manners and ethics, as you will later see.

The industries minimize or ignore what's important to flyfishers and in unrecognized actuality, themselves. They also pay zealous lip service to primary concerns of knowledgeable, concerned flyfishers but take minimal, concrete action (money donations) to improve flyfishing. Judge the industries by what they *do*—not what they *say.* Real flyfisher disgust and frustration festers, revealed only when someone asks numbers of flyfishers what they think about flyfishing's sellers. That happened in the upcoming survey and was partially revealed in question No. 66. In the industries' defense, I've recently read of money from a couple of big catalog sellers finding its way to help in rescuing beleaguered rivers. It's a mere drop into a large bucket of need.

Industries need and want more business from new and existing flyfishers. Question No. 66, however, tells us Elite shops offend, mislead and discourage existing flyfishers as well as persons considering flyfishing who might visit an average fly shop. The industries say they stand and fight for our fish and fisheries yet contribute *diminutive* dollar amounts to fish welfare, sell stainless steel hooks, 1- and 2-weight fly rods, hard-finish nets and stomach pumps. Such actions have definite potential to harm fish. It all has consequences.

Elite shops are minimally patronized by flyfishers cognizant of shops' flyfishing damaging actions and attitudes. The sales boom now enjoyed by the industries will fade. Industries' big shots know that. Many are probably socking enough easy and gullible money away, planning to sell out or retire before the bubble bursts. Unenlightened and uncaring "flyfishers" *actually aid* those responsible for many of flyfishing's troubles. The Elite could change but most likely won't. Changing would require admission of embarrassing mistakes and changes of emphasis and attitudes. Changes of leadership would be required. That, however, would cause a loss of power by existing "leaders." Moves would be required that selfish, arrogant leadership seldom make until it's too late, perhaps not even then. I wish there were more of industries' people in power like John McBride:

> "As a manufacturer's representative in the flyfishing industry, I found the results of your survey enlightening. The flyfishing industry needs a wakeup call if the industry is to remain healthy. Your survey has certainly opened my eyes in more than a few areas. I was quite surprised by the majority of the responses. On the other hand, a few were predictable. You have done the flyfishing industry a great service. Let's hope the manufacturers and the magazine editors listen to what flyfishermen are saying."

That's encouraging, and we can hope those needing to listen and change will. Don't hold your breath.

The Root Problem

Ultimately, and without excusing either industry their massive shortcomings, *flyfishers are responsible for most of flyfishing's problems.* Flyfishers allow, even encourage, the industries to operate as they do. Uninformed flyfishers failing to exercise buying discretion when, where and in amount needed empower the pillaging industries. Flyfishers failing to acquire, then use and defend, accurate and adequate understanding of flyfishing thereby threaten the soul of the sport. Flyfishing despoiling "flyfisher" actions, however ignorant or innocent, are still despoiling. They're commonplace and exasperate those fighting to remain apprised, considerate and protective of flyfishing.

Flyfishers seem somehow conditioned to expect, then excuse, the actions of uncaring flyfishers and the treatment of the industries. Is it some goofy aura seen to surround flyfishing that causes people to be willingly abused, accept flyfishing's tarnishing and be herded like sheep? Or is it simply flyfisher ignorance and apathy?

Uninformed, shallow or "correct" flyfishers look for guidance from those they believe or assume enjoy expertise. It's trendy and easy to lean on low technology over skill and to live in fantasy worlds. Highly touted, popular and "new and improved" rods and reels, lines, flies, leaders and on and on are seen as strings of panaceas capable of replacing flyfishing understanding and ability. Fat wallets and skinny flyfishing intellect or discretion are proffered to often unethical or misguided but always voracious sales forces.

Using flyfishing *knowledge known correct*, heritage acceptable and ethical, *with discretion and buying power*, will protect flyfishers and flyfishing. It's possible numbers of us could change things for the better—for everyone. Enlightened flyfishers need to help educate those deserving and tolerate the rest until they leave flyfishing—or drown. It's not always big chunks of clearly identifiable damage done by the avaricious or unknowing but subtle, creeping and cumulative degradation done flyfishing. Some call such insidious, degrading change "progress." "The problems we have created cannot be solved with the same thinking that created them," unless you question the intelligence of Albert Einstein's thinking.

Elucidation

Each chapter following examines a basic of flyfishing. Misconceptions and inaccuracies revealed facilitate understanding and changing as needed to maximize effectiveness and consequent enjoyment. We'll identify dangers and avoid or solve problems. The next chapter addresses flyfishing leaders. You could start there now if uninterested in what follows further showing the character of the flyfishing industries and supporting statements earlier made.

The following is from Tom Meade of *Fishing Tackle Retailer (FTR)* writing about flyfishing:

> "The products are designed to lure customers who are as fascinated with the idea of fly fishing as they are with fly fishing itself"; and, "Fly fishing vests have become fashion items worn to look cool"; also, "Western spring creeks are being crowded with new fly fishermen flailing away with $1,000 outfits, their Saabs

and BMW's parked nearby"; and finally, "Nearly 75% of consumers generally believe the information contained in manufacturers' ads."

From *Fishing Tackle Trade News (FTTN),* quoting an Elite industry retailer:

"The goal is a 100 percent margin on flies"; and, "When a customer comes in to buy a new fly line we try to sell him, if possible, a new reel, backing, leader material. But what generates the most income per square foot would be leaders and tippets."

Bill Hunter of *FTD:*

"Many of the fly-fishing industry's most knowledgeable people are now saying that the growth of the sport and the industry is dependent upon the dealers"; and, "Would a mass merchandiser's success usurp too much of the control fly-fishing manufacturers now enjoy?"; also, ". . .expand their customers' 'useful shop life?'"

From Paul Marriner, also of *FTD,* concerning fly shops and pro-shop programs:

"It's a dealer-only market, the margins are much higher (than conventional tackle) and manufacturers protect territories."

Mr. Archer Mason in a letter to the editor of *Flyfishing:*

"Do you have any notion what percentage of revenues generated by magazines, rod makers, resorts, retailers, et al. is set aside by them for this advocacy? [Stream, fish improvement etc.{sic}] It is a tiny, appallingly tiny, fraction. (We're talking a number well to the right of the decimal.)"

Mr. Mike Hayden, President of ASA, (you saw ASA's fine written goals for general fishing earlier) from an interview published in *FTR:*

"The [NAFTA] board of directors is so paranoid about mass merchants, they can't get beyond that."

That reveals the Elite's numbing fear.

Chapter Three: Flyfishing Leaders

Leaders might seem a strange place to start a discussion of tackle rather than the near obligatory fly rod. Leaders are considered first because they are simply most important. The only other possible choice for first place is the fly line. Lee Wulff, a most knowledgeable and experienced flyfisher, believed a leader's purpose is to fool fish. Important leader qualities must be present and work together to accomplish that and other necessary ends. A leader must be able to accept and then continue power from the cast line, roll out and make the vital presentation of the fly before it can fool fish. It must then hold the fish once fooled. Leaders must be durable yet pliable with contradictory characteristics of strength and daintiness.

Basic Leaders and Diameter

Rudimentary leaders are usually short and made of a single

piece of level monofilament. The most used leaders, however, have a decreasing diameter along their length from butt to tippet, hence the name tapered leaders. Tapering is accomplished by tying pieces of material together or in manufacturing to produce knotless tapered leaders.

Correct leaders have long and stiff butt sections—longer and certainly stiffer than historically found on most commercial knotless tapered leaders. The mid-section of a tapered leader is for rapid diameter reduction and the end, tippet portion, is most devoted to fooling fish. There are several proven tapered leader formulas. Others having reverse or bizarre tapers cause me wonder; maybe they work in certain obscure situations. You won't go wrong by tying or buying leaders of the proven 60% stiff butt, 20% graduation and 20% tippet formulation.

Stiffness in leader butts allows the necessary power acceptance and continuation from the fly line. It's generally recommended that butt diameter be two-thirds the diameter of line end. In the most fished lines, 4- to 8-weights, that translates to leader butts of near .020 of an inch in diameter. In fact, much concerning leader qualities centers around diameter. It's absurd. Baling wire and a strand of cooked spaghetti have the same diameter. Misunderstanding of or false reliance on diameter causes lots of flyfishing problems.

Smaller diameter leader material is regularly stated as being a certain "X" size (2X, 3X, etc.). The "Xs" correspond to almost ancient and confusing gauge measurements. Material of many sorts (wire, silkworm gut, etc.) drawn through holes of certain diameter was given an "X" designation up to the largest of 0X (ought X, about .011 inch). Then designations change to numerical. Most "X" spouting, old-time gauge using, diameter dominated flyfishers are only partially informed. Ask them the correct gauge size thought to be correct for leader butts (1/5) or the correct gauge size for .014 diameter material (8/5), few will know. Leader material diameter is minimally useful to know and should be stated in thousandths of an inch by its manufacturer for all material. It is more often these days. (If for some reason the "X" size of a piece of leader is wanted, subtract the diameter in thousandths from the number 11 [e.g. 11 minus .006, or 6, equals 5X.] Of course it doesn't work for diameters over .011.)

Diameter is used, incorrectly and unsuccessfully, as a surrogate for stiffness, particularly in larger leader material sizes. What is important is *relative* stiffness. Stiffness of different types or brands of similar material varies considerably even though diameters are identical. I've tried to measure relative leader and fly line stiffness a few times. Extending equal lengths of fly line and varying leader brands, of same approximate diameter, over a horizontal table top, I've tried to observe the amount of sag or drop. It doesn't work well. Leader from spools has small amounts of seemingly permanent curvature that affects the sag test. I've learned, through trial and error, what materials have requisite stiffness and other desirable qualities allowing maximum fishing effectiveness.

False diameter worship has its roots, as other flyfishing falsehoods, in a tendency to think fish see things, perhaps even think, as humans. Excursions into anthropomorphism result in flawed conclusions. Nonetheless, such excursions are common, easy and provide supposed reason to our flyfishing methods and theories. Smaller diameter means less fish visibility—right? I'm not sure but doubt that's the case. Besides, for on or near surface fishing, it isn't necessarily the diameter of leader or its visibility that's our undoing but the leader's shadow or shine. Both are variably magnified by water and light as leader lies on, above and in the case of shine, perhaps below the surface. Leaders or shadows are probably seen by fish as cracks in the water's surface. That's abnormal, as is leader shine.

Capable and researched fishing minds believe game fish have ability to see all leaders. Because fish may have such ability doesn't mean they always do see leaders. Fish may be excited, made less cautious by close competition or fooled by an angler to mention a few possibilities. The fooling them part, done by clever angling, is most rewarding and defines the very root of flyfishing. It requires angling knowledge, skill and some luck. Fooling fish isn't dependent or even aided by using someone's wonder material that won't hold knots, present a fly correctly or survive even moderate abrasion despite glowing advertising and seemingly knowledgeable rhetoric.

Abrasion Resistance

Damaging leader abrasion has many sources: brush, rocks,

knots or even teeth and body coverings of some fish. Soft leader material, continually worked against something rough, as a hook's steel eye, abrades. Results can be disastrous. Who cares about leader's diameter, suppleness or supposed strength if it easily abrades and therefore can't do its job? Abrasion resistance wields control over material's advertised breaking strength. Even slightly abraded material can lose much of its strength.

Once you vanquish the diameter bogeyman to rightful near irrelevance, you will find there are excellent materials having high abrasion resistance and strength available at a cost of only one- or two-thousandths of an inch greater diameter, maybe less or no difference. Abrasion resistance, therefore strength, varies markedly among various brands of material. It's a function of material's chemical makeup and manufacturing. Abrasion resistance is synonymous with toughness and durability and is desirable in any leader material. You don't want the best or only fish coming at end of a long day to escape due inferior material that abraded or suffered an abrasion-causing and uncorrected wind-knot.

Knot Strength

Knot strength and materials that supposedly "have it" are highly touted. Knot strength embodies several variables; *most important* is the person doing the knot tying, and we all occasionally tie bad knots. Knots correct for material used and application at hand are important. Some materials, particularly the newest, are slick and require careful tying with extra wraps or loops, even special knots. The same is true of most materials as diameter decreases. You won't need to worry about new knots if you stick with proven and reliable leader material. Knots are covered in detail in Chapter Eight.

Knots generate heat in tightening and slip before they fail. Some materials create excessive heat abrasion when knotted. Don't use them. Test before purchase or employment, knowing softer materials are most easily damaged. Do tie knots tightly and avoid materials that defy solid tightening, the too slick or the "new and improved." Numerous knots are designed for purposes other than those of flyfishing, but flyfishers try to use them anyway. Proper knots, tied correctly are more important than reliance on materials with nebulous, supposed or advertised knot strength.

Suppleness and Stretch

Significant leader suppleness is considered important, by some, in lots of flyfishing. Limpness has a hand, but is not definitive, in allowing a dry fly to drift naturally or an unweighted nymph to seductively wobble and suggest life. Excess suppleness, or too long sections of limp material, often cause leaders to land in a tangled mess at cast's end. Incorrect fly to tippet balance (too limp material for a large fly) causes the same problem. Wind, long or poor casting aggravate supple leader collapse. A correctly designed and tied leader of stiffer material eliminates many problems.

In my experience, you won't find high abrasion resistance in supple materials, despite producer claims to the contrary. You will find minimal diameter per supposed breaking strength; however, my experience again fails to collaborate manufacturer claims about breaking strength of supple, abrasion prone, materials. We need toughness with useable, but not excessive suppleness. Limp, abrasion-prone, material might work in easy, snag free water, for fussy fish that are smallish. If larger fish were present (small and large are relative to species, place fished and tackle used) try to hook them first with stiffer, tougher material using correct approach, casting angle and line mends. Quests for suppleness cause other mistakes.

Some flyfishers use different brands of tippet material for different situations. It's safer to use one, proven tough, brand. Simply drop down in pound test and diameter if more suppleness or supposed lessened fish visibility is thought needed. Your knots will tie and your leader perform best. If you elect one brand, don't pick a supple one; your butt sections will lack required stiffness. You would also sacrifice abrasion resistance, therefore strength.

Leader material stretches, some more than others. It can't be avoided and probably shouldn't be. Stretch protects against over-exuberant strikes and mistakes made in fighting fish. The larger and faster the fish the more important stretch becomes. Stretch hinders hook setting, but that may be minimized by controlling slack line, keeping hooks sharp and barbs low or nonexistent. Excessive stretch is usually found in conjunction with, you guessed it, leader suppleness. Stretch inhibits ability to move sulking fish and complicates extricating flies from snags.

Kinks and Memory

A kink in a leader damages casting accuracy and presentation. It's one thing to intentionally place a curve in your leader by luck and canny casting—to achieve some desired effect—and quite another if the leader has a kink induced, curve-throwing, mind of its own. You, not the leader, are to be in control. Memory in leader is like a near continuous kink. At best it can never be completely removed; at worst leaders jump into remembered coils or kinks at every opportunity. Many materials do after we erroneously reel the leader butt too tightly over rod tip and some after winding the whole leader onto the reel. More frustrating are little curls remaining in the tippet after affixing a fly. They cause your fly to appear connected to a coil-spring. Use material that doesn't allow curlicues, resists kinks and has poor memory.

Memory and kinks in a leader, except those at the fly, can be removed by abrading the leader with a piece of rubber. You have probably heard that before, and carrying a small piece of tire-tube in your kit is usually recommended. It's just another piece of junk to lose. There is a simpler solution. My favorite leader material, Maxima Chameleon, lies ramrod straight after slight stretching. Kinks and set are easily removed, and it doesn't tie curlicues even if you try. It has unmatched abrasion resistance, minimal stretch and a host of desirable characteristics.

Shine and Color

Leader shine may spook fish as noted. A high degree of shine is usually found in slick materials that are again, supple. It's safe and easy to lightly rub leaders with a piece of abrasive material to remove shine. At a friend's suggestion, I carry a piece of green polishing cloth in a vest pocket or float-tube at all times, and yes, do lose them occasionally. They are easy to replace from a sheet kept at home. A piece of Chore-Girl or Brillo pad works, and in a pinch, river mud or the gunk that accumulates in the bottom of a boat will serve. Shine is muted by leader color, and clear, or near clear, materials shine most to my eye. Clearer leader material may actually intensify, then transmit light underwater—disturbing to contemplate. What of color?

Leader color gets lots of lip-service. Flyfishers of yesteryear often dyed their leaders, usually brown or red-brown. It's always wise to learn from earlier knowledge. The idea of a material that more or less matches the color of the water or blends with surroundings being fished is engaging. Backgrounds found in water and bottom colors change; my first choice for leader material doesn't. I've ceased worrying much about color match, and success doesn't seem to suffer.

More consideration might be given leader color in very clear water with discriminating fish, but that would suggest their vision can be fooled. Perhaps it can be handicapped. Too much shine or reflection isn't acceptable; color divergence from that of water fished is. The makers of Maxima Chameleon claim their reddish-brown material absorbs rather than reflects light. It sounds reasonable and if true, fine; if not, I'll still use it. They also claim it takes on the color of its surroundings, hence the name Chameleon. I believe it true. Drop a piece of Chameleon on the ground and then try to find it. I hope your eyes are good.

Other Considerations

We are told leader material loses strength as it absorbs water. It's probably true, but I have never tested it and don't much care. It's reported to be minimal and nothing can be done. A leader gets wet.

To avoid deterioration, keep extra leader material away from light and heat. Time also causes deterioration. You will encounter a spool of bad material now and then. Perhaps trustworthy material may be found deeper in that spool; it's worth a try before you discard the spool, but don't take chances. Test material by tying a simple Overhand knot and pulling until it breaks. You will develop a feel for what's "right," or wrong. Test several brands. Old age, light damage or lack of abrasion resistance cause some brands to break easily under this test, even new material. Most leader vendors display leaders and material under bright, often natural light; that's damaging. Buy the spools hanging two or three deep on the peg or ones appearing freshest, perhaps after testing.

It's normally necessary to test only proposed tippet material and a couple of leader steps just above in the case of knotted tapered leaders. The butt and most of the graduation steps will be stronger than your several tippet choices, but it's a good idea to test the whole leader by jerking on it once in a while. The people tying tapered leaders for a living must get exceedingly bored at times, and knotless tapered leaders may be damaged in manufacture or use. Whatever, I've seen lots of bad knots and strange things happen to leaders above the tippet. Discover them before hooking a dandy.

Correctly functioning, trustworthy leaders are critical to successful flyfishing. There are commercial leaders by more than 20 manufacturers for specialized purposes galore, some more imagined then real. I've experienced problems with nearly all commercial leaders I've tested, as have people with opinions I trust. Generally, commercial leaders are too light, short and soft of butt and of too soft material overall.

Any knotless tapered leader I've used in the last many years usually saw only the graduated part of the leader used. I used to attach it to my correctly stiff butt section and then added tippet of my choice. It's a poor practice, allowing varying material problems of knots, diameters, stiffness and performance. Perhaps the newest commercial leaders, knotted and knotless, are better. I haven't tested them all and don't plan or need to. I do know commercial leaders are expensive. One other thing is sure, you can ensure having what you need and know will work by tying your own leaders.

Leader Kits

Several leader tying kits are sold. I've had a Chameleon one in its original and now dog-eared box for over 20 years. I purchase new material to replace spools used. A leader kit should be full and complete at all times, or it's of little use. Don't steal from it to supplement on-stream supply or regret will follow. Keep extra spools of most used material on hand to refurbish your vest or whatever you use, but don't buy too much at a time to avoid deterioration. You need a kit that fits your fishing.

My kit originally contained spools from 1- to 25-pound test. I jettisoned the 1- and 2-pound and added 30- and 40-pound years ago. The kit is always in my fishing vehicle or duffel, and my vest or float-tube contain several basic pre-tied leaders. I keep my most used sizes of material, mostly tippet, with me. The kit is carried to replace leaders I might use or give away, something occasionally done upon meeting frustrated persons astream fighting poorly designed or functioning leaders. Their lack of success can be due many causes, but a poorly functioning leader is high on the list of probabilities. Leader kits are available from several makers.

Mason, Orvis and others make leader kits. Mason material once had a wide following among saltwater flyfishers—before they discovered Chameleon. Some of them tell me they now consider Mason material to be markedly inferior. I agree, never being able to get the kinks and set out. Orvis material always seemed too soft, supple and abrasion prone to me. Manufacturers don't promote kits or leader tying aggressively. They would rather sell finished leaders and lots of different kinds of tippet material. Doing so is much more profitable. (Remember the dealer quote from Chapter Two declaring leaders and tippet to be "by far" the most profitable items for dealers?)

Ideal Material

I don't care to do commercials for anyone. It's just that you seldom find something so effective, dependable and unfailingly deserving of reliance and continued year after year use for such an important need, as Maxima Chameleon leader material. We have discussed the characteristics of leaders at length. When it comes to having what's needed for any flyfishing and what will get the job done, Chameleon outperforms any material of which I'm aware.

Chameleon is sometimes criticized as being too stiff or overrated. By overrated, pound-test and diameter stated on its spools are not in agreement with actual measured diameter or breaking strength. It usually measures a thousandth or two larger and has more breaking strength. So what? Knowing material will not test over what it is supposed to test is only important to those strange types worried about class tippet records. Pursuing "world record" fish is thankfully avoided by most. That aside, diameter matters little; Chameleon is stronger than similar diameters of different manufacture—allowing use of smaller diameter. It has needed toughness in all sizes. Material I've measured of other manufacturers varies just as much in diameter without increased breaking strength or durability. Chameleon is so tough it will break competitive materials of larger diameter and higher stated breaking strength when they are tied together and pulled to the breaking point.

That last fact causes derogatory comment from some trying to knot a piece of wimpy, perhaps pet, material to Chameleon. It usually destroys the material they were told, or may believe, to be "the best." The hard surface and stiffness of Chameleon cuts soft and easily abraded material. Many experiencing such results—rather than recognizing the inherent superiority of Chameleon and embracing it—in a fog of ignorance, only berate the superior material. Chances are people read and believe too much industries' exaggeration about *supposed* abrasion resistance, thin diameter benefits, strength (knot and otherwise) and haven't spent enough time fishing and testing differing materials.

Don't be deceived by other models of Maxima leader. While Ultra-Green, Clear or Silver Maxima are as good, maybe better, as any soft material, they are not capable of Chameleon's performance. It was the original and still the best. It's been threatened by its makers, for a number of years, to sell knotted, ready-made leaders. I tried, repeatedly, to buy them when I owned a fly shop and never could despite their being advertised as available. (I tied and sold my own leaders of Chameleon.) Perhaps they are obtainable now. The current year's catalog by Maxima's distributors show the new knotted leaders will come only with tippets of Ultra-Green. It seems Maxima's providers have succumbed to prevalent limp tippet thinking. If formulas used are correct they will still be fine leaders. Replace the Ultra-Green tippet with Chameleon before use.

Legions of flyfishers will continue to use materials and leaders that destroy casts, scare fish, kink, curl, abrade and generally under perform. The fly shop guy wouldn't have sold them wrong—would he? Besides, it's "top" brand; it has to be good. Inferior materials will be used and forgiven their grief-causing for numerous flimsy reasons.

"Super" Materials

Few are immune to claims that a new material has nearly twice the strength for a given diameter of other material. After reading that the then new Dai-Riki had such attribute, I bought a full range of sizes. I was doing lots of steelheading and guiding at the time, fishing 10-pound tippets on dry flies and 8-pound on wets. Dai-Riki in the same reported diameter as 8-pound Chameleon tested a reported 15 pounds. I used my standard interlocking loops to attach the 15-pound miracle stuff where my favorite 8-pound would go and promptly lost the first three steelhead I hooked—all due to knot failure or wear-through at the fly eye.

I have the last loss video-taped as it happened while filming an instructional video to use in conjunction with my speaking engagements. This 10-pound fish, nearly whipped, wouldn't quit and swam in repeated tight circles beneath the rod tip. It slapped the leader with its tail on every revolution and was constantly changing the angle of pull on the fly imbedded in its upper jaw. It wore the Dai-Riki through at the hook despite its reported 15-pound breaking strength. It had poor abrasion resistance. I've caught quite a few steelhead on the fly rod and do not believe any of the three fish would have been lost using Chameleon of 8-pound test.

Leader Design and Loops

It's simple, efficient and cost effective to tie and experiment with your own leaders. You will probably have a good one when you can cast it easily and see it turn over flawlessly using only your hand and arm. In building leaders I use 40- and 30-pound test for the butt on 8- to 10-weight lines, 30- and 25-pound for 6- and 7-weights and 25- and 20-pound for 4- and 5-weights. Again, tying procedure and knots are covered in Chapter Eight. For now let's discuss why leaders are constructed in certain ways.

My butts are two-piece, first 3½ to 4 feet of the heaviest material and then 2 feet of the lighter. Next come 6- to 8-inch lengths, in .002- to .003-inch diameter steps, down to the size just above the tippet. I leave the last step above the tippet about 10 inches long. All connections are made with Blood knots. In larger sizes (40- to 20-pound test) two or three wraps, rather than the normally recommended five, hold securely and tighten easily. Take one wrap less with the heavier material being joined (e.g. two with 30-pound, three with 25-pound). The resultant knot is smaller, has a pleasing and functional taper and is plenty strong.

The final step section of our leader, you will remember,

was left 10 inches long. Say it is of 6-pound test. In its free end, tie a Perfection End Loop. Now take a 30-inch length of your desired tippet (it could be 6-, 5-, 4- or even 3-pound test Chameleon) and tie another Perfection Loop in one end. Interlock the two loops so they look like a Square knot when tightened. Do so by first putting the tippet's loop *over* the loop in leader end. Then thread the loose tippet end through the full leader's end loop and tighten. The described leader will be between 9 and 10 feet long.

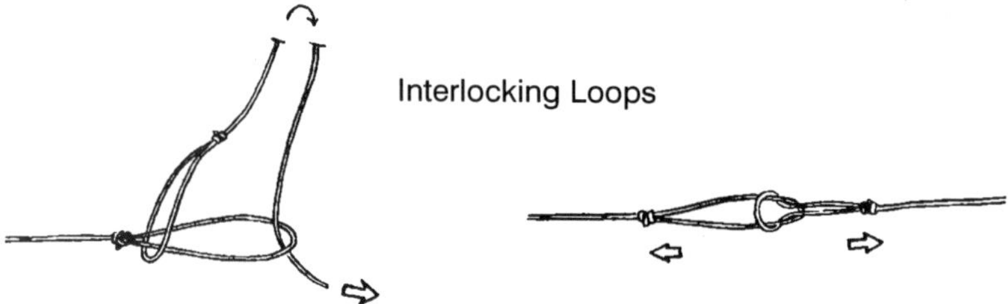

I have fished long, hard seasons with only one or at most two of my leaders per fly line. When forced to change tippet due to wear or cannibalization due to fly changes, simply add new tippet to the existing loop. It's fast and easy. But more importantly, you are not tying repeated knots in the final leader step quickly shortening it, destroying leader balance and requiring frequent retying of sections on up the leader. If you use purchased leaders, employing interlocking loops will find you using fewer of the too expensive things. Enjoyable and efficient flyfishing thrives on economy, simplicity and durability such as this looped-leader tippet system allows. Loops accommodate the use of differing brands of material as well and probably better than tying Blood or Surgeon's knots. Variations are easily accomplished.

The last leader section above the tippet would be of 12-pound test if you were building a leader for most steelheading, Atlantic salmon, bass or fish of larger size or requiring larger flies. That would include larger trout. This leader will handle tippets from 6- to 12-pound with 8- and 10-pound being ideal.

The leaders described are easy to modify if more or less length is needed. Lengthen or shorten the second butt section. In a pinch, and to lengthen a leader, add extra of the last section above the tippet (it's always with you) and then an extra long tippet of one or two sections. I use these methods if I want to fish a fly very deeply or present small flies to spooky fish. There are many other possibilities.

A System That Works

I guided trout-fishers from a drift boat for many years on Idaho's upper Salmon River. The casting was along and under brushy banks for wild rainbows and cutthroats. Fishing from a moving boat, casting to brush protected pockets, is never easy as some think, even for the best of casters. Believe it, I've had Steve Rajeff, the many-time world champion caster, in my boat. Before starting any float I ensured my supply of loop-tippeted, floatant-dressed (if required), flies of appropriate patterns, was adequate and handy. I would hang them on a small net hammock near my rowing seat. The other required action was to place a Perfection End Loop and appropriate tippet at the end of each client's leader, often after replacing their entire leader.

The stretches of the water I fished seldom allowed pulling to shore to fiddle with a broken leader. A fly broken in streamside brush means somebody will miss a lot of prime fishing unless you can get a new fly back on the water quickly. Since breaks would come in the lighter tippet, I could momentarily drop the oars, grab the client's leader, remove the broken leader and affix a fresh prerigged, prefloatant dressed fly and have the client back fishing about as quickly as you have read this sentence—maybe a little longer. If you want to become as adept at flyfishing as you can, you *need* control all the problem causing details and time wasters you possibly can. Leaders are the place to start.

Leader Tests

There are continuing research and testing results that circulate concerning the superiority of differing brands of leader material. One such landed in my mailbox just as the final work on this book was being completed.

This report included an eight-page "Independent Research and Testing Results" booklet. A full color advertisement enclosed with the report showed a bar-graph of eight popular brands of monofilament revealing their tested abrasion resistance. Maxima Chameleon ranked second; the promoted brand, Silver Thread Excalibur (registered trademark), ranked first with a ranking of over *nine times* more abrasion resistance than Chameleon. My curiosity was piqued.

I've read sensationalistic material comparisons before (remember the Dai-Riki example) and immediately called the Executive Director of Sales and Marketing for PRADCO, maker of the new wonder mono. I asked for small spools of material to test. They sell only large spools and offered to send those. I asked for 6- and 12-pound test. It arrived today.

My caliper showed the material's listed diameter as accurate. A quick test with a cutting, single Overhand knot in the 6-pound material showed the material broke very easily. Lubricated with saliva, the knot still broke easily. I then retrieved a spool of Maxima 6-pound test from my stash. It measures only one-half thousandth of an inch (.0005) larger in diameter but, nonetheless, feels finer in your hands. Perhaps the roughness of the new Excalibur makes it feel larger than Chameleon.

I tested the Overhand cutting knots in the 6-pound test Chameleon. It took markedly more pressure to break dry knots. Using a lubricated knot I couldn't break the Maxima, even by jerking on it, without cutting my hands. Interestingly, Chameleon beat the other seven materials in the "Independent Test" in the "Dynamic Load Impact" (jerking) test.

The only criteria wherein the eight lines were tested that Maxima ranked first among was the jerk test. As mentioned Maxima Chameleon ranked second in abrasion resistance testing. The eight tests were: diameter, abrasion resistance, wet knot strength, wet knot ultimate tensile strength (?), dynamic load impact, limpness, castability dry and castability wet. I'm not sure what all those fancy terms mean, if anything, but know some have little connection to flyfishing leaders. Maxima, despite two high ratings, finished dead last in the test.

I further tested the two materials by tying them together with five-wrap Blood knots then pulling until something broke. It was 50-50; the Maxima broke as often as the Excalibur. Then I tied Perfection End Loops in both materials, locked the loops together and pulled to breaking point again. The Excalibur knot failed first every time. Further, when I would grip what remained of a broken Excalibur loop with the pliers and continue to pull on the unbroken Maxima the Maxima would cut through the remaining Excalibur loop without breaking. Does that sound like nine times better and useful abrasion resistance to you? I also tied Turle Replacement knots on a turned-down eye hook with both materials. It took considerably more effort to break the Maxima thus tied than the Excalibur.

I've asked you to believe Maxima Chameleon to be superior material. Despite all the test comparisons you might read (and there are plenty), when you test what is important to flyfishing performance Chameleon shines through, it always has.

During my banking years I saw bogus reports and appraisals galore, often done by licensed and "professional" organizations or individuals. If you believe results of "independent" tests copyrighted and paid for by the winners of such tests you deserve what you will receive. I have biases as clearly stated in Chapter One and they include tackle preferences, however, I'm not paid by Maxima or trying to sell Chameleon—only trying to help flyfishers. Believe what you will.

Closing Thoughts

What of the new fluorocarbon leaders? Their diameters are not much smaller than similar strength Chameleon, and I've found you must be careful with or use knots different from the simple ones I prefer. Maybe the clear color of the Umpqua and Climax stuff I've been testing (after floating a loan to buy a couple of spools) is a help, as they postulate, but I doubt it. Time will tell.

There are many flyfishers without correct leaders or leader understanding. Leaders are responsible for final delivery of the fly. They must perform correctly and *repeatedly,* under adverse conditions and are responsible for a portion of fish fooling. As the weakest link in a chain, leaders exercise critical influence over the eventual capture of fish. You'd best know what you are about with them.

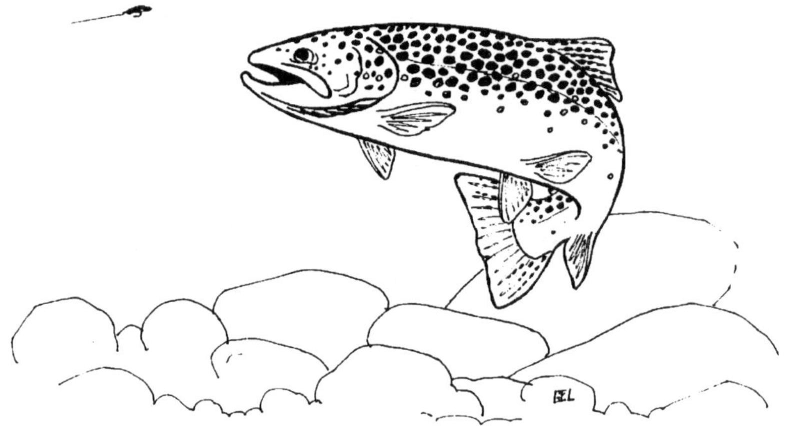

Chapter Four: Fly Lines

Since leaders are the most important tackle variable concerning effective flyfishing equipment, it logically and truthfully follows that fly lines are next in importance. Nearly any rod will cast a line—it being most dependent upon angler skill. And the best fly in the world is useless if the fly line and leader won't perform. The selection of specialty lines, sink rates, tapers, colors, prices and weights today is dizzying and unneeded. Most are of weight forward (WF) taper design. Created demand for differing lines means more profits for the flyfishing industries. But to what extent?

Most buyers of extra fly lines will want a new reel or spool, maybe reels and spools, and certainly more backing and leader. New rods find their way into line buyers' hands. If a "specialty" line is thought needed for certain situations or specific fish, is it unreasonable to think or be told a special fly rod will work best under also certain circumstances and with a specialty line? New, different or specialty fly lines account for a whole lot more tackle being sold—much unneeded. So what is needed? A light colored, double taper (DT), floating fly line, or several, best handle most flyfishing. Yet, many flyfishers will not believe. It's too simple and contrary what you're told or read elsewhere.

Line Disease

Most flyfishers have acute "weight forwarditis." It's not surprising; the flyfishing industries work to see you remain afflicted. Sell-siders know that over your "useful shop life" (remember that's the industries' view of you), you will buy twice as many fly lines if kept using WFs. Flyfishers, lacking knowledge of WF shortcomings, fall for ego massaging "distance line" nonsense or supposed special needs "requiring" the many WF specialty tapers. Many others, ignorant or oblivious, simply follow recommendations and end up with WF lines.

WFs can't be turned around like DTs when one end wears; you get to shell out $25 to $60 for another line—in half the time. Fly lines reportedly last for 200-250 hours of casting. Beginners and poor casters destroy fly lines more rapidly. They contribute heavily to industries' profits, *if* they notice or care their lines are worn. If not, their casting and fishing suffers. Even that enormous, cumulative, extra and unneeded cost to flyfishers palls in the face of other shortcomings and negative aspccts of WF use.

Maybe you don't care about cost or prefer to use "correct" WF lines. Let's see. You have been told or read that DTs are primarily for close and especially delicate presentations. That's false. Until recently—we will examine changes later—WFs and DTs had nearly identical front tapers.[1] Using casts of

[1]I use the length and diameter definitions for WFs and DTs shown in *McClane's Standard Fishing Encyclopedia* (1965). Doing so avoids the differentiations of the several line manufacturers and provides solid reference. WF limitations remain through producer manipulations to minimize them.

50 feet (35 feet of line plus leader and arm reach) or less, there is no measurable difference in delicacy. There can't be with identical front tapers. You can't cast or fish to long distances with a DT—wrong again. Nearly any caster can cast further, faster, more quietly, accurately and with considerably less work using a DT rather than a WF, certainly under fishing conditions. Again, that's further, faster, more quietly, accurately and with less effort. But that isn't what the "experts" say or what you have been told. Not always.

"Many times I have watched my friend Joe Humphreys, for example, cast the entire length of a double tapered line which makes me wonder just how much advantage there is to using weight forwards," says Ed Shenk, from *Fly Fishing Quarterly.* From a Fenwick Co. Tech Sheet: "Double-tapered lines are still preferred by many anglers because of the control they afford in achieving casting accuracy and their ease of manipulation while airborne and on the water." The last quote could give the impression that some idiots are "still" using DTs. It doesn't recognize the distance casting abilities of DTs as does the first, although it does recognize a DT's superior accuracy and controllability.

But we know Fenwick wants to sell all the fly lines possible and lots of industries' people writing sales spiels really know little of flyfishing. To wit: The most recent marketing booklet put out by SA says level lines have "no performance characteristics." Now what does that mean? The line won't bend, cast at all, it breaks, what? It's reasonable you require more proof of DT superiority; "weight forwarditis" is very hard to shake.

A Stillwater Situation

Imagine yourself in a boat or float-tube on a calm lake. You're fishing 65 feet of WF floating line; the line plus 10 feet of leader and your fly are on the water in front of you. You now wish to present your fly to a large and spooky, just visible and very soon to disappear fish. It's about 75 feet away but 45 degrees left of where your fly line lies. WF use requires you strip in at least 20 feet of line and leader. That's four or five noisy, time consuming strips, minimum. Stripping is required because a WF's skinny shooting line, when outside the rod tip, can't lift or support its heavy front taper during a pickup cast, let alone do it quickly or quietly. Nonetheless some try. A very few might be partially successful. They spook lots of fish. We continue.

After stripping in the running-shooting line, you lift the remaining line from the water and extend eight feet of running line on the first back cast—many can't. You plan to shoot the remaining ten feet or more of running line on the forward, presentation cast. Many can't do that either, necessitating several false casts to both extend needed line *and* complete the 45 degrees of angle change. Does the neurotic running line choose this time to snarl?

Small diameter WF running line has a nasty tendency to tangle on things or itself in a pressure situation. It's a problem accentuated by false casting. False casts are always time wasting and in this instance fish spooking and fraught with danger. At long last, you make your delivery. Is the fish still there? Did false casting spook it? Did the line tangle? Did the heavy, unsupported taper of the WF crash to the surface spooking the fish, as is typical? Too many things can go wrong and way too much time elapses using a WF.

Now watch, with your mind's eye, as a decent caster using a DT casts to the same fish. He sees the fish and (being a knowledgeable flyfisher knowing the casts would be long and requiring delicacy had rigged his rod with a DT one line-weight lighter than usual) merely picks the full extent of line from the water after starting it moving with one strip of his nonrod hand. On the back cast he adjusts for most of the angle change, corrects for the remainder on the forward cast and deftly presents the fly. It literally takes less time to do than read about. Perchance our caster is not the best or had not under lined the rod, he would strip in five to ten feet of line, easily lift the remainder from the water, back cast as described and shoot the stripped in line on the presentation cast. It's still very much faster, quieter and less obtrusive than WF use with much higher probability of hooking the spooky large fish.

The longer belly portion, beginning about 20 feet up a standard DT and continuing for about another 50 feet, has much greater stiffness and ability to lift and support more line weight and length than a WF. The long and thick portion of a DT line does not tangle as easily as does skinny WF running line. We've seen those attributes demonstrated, but there are many more. The longer, stiffer, uniform belly of a DT "hangs in the air," giving softer, quieter fly delivery. Extra weight and the longer, thick belly diameter provide elongated mass and inertia to buck air resistance and gravity. A DT defeats wind much better than a WF. The large and uniform belly of a DT increases accuracy of casts markedly. Uniformity of a DT's belly diameter, without a WF's extra taper changes, allows you to place the line as you want with greater precision. WFs accentuate other problems.

We've seen DTs allow long lengths of line to be lifted from water's surface. Trying to pick up long lengths of WF taper is natural and needed, but laws of gravity and physics won't oblige. Such need and the fact that most flyfishers use WFs have contributed to the many too-stiff fly rods. In vain attempts to overcome WF limitations, misunderstanding fly-fishers try to lift and carry long lengths of line by using ever stiffer rods. It's scientifically unsupported procedure, hence unsuccessful, discouraging and detrimental flyfishing success and enjoyment. There's further misunderstanding.

It's advantageous and important that false casts may be less precise using a DT. An example: Anyone using or understanding shooting heads (30-foot lines backed by thin running-shooting line) knows they drop like stones on forward or back casts if timing isn't near perfection. Shooting heads are anything but delicate of presentation since their thin and soft running line can't support the heavy head in the air. *Precisely the same unsupported collapsing and rapid drop happens to a WF* on casts with more than about 40 feet of line. It doesn't happen as rapidly with a DT. You have more time with a DT where fractions of a second count. Gravity and physics aren't ignorant or wrongly biased as are many fly tackle sellers and WF users.

WFs place a premium on precise timing and slack line control. To cast long effectively with a WF, the "distance" taper, the average caster can only extend line on the last back cast. Pray for absolute perfect timing and hope to shoot a lot of running line, unless you are a very good caster with consistent, excellent timing and superb slack controlling hands. Most aren't. Casting and particularly slack control is difficult when wading in current, when the winds blow or with problems like bushes or boat cleats. Razor-sharp timing requires regular, frequent practice.

On a good day, I will cast a full, 90-foot, DT under fishing conditions. It takes a couple of back casts, but extreme lengths of line may be carried in the air compared to that possible with a WF. It's not as difficult as may be thought. Carrying long lengths of DT in the air will prove easy for most casters. Shooting controllable DT line is easier than WF's tangle prone running line—easier because weight of the extended DT works for, not against, you. Force of the moving and extended DT wants to rip line to be shot from your line hand despite its being easier to grip than skinny WF running line. Potentially higher line speed of a WF is useless when shooting line tangles. Only the heavy front portion of a WF is capable of retaining maximum speed, and it can't always drag the "shooting" line behind.

The presentation comparison of the example is germane to most on or near surface fishing for near still-water, be it river, lake or ocean. Disagree or doubt all you want. But be prepared to disprove the laws of gravity and physics as they affect cast fly lines when you do. Let's look at a floating DT's even greater advantages fishing flowing water.

Flowing Water

This time imagine yourself wading thigh deep in a favorite river, perhaps stalking finicky small mouth bass or tossing giant stonefly dries to heavy water rainbows. I envision swinging a barely submerged, sparse Claret and Black through a greasy slick—a known steelhead lie. It's mid-fall and the last hour before dark. The evening is quiet, the fish known present and the shadows long. It's not a matter of if I'll hook a fish, only when. If I do my part correctly the steelhead will. If you don't mind, set your vision aside for a moment and wade with me.

We'll start at the very top of a long and wide run, just below the riffle spill. The water is submerged rock-studded there, beginning to get dark and secretive. Casts will be 80 to 85 feet once we get going; that's 65 feet of floating DT, 10 feet of leader and 5 to 10 feet of rod and arm reach more or less. You are on my left, upstream, side. We begin with 20 feet of line. Experience, here and elsewhere, causes me to make the first casts and swings short. You never know for sure where fish might hold in water like this. I will extend each cast by five or six feet until the needed 80 plus feet are reached. Then we will start the two short steps and cast steelheaders' waltz.

Each new cast, after reaching 85 feet, begins by pointing the rod downstream at the hanging fly, stripping once, then again faster while simultaneously snapping the rod into a high back cast. The line and leader, 70 plus feet, straightens behind us. I haul lightly on the line with my left hand *just* before starting the forward cast and easily shoot the stripped-in line to place the line on the water across stream from our position. Now the critical part.

Before the line or leader can settle, I mend, strongly, (it's more a modified roll cast) clear to the fly if I can. That sets the line and leader several feet upstream from the fly. I mend again, immediately, setting the middle portion of the line upstream and then again, more gently this time, to position the line just beyond the rod tip. Those mends, quickly and correctly executed, are critical to our success. They slow the speed of the fly. Such slowing is customarily needed for a steelhead run's character and current speed.

With the line situated I either lead or follow the fly with the rod as current dictates. No other mends or line manipulations are made, for I have a recurring nightmare of long standing. It invokes a holding steelhead, a large and tense male watching a swinging, near-surface fly. With malice in its heart, it's making precise calculations of the fly's speed and angle of travel planning an uncivil interception. Then the fly darts unnaturally upstream. Someone *mended*—destroying the steelhead's target solution. He decides he'll let the fly pass; something's wrong.

We proceed, forced by deepening water to wade close to the shore, continuing our probing of the run to a point where a sudden line of willows, 15 or more feet high and extending the full remaining 50 yards of the run, rises behind us stopping all possibility of future back casts. Then, at mid-current, there is a disturbance—more accurately a large upsurging of water—near the fly. No touch or weight is felt through the line. I hear you gasp audibly and figure you've never steelheaded before. The fly is allowed to complete its swing. Steelhead are prone to follow a fly they have examined. They loop, after turning out-current, below the fly, and sometimes take as the fly approaches the end of its swing. It's particularly true if the water is deep enough at swing's end to allow them comfort. Not this time.

We know the fish is out there and excited. I repeat the cast, nothing happens. Steelhead, having risen and refused a fly, often move out and down current from their original position. We take the two steps downstream, but now a normal back cast is impossible because of the willows behind. Not to worry, as the line hangs downstream I make three rapid retrieving strips with my arm and rod pointing as far downstream as possible. As the third strip is started I use the rod to heave the line as far up- and out-stream as possible. Pivoting one's body helps.

The rod is immediately lifted. In so doing I feed a *little* of the stripped slack back out the guides, simultaneously dragging *more* line, on the water, beyond the rod tip, back toward us. That's done to get cast killing slack under control while keeping all the line possible on the water in position to be cast. I continue to raise the rod to a vertical position, right hand near right shoulder. The waterborne line is rapidly drifting downstream, and the airborne line, beyond the rod tip, is bellying behind me. When the drifting line is in front of me I snap the rod tip down, hard, into a roll cast. Remaining slack line is snatched from my hand by the line and leader rolling out to the full 75 plus feet. The first required mend is made even before the rod fully recovers from the roll cast followed by the intermediate and short mends. Now we're fishing.

No boil comes, only a muted underwater flash of silver-pink is seen. Simultaneously, and for only a second, the line feels somehow heavy, different. Then the line snaps upward, throwing spray, guitar-string tight. The rod plunges, the reel sounds, and my rod hand's middle finger tingles again where line or backing always rips across. That lived for, exhilarating feeling of being totally, if only briefly, out of control inundates. I think I hear you yell. We both see the large hen steelhead jump, heading down and out stream, as the old Hardy and proven Lamiglas gain predictable, if too rapid, control.

For many circumstances and fish species, unobtrusive, efficient, correctly angled presentations of proper speed are crucial to success. Long casts and near equally long and precise mends are needed even after attaining the best casting position. Of the two, mending is recurrently more important. There is no way a person using a standard WF could have correctly fished the run just described, or many others. If there were always back cast room (there isn't), long mends are still required. It's impossible to roll cast or mend a WF as needed, beyond 45 feet or a little more. A WF's thin running-shooting line can't move its heavy belly section as required in mending and roll casting.

The run I described exists. Persons fishing it, and others similar, handicapped by WFs can't fish correctly. If they could reach the distant fish holding slots, they can't mend as required. WF fishers make such disturbance trying that they hook few fish—even the ones that hold close.

Other Possibilities

Use one of the new long-belly or strange taper WF lines you say. Sure, they might work in some places, but you still fall prey to "force them to buy another line—soon" schemers. Long-belly WFs are nothing but inferior DTs, without the beneficial feature of reversibility. Don't allow overwhelming by the specialty WFs now offered (bass-bug, bonefish, bill-fish, steelhead, pike-muskie, multicolor, differing stiffnesses, etc.).

Another possibility is to use a Spey or two-handed rod to fish what many would consider difficult water. Spey rods are cumbersome and heavy (despite two-handed use) and give undeniable grief in fighting and landing fish. They're also expensive and ugly. There are worthy reasons Europeans, inventors of two-handed rods, have moved away from two-handed rod use that shouldn't be forgotten. A few casters may have physical limitations favoring rods needing two hands to operate. Many flyfishers are gullibly sold or in ignorance desire the "benefits" of WFs and now Spey or two-handed rods. The sizable, undeniable and unconquerable negatives of both are ignored or unknown.

Wrong line and rod use so often stems from angler ignorance or worse, "expert" recommendation backed by half-knowledge or sales gain. I suspect Spey rod users will largely return to single handed rods when negatives are discovered, but it will take a while. It might not be all bad; super long, heavy and goofy Spey rods are usually rigged with DTs; their users should come to understand DT superiority. Single handed rods, *DT equipped,* get jobs done admirably with less grief, cost and earned feeling of ability and accomplishment.

When it comes to two-handed rods (and many other things), the allure is great: Flyfishers paint and carry wishful, if illogical, mind pictures, want to be on the supposed cutting edge, gain advantage over fishing competition, mysteriously improve casting skills and effectiveness, listen to too many experts and are perhaps too easily awed by a two-handed rod's potential to cast far. Casting far is seen as Mecca by many while mending is ignored. In truth, it's almost always counter productive to cast far if you can't control line and fly as needed once on the water. Many flyfishers stubbornly or stupidly fail to recognize or admit such. Try to accomplish *quick, nonfly-disturbing* mends with a 12- to 16-foot telephone pole of a rod. It's more than likely flyfishers failing to admit truth or practice to obtain competency casting single-handed rods will do any better with one requiring two hands and even more practice. Successful flyfishing requires certain actions.

Persons knowing or intuitively sensing what's needed in certain fishing situations are often equipped with inappropriate tackle, particularly leader and line, often rod. Inappropriate tackle defeats intuition. It's a sad case of tackle limiting user. Tackle used was probably recommended to be the latest, best, correct, what was needed or what some famous author or expert and just everybody uses. In that "everybody" are a good many of the 90% who catch only 10% of the fish, possibly the famous authors and experts. (It's certainty many of those selling and recommending tackle are among the 90%.) I fish to catch fish, learn, enjoy myself, nature and friends, in about that order. Thinking for yourself and using basic sense and reason is required if becoming the best flyfisher you can is your goal. Ignore ignorance.

Keep an open mind and ponder any advice, including mine. Question advice, articles, books and conversations until you see—with clear understanding—that simplicity, common sense and basic truth support theory or practice. Much advice regarding lines and other things isn't so supported. Ego, lack of *meaningful* experience, any profit or sales motivation, hero worship and sophistication account for lots of wrong-headed advice. Believe it and suffer. Ask lots of questions and contemplate answers.

Remember a vociferous DT spurning, but "correct," or "expert," WF user enjoying some success by virtue of living near the water, gullible fish, simple casts, numerous hours fished or knowing exactly where his limited tackle works probably never considers what could have been done and learned or *fish uncaught*. You might.

Lines Compared

Comparisons of DTs and WFs always concern lines of equal size (i.e., 4-weight, 7-weight, etc.) unless noted. DT lines have negative aspects, minor, compared to their superior attributes.

Your reel's backing capacity will be reduced by 10 to 15% (according to a recent Winston Rod Co. catalog). But backing capacities shown by reel companies are notoriously suspect and all save one or two show capacities only with WF lines. That latter fact gives the impression that using a DT line is somehow wrong. Manufacturers actually do it to show larger supposed backing capacities, appear correct and sophisticated and of course to sell more WF lines. When was the last time you, or anyone, was dependent on the last 20 or 30 yards of backing? If you hook something nasty enough to clean your DT and backing, it will also take the last few extra yards of backing behind a WF—if you could have hooked it in the first place using a WF. Hope it happens. You will remember such occurrence when fish caught are long forgotten. It's wise, however, to always use correct tackle that is well maintained to land such a fish when it comes.

Water resistance on the line may be greater when fighting a fish with a DT's longer, greater diameter. The fish would have to take and keep a lot of line to notice much difference and that would be partially negated by the DT's shorter length compared to a WF. It's a minor, if any, problem.

Wind may get a larger purchase on the larger diameter DT belly line; but it will move the skinny running line of a WF easier. Advantage in wind lies with the DT's ability to buck wind due to its greater weight. Heavier weight retains velocity longer and is less affected by wind. That's precisely why long range rifle shots use heavy bullets for bore size.

Lifting long lengths of larger DTs (8-weight and over) can be difficult for casters without developed arm and back muscles. Practice will develop muscles while improving timing. Heavy line weight is beneficial to distance casting. Many new users of two-handed rods, incapable of using a DT 8-weight on a single-handed rod due lack of practice, will find the stresses of a two-handed rod worse. Nor will lack of practice facilitate timing dependent WF use.

Possible WF use lies in limiting yourself to water where less than 45 feet of line is used or where back cast room is always ample. Some smaller waters favor such distance limitations, but few always offer unimpaired back cast room. Persons looking for uncomplicated situations on larger water will find any easy water limited, full of people and with spooked or nonexistent fish. Without ability to make long casts and mends, often needed in pressured modern fisheries, people hook far fewer fish than they might. It's true some fish will respond to poor casting and "wrong" presentations common to WF use. The 37 people who already fished the easy water earlier in the day or yesterday probably hooked or spooked those sophisticated fish. I see numerous flyfishers trying to make a flyfishing life on the backs of the easy fishing places, naive fish and WF lines. Maybe they're happy and don't consider what could be or options available, including those concerning lines.

Color, stiffness, weight—what can be had in one taper is usually available in the other. Light colored floating DTs are preferred. They are most visible to humans in low light, blend best against most sky conditions and are less visible to fish—in theory anyway. The Department of the Navy paints the bottoms of its ships white. Their tests show white is least visible from below, at least to humans.

Should you use a stiff or soft line? Stiffer lines perform best for distance casting, and each bending of a fly line (or a fly rod) destroys some small fraction of original stiffness. Don't start with something too soft. Cortland lines have always seemed limp compared to Scientific Angler (SA) lines. Cortland gives a $1 rebate per line to people selling their lines. SA doesn't. That's why lots of Cortlands get sold. Cortland lines I've used, besides being soft and limp, always feel sticky, and it never goes away. If you checked a new Cortland line today, I'll bet the coils of line would be stuck together. The same goes for one wrapped on a reel for a while. Stickiness, as limpness, robs distance from casts. Stiffer lines may take a set or remain in coils more than a softer line, but a well stretched and broken-in stiffer line gives few problems.

Some say a limp line works best in conflicting currents for fussy dry fly or nymph fishing. Soft lines may also lend themselves to shorter casts. I say may, because far more knowledgeable flyfishers I know use stiffer SA lines for all purposes than those using Cortland or other brands. There are also lines of decreased stiffness, even by SA, for "special" purposes. They aren't needed. Producers and sales people will disagree as they want to sell more lines by capitalizing on minutiae, real or imagined. If you desire the most delicate of presentations and protection from complex currents, *modify your leader.* Continue to use a stiffer, light-colored double tapered line.

Achieving the Most for the Least

Suppose you have floating DT5-, 6-, and 7-weight lines for your favorite, and *correctly designated,* 6-weight rod. You have tremendous versatility with this arsenal. If the casts are long, the fish spooky, the leader light and the flies small, use the DT5-weight. If you expect average conditions with mostly moderate casting distances and a variety of fly and tippet sizes, use the DT6-weight. If the casts are to be short, the flies quite large and heavy or wind is expected, use your DT7-weight. You will be able to make more accurate, longer casts and mends or buck windy conditions better than you could with a WF6- or 7-weight. If you use the DT5-weight for the needed long and delicate casts, they will land softer and more accurately than a WF could present them.

Unlike removing the tag from your mattress, there is no legal penalty for using lines other than 6-weight on a 6-weight rod. If desiring only one line, choose a DT over a WF to procure advantage. It's a darn shame that poor equipment limits so many people, doubly so when someone unqualified or too "expert" recommends a WF over a DT floating line. You can bracket any rod's true (not necessarily designated) line weight with floating DTs as per the example quite reasonably compared to buying extra rods, reels and lines. Some flyfishers may think they don't need or can't learn to use DT's advantages. If so, they should also remember continuing WF use limits, slows and may prohibit flyfishing improvement. Let's see what the industries are doing.

The front taper section (9 to 10 feet) of WFs and DTs were near identical for many years. Recently some manufacturers altered those of DTs, lengthening them, for greater supposed delicacy. Such alterations were unneeded but do not affect the superior performance of DT lines. The belly *plus* front taper portion of a standard WF was, for many years, about 30 feet in length. Now producers are altering the belly length, increasing it by several feet. Hallelujah—they're going to make DTs out of WFs. Well, it's a start anyway. I suspect the reason is a clumsy response to the many too-stiff rods sold or perhaps recognition of DT superiority (the latter is my attempt at a joke). If you have a newer rod that seems a better fire-poker than a fly rod, you'll find a DT will work better. It will force a stiff, wrongly labeled, rod to bend as longer lengths of DT are extended increasing cast line weight.

New Lines

Needing to originate and differentiate minor line manufacturers have introduced radical line designs. RIO Products, an Idaho firm, is just marketing WFs with 30-foot front sections of one given weight and belly sections behind two line-weights heavier, as I understand their advertising. Such design is decidedly DT-like. I think RIO has problems correctly identified. Such lines would better load too-stiff rods and buck wind better. But WF brainwashing of flyfishers always seems to dominate. Would this new and special WF design work any better than using different weight DTs? Not unless their belly sections were very long and then only for applications where more, not less, weight is needed. It's a step in the right direction, however.

Line Care

It's wise to obtain all the use you can from fly lines. Follow manufacturers' suggestions for maintaining fly lines. Substances, like insect repellent or solvents can damage a line's finish. When gunk accumulates on floating lines, I strip them into a sink and first soak then scrub them gently with dish-soap. It works best if you catch accumulation before it gets heavy. Drying then dressing a heavily used line, even astream, is a decent idea. It may not markedly aid casting, but it will increase mending ability. Strip the line from the reel;

hang it over trees, bushes, whatever is handy. When it has dried awhile, dress lightly with Mucilin. Off the subject, Mucilin is another of flyfishing's old but proven "good things." I have used it for years as fly floatant as well as line dressing. I now mix about two parts of Mucilin with one part of the additive black-powder shooters use to keep their powder dry. It's the "dryingest" stuff I've ever seen.

Sinking Fly Lines

Full or partially sinking fly lines of any taper aren't much needed and are very often counterproductive flyfishing effectiveness. Few modern flyfishers will admit seriously thinking about it, let alone agree with me. Exceptions are use in still or very slow water. Despite personal bias that learning stymieing technology is a cheap substitute for simple tackle alterations, knowledge and skill, there are other reasons to avoid sinking lines—reasons particularly germane to any water moving by effect of wind, gravity or tide.

Problems in Current

Successful flyfishing (tradition supporting, ethical, efficiency catching fish, learning and enjoying yourself) boils down to: Fishing where the fish are then exerting control over line and leader at all times causing flies to fish correctly. Once line sinks below moving water's surface, a flyfisher relinquishes nearly all control. Whim of current dictates. The same is true when leaders sink. The greater the amount or depth of sunken leader and line, the greater the loss of control. Why won't more flyfishers admit such basic truth? If they will admit it, why won't they learn and change to their advantage? I wish I knew. I suspect lots of flyfishers can't handle truth that disturbs their feelings of well-being or correctness. They don't take flyfishing seriously. That doesn't keep such types from complaining about success or rendering opinions, however.

Flyfishers often have poor understanding and an inaccurate mental picture of what happens to sunken lines, leaders and flies in current. Lines do not drift along straight, evenly sunk or sinking. Actually, tremendous bellies or bends, often conflicting, develop causing flies to fish head-downstream with excess speed. It's always so. Water near surface almost always travels faster than water near bottom. Placing line in differing flow speeds, horizontally *or* vertically, must cause bellies. From beginning to end of a sunken line's down and across, obstruction uncomplicated, current swing the fly gains speed. It's analogous to the end person of the chain in the childhood game of crack-the-whip. Such action causes sunken flies to rise, often when flyfishers think, or want, the fly deepest. Review the diagrams on the next page to see what happens in fishing situations with sinking and floating lines.

To minimize bellying and whipping (it can't be eliminated with sinking lines or wet-tips and casts over a few feet in length) a fisher must make casts at downstream angles. That drastically reduces water that could be effectively covered (up to 75%) and time available for fly sink. The solution, to better water coverage, is seen as faster sinking lines and more heavily weighted flies. Flyfishers go to extremes trying to fish flies deeply, ignoring the law of diminishing returns. Downstream casting, miserable heavy flies and equally miserable sinking lines hinder effective, enjoyable casting and fishing. Fishing inefficiency reigns for want of learning to cast, use and mend a floating DT. Then you could both sink *and* control flies on a long leader for extensive water coverage. Flies must be controlled for good reason.

Think about items of living fish food freely drifting in current and actions of mobile nymphs or baitfish. Such things may drift or swim head-downstream at times, but it isn't normal—they probably can't breathe well. They may also rise naturally toward the surface. Freely drifting things *never* move faster than the current. Flies on sinking lines or wet-tips nearly *always* do. If swimming fish food moves faster than current, it does so by only small amounts or in brief spurts, nothing akin the crack-the-whip increasing speed flies fished on sinking lines develop. Even credulous fish or those that strike for reasons other than feeding are poorly approached with flies zipping along, head-downstream. Stripping sunken, impossible to pick up, lines back to yourself in stream situations causes snags, fly losses and wasted time.

Flyfishers waste tremendous time and effort, damaging their own and other's flyfishing effectiveness, spook and catch fewer fish by muddling with sinking lines in current—certainly in water no more than six feet deep, often deeper. Such damaging mistake is second only to that of using WF rather than

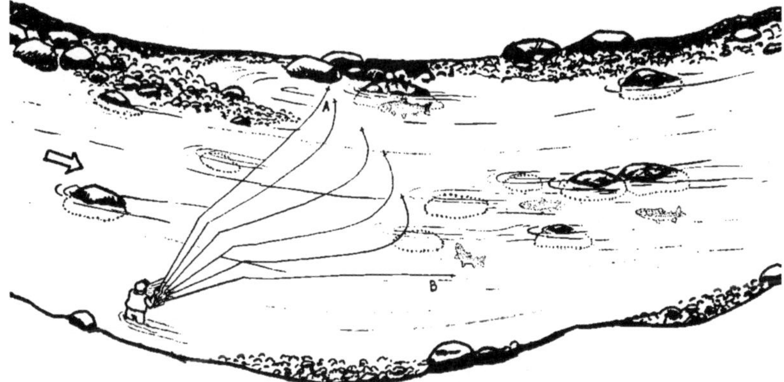

Wet-tip line. Fly gains unnatural, belly-caused speed from A to B, resulting in fish refusals.

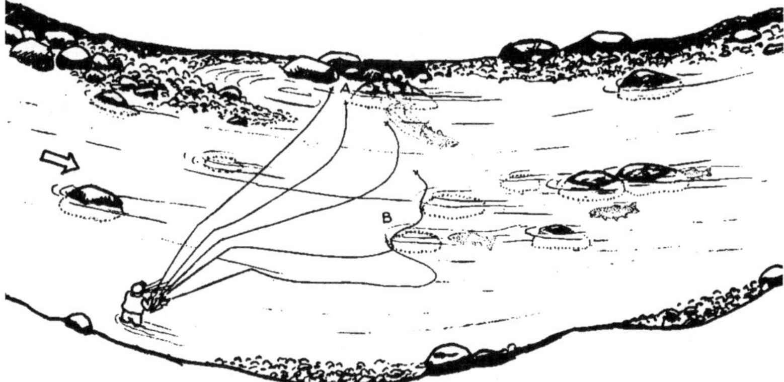

Sinking line. Shallow water fish near A spooked by dragging fly. Fly snags solidly at B.

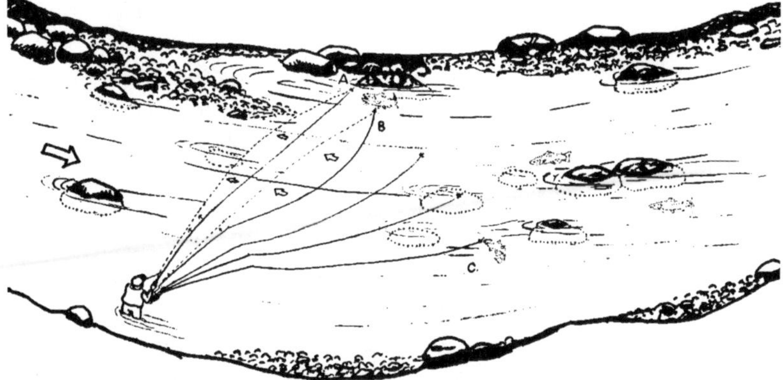

Mendable, floating DT line. Fish commonly take between A and B and anywhere from B to C.

DT lines. If flies must be fished deeply, more success would be enjoyed with a floating, mendable (therefore controllable) DT, a long leader, sparsely dressed fly and perhaps a bit of weight added to the leader (where legal). It's also possible to use short pieces of lead-core line looped into leader butt. Since flies fished on sinking lines in current commonly fail to fish as deeply as users think or want, the same or greater depth and more effectiveness can be attained more easily, enjoyably and effectively with a floating DT. Validly experienced and more accomplished fishers are more likely to understand DT advantages.

Sinking line and wet-tip usage in flowing water is widely recommended and practiced today. Proponents are often neo-flyfishers or sophisticates. Advocates listen to modern experts, read books and articles or believe industries' sales spiels and rely on technology's "quick fix" rather than skill. That damages potential effectiveness. Many flyfishers don't want to hear or believe facts, admit lack of ability, understanding or mistakes. Many of them will doubtless think me wrong recounting opinion of "experts" to "prove" their method's validity despite factual support of what's presented here. About now some readers could be considering all the fish caught on sunken lines in current. They should also consider the *extra* fish that could and should have been caught and the increased ease and enjoyment of catching *all* of them. Bill McMillan, a fine flyfisher and author, noted the advent of sinking lines set flyfishing back 20 years—and that was over 20 years ago. Will people never learn? Is modernism worth any cost to heritage, tradition and possibly flyfishing ethics?

Fishing flies deeply and effectively in current via skill and knowledge, not inefficient technological cheating, is extremely rewarding and builds better flyfishing skill. Fishing deep with a floating DT isn't difficult, only misunderstood. It requires assuming best casting position, casting well upstream, stacking and mending slack to allow fly sink. Strike indicators aren't needed. Paying close attention, roll casting ability and controlling slack is. As for "expert" opinion mentioned above and held out to support sinking line use in flowing water, one only needs reference other expert advice—stock market experts, for example. They commonly cause those following their advice terrible, catastrophic and devastating financial loss. Stock market soothsayers have been outperformed by monkeys throwing darts at lists of stocks to buy. Flyfishing experts can, however, cause excruciating loss. Not catching fish you should is very much more serious than mere loss of money. There are other reasons to avoid sinking lines.

Sinking lines are thinner than floating lines and made of different materials or by different processes. They have different casting dynamics and "feel." Few, even their proponents, consider them enjoyable to cast. Combination floating-sinking lines undergo a change in dynamics somewhere along their length at the float-sink junction causing an irksome hinging effect. Casting a tight loop (generally desirable) results in a stacked-up, collapsing and splashy mess at the end of casts made with combination lines. Sophisticated flyfishing pedagogue, Lefty Kreh, even believes that. Most casters compensate by modifying their casting, possibly acquiring hard to shed bad habits. I did. It was back in my unseasoned youth when I was pursuing flyfishing's Holy Grail and following all the Gurus I could—what a bunch of horse manure and wasted time that was. Perhaps not all was wasted. I learned of things said to work that did not, being unable to refute nature's laws.

Only a few DT sinking lines or wet-tips are made. If I were forced to use a wet-tip in flowing water, it would be a DT. With it I could still mend, albeit with decreased effectiveness, and certainly pick up more line, including the sodden tip—distinct advantages.

Sinking Lines and Still Water

Sinking lines are for still water. I use an oddball bunch of them made by cutting and then splicing loops into the ends of sundry lines. Most are some form of shooting-head. You can buy sinking or combination lines with many, too many, sink rates. Manufacturers claim they can make the varying diameters of a tapered line sink at the same rate. Maybe. Floating lines should float high and sinking lines sink, not dawdle down. I use faster sinking heads, controlling fly depth and how it fishes by varying leader and cast length or sinking time allowed. "Intermediate" lines, popular with the sophisticated, are agonizingly slow sinkers or deathly inefficient floaters. Intermediates might defeat wind-caused belly for near-surface fishing, but made only in WF configuration, they're as useless as other WFs for distance work. If I fished a good deal over sunken lake weeds, I might consider a slow sinking line. Still water has certain easy fishing characteristics.

In still water, unlike flowing water, you can, more or less, count on sinking lines and leaders staying straight from you to your fly. Subtle currents, wind and varying sink rates along the line alter straight lines. You can't always tell to what extent since a sunken line can't be seen as may a bright floater. It doesn't seem to cause much problem in my fishing. It's possible to correctly fish a deeply sunk line and fly in current-free water, and responding to unannounced pulls of who-knows-what has allure.

Of late I've been doing some lake fishing. Streams are high with runoff, and those close to home are primarily westslope cutthroat inhabited. I like cutthroats, grew up catching them, and have caught plenty. While pretty fish, easy to catch and living in super environs, I'm burnt-out with them, so I've been on a hunt, encompassing three states, for large brook trout. The best are found in a very few lakes, and the largest brookies hold deeply, near drop-offs.

Extensive driving time to lakes and sitting in a float-tube waiting for boring sinking lines to gain, or is it lose, 15 or 20 feet of depth causes significant consideration of sinking line fishing. It's tedious drudgery but necessary when targeted fish are deep and refuse to respond to near surface flies. Fat, lazy brookies are often like that. Lifting sunken line into back cast puts heavy load on rod, wrist and arm. Ripping and efficiently lifting any serious length of heavy sinking line free of water, while sitting in a float-tube, is nearly impossible. The load on the rod, created in trying, must equate to something near false casting a chunk of line 5 or 6 weights too heavy for the rod, maybe more. Sinking lines need be stripped nearly to yourself before pickup, but that's offset by the fly sometimes being in fishy water. It's always slow fishing with a sinking line. If my sought brookies would come to, or were found in, water even eight feet deep I could catch them with a floating line and enjoy faster, easier casting and fishing.

Other Problems and Solutions

I question sinking line colors being as desirable as they could be. Near the surface, dark lines must be very visible to fish looking upward. I have a clear sinking line, seldom used, and wonder if it magnifies or transmits light to appear fiber-optic or neon bright underwater. Sinking lines are usually shades of green, brown or black. Their colors are quite homogeneous, so it doesn't pay to worry. We don't have the hue choices available in floating lines. Sinking line's boring tendencies are far reaching.

People fishing sinking lines, particularly in current, are of wearisome single dimensional ability. If told that, they may recoil and quickly assure you they always have extra lines or heads with them and can change lines as situations dictate, "any time they want." So who really suffers the grief or takes the time away from fishing to *frequently* change lines? If flowing water is being fished and the angler moves or wades, need for differing presentation can change frequently. Nothing beats the speed and versatility of a floating line.

A DT facilitates fast pickups, all casting, mending and water coverage. Only a floating line allows effective, easy alteration of cast angles and mends with varying fly weights and types to quickly meet changing requirements of fly presentation *while* providing the fisher maximum fly control.

If water is anything but very small in stature, then a DT rather than a WF is needed to accomplish long mends, roll casts and slack stacking. Large or small water can be fished with a DT. A WF is marginally suitable for only small water. Why would anyone then consider anything other than a floating DT? You get twice the lines for the your money and gain extensive potential to be effective. Floating DTs are the most effective, versatile, and economic of all lines, but more WFs, floating and sinking, are sold. You know why.

The tip of new lines may be ineffectual in transferring the power of the cast to the leader. They often seem too limp or small of diameter. I cut 12 to 18 inches from new lines to reach stiffer material before attaching leader butt. Examine some new line tips yourself. See if you find the same problem. It's similar to leader problems, more felt limpness than measured diameter deficiency. Perhaps recent or "new" lines are better.

Despite feeling the "new and improved" features of modern lines are mostly bogus, I occasionally test some. I can't see where newer floating lines perform any better than the Air Cel and Air Cel Supreme lines of 30 years ago. Perhaps memory fools, but floating fly line materials or at least manufacturing haven't changed significantly since the 1960s. Most of the distorted or supposed improvements in lines of recent manufacture, like so many things in flyfishing, are minute, arcane, contrived, superficial or nonexistent.

Backing

This seems the correct place to discuss backing. Backing's first purpose is to fill reels to level for optimum performance. Nearly as important is safety when large or strong fish are encountered. Flyfishers have long used braided dacron for backing. It's thin in diameter, allowing more to be used. It doesn't rot or stretch much. If backing material stretches, as when fighting a large fish and it is wound back onto the reel in an elongated condition, it will eventually return to its original, shorter length. That can and does happen with enough constricting force in the many layers of backing to bend reel parts. That usually ruins the reel. Don't use monofilament or nylon material for backing, it stretches. Dacron abrades quite easily. Inspect it frequently paying most attention to that portion near the backing's junction to fly line.

Line Costs

I have a copy of a late newsletter from the Gink Co., maker of fly floatant among other things, that states the recent cost of making a fly line to be between 87 cents and a little over one dollar. Would you care to speculate why lines cost up to $60.00? What benefit some of those excess dollars could achieve for our fish and fisheries. I'm certainly not anti-capitalist and just as certainly against price gouging. I make my fly lines last and last; damned if I'll contribute to profiteering. I build rods, tie flies and leaders and have considered making my own lines, somehow.

There's more to say about fly lines that will be covered in Chapter Six on rod-line balance. For now let's look at fly rods.

Chapter Five: Fly Rods

Fly rods are "the icons" of flyfishing despite relative unimportance. They are certainly unimportant compared to understanding and using correct leaders and lines and unimportant compared to a person's ability to *use* a fly rod. But casting practice, lines and leaders aren't so engaging, and people want to believe fly rods are important. Fly rods are different from other rods in use and appearance and perhaps mysterious of construction materials and hardware. Persons giving them unjustified importance understand them least. Fly rods are simple levers, extensions of the arm, flingers and propellers of line for those who know how to use them; nevertheless, fly rods are needed, and good ones have desirable characteristics.

Desirable Fly Rods

Describing desirable characteristics of fly rods is mildly perplexing; it leads to the unavoidable land of elusive and vague terms. Notwithstanding, a fly rod should posses "lightness" in the hand compared to rods of similar line rating even in the heavier 8-plus-weight rods. As important is a bending or flexing pattern, sometimes called "action," that accommodates an easy casting style. A rod's action must be neither too stiff or soft and exude power, subtlety, along its full length under moderate flexion. You need feel the bending of the rod blank under your hand on the grip. The desirable attributes of lightness in hand and pleasing action contribute heavily to fly rod "feel." All rods have some kind of feel but not "the feel" we want or can best use.

While "feel" as used so far is vague, all desirable and cherished rods are possessors of whatever it is. I've experienced correct feel in rods of all materials: Fiberglass, graphite, boron and bamboo. Rods lack feel for a variety of reasons, and there are a number of identifiable attributes that contribute to feel, besides the dominant two discussed. I won't leave you with something slippery and undefined. Discussing all characteristics of rods that contribute and add up to desirable feel is the main topic of this chapter.

Soft and slow rods are often heavy, or at least seem heavy in the hand. Very light rods are likely to be stiff or too short and small in stature, but not always. Excess felt weight and stiffness limit effectiveness and joy of use. Increasing stiffness in every year's line of new rods has been the recent rage until a couple of years ago. It seems major rod company sages who shamelessly promoted ever stiffer rods suddenly realized their mistakes and started backpeddling, or maybe they had nothing left for an encore after rods became so stiff as to be better froggigs or wading staffs than flyfishing tools.

Rod companies experienced growing numbers of broken, returned rods. Those actions increase their operating costs. Costs, regardless origin, are almost always passed along to consumers via higher prices. Stiff rod users found double-time, arm-damaging, goose-step casting strokes needed to run unfeeling "experts'" rods not as pleasant as told or envisioned. Supposed "power," "aggressive" or "advanced" caster actions be damned; such things only play on flyfisher ego or naïveté. Stiff rods are not pleasant to fish; neither are very soft ones. Lots of stiff rods found their way into the hands of "not so advanced" flyfishers.

Professional golfers, I understand, use clubs with very stiff shafts. Pros have tremendous experience, developed timing and strength to utilize such clubs. Golfers from duffer to advanced want to mimic the pros, but it's fool's play. Few golfers have the skills to use stiff clubs. A golf club comparison to fly rods isn't precise. It's similar for sure, but I remain unconvinced that even the "best" casters are better off with stiff fly rods. Stiff, brittle, fragile and difficult casting rods have too many negatives. Decent or better casters, I tend to believe, stress lightness and moderate, restful action. Please don't be fooled by industries' damaging yammer.

It's easy to get into all kinds of esoteric, modulus, hoop-strength, contraction, material and construction arguments or discussions concerning fly rods. Why? Let the "experts" wallow in those mud-holes. Such terms, descriptions or specifications are biased, always variable and indistinct at best. They're mostly superficialities, confusing differentiations and misunderstood sales gimmicks used in trying to prove superiority of one brand over another. The "experts" like to flog each other with sophisticated terms. You needn't participate. If a rod is suitable to your planned use and budget, use what pleases you. It's nice to test cast rods if possible, but it isn't necessary. When you find correct feel, decent fittings (more later) and an acceptable guarantee, who needs know more? Those devoid understanding of correct feel or fittings do.

A newcomer should buy a correctly appointed, affordable rod on the softer side of the middle of tested actions—one that definitely feels light in the hand. Beginners, or others, may not be able to escape the rod salesman-expert's technical diatribes. It's best to listen, occasionally smiling and nodding your head with dumb-struck wonder; then buy what feels right and what you can afford. Trust instincts.

Rods Old to New

Let's examine some fisherman-proven, desirable rods.

Bamboo rods often have near desirable feel but are heavy and expensive. Shorter, lighter ones for light lines (7 to 8 feet long for 4- or 5-weight lines) are, if correctly appointed, fun and enjoyable to fish. Longer bamboo rods encroach heavily on our first criteria of lightness in hand. Other materials are much lighter. Don't try to use some old bamboo rod of poor quality (there are many around) if you are serious about flyfishing.

Following WW II fiberglass was used almost exclusively in fly rod construction. There were some decent fiberglass fly rods. Shakespeare's "Howell Process" rods were acceptable, but fitted with metal ferrules and of thick fiberglass wrap construction, they were heavy and slow of action. I fished several of those white-spiral rods in my youth. They were market leaders, for their time. Fiberglass construction got much better.

Don Green has designed and manufactured a number of great rods that by his own words had the same characteristics. "My goal was to achieve line contact; to achieve feel." He first achieved it with fiberglass rods from his Grizzly Co. founded in 1954. Green's Grizzly Co. merged with the Fenwick Co. in 1969, and Don went along. Rods called Grizzly-Fenwicks were produced with the truly revolutionary addition of a glass to glass "Feralite" ferrule designed by Fenwick's Jim Green (no relation to Don). Prior to using such a ferrule, multi-piece rods were usually joined using metal ferrules. Grizzly-Fenwick rods evolved to carry only the Fenwick name. Both rods were relatively light, well-made, moderately priced and had the "feel." They were the first really decent, modern rods available to the masses. Many old glass Fenwicks are still in use.

Don Green attempted to translate his intuitive "feel" in rods to graphite material when it came along, but not without problems. Some of his earliest, gray-colored, Fenwick graphite rods suffered excess breakage. I have several older ones built from blanks and fished them extensively for years. I still fish them some; they have served me well for 25 years or more, but they are softening from use.

Fenwick, and its fine rods, incurred the wrath—still predominant today—of the stupid part of the flyfishing industries by selling to retailers like K-Mart and Payless Drugs. To ordinary flyfishers that meant fine tackle was available at reasonable and competitive prices. To many in the industries it meant continued price gouging was difficult. Flyfishing's sophisticated upper crust would have you believe selling decent tackle at sensible prices, by discount stores, somehow leads to poorer quality tackle. That's flawed reasoning in the short run and perhaps the long. The Fenwick fly rod sold for $49.95 by Payless was identical to the one sold by a fly shop for $79.95. Any time the less expensive rod ceased to be identical or suffered quality degradation and fishability loss compared to the more expensive, many in the buying public would stop buying them. You know Payless didn't pay Fenwick $30.00 less for its rods than the fly shops. Don't worry too much about true long run rod problems. Lord John Maynard Keynes correctly stated: "In the long run we'll all be dead."

Don Green left Fenwick in 1979 when it was sold to Woodstream Corporation (then to Berkeley Tackle Co.) and founded the Sage Rod Co. His intuitive sense of correct rod feel was somehow compromised there. I was custom building lots of rods from Fenwick and the new Sage blanks at the time using both glass and graphite blanks. The Fenwicks were my favorites. They simply have better feel. Sage and other companies now produce many rod models and blanks that are just too stiff. Recently Sage Co. seems to have recaptured feel. Don Green's ideas once again surfaced, hopefully to prevail forever. The Sage SP (Smooth Performance) models, the green, very expensive ones, are decent fishing tools. Sage seems to have admitted its earlier mistakes by producing this rod model. Other rod companies simply held the "correct feel" line through the wild design rod years and weathered the storm.

Winston Rod Co. references and builds "smoothness" into its fine rods. They know slower, softer, uniform bending rods cast and mend line best. Such rods fish most enjoyably, hour after hour, and are always smoother than stiff rods. Contrarily, Sage Rod Co. believes less casting stroke is needed to "load" a stiff rod. Sage is also right, but feel, fishability and smoothness are impaired. Following Sage's rod "loading" thinking, a quickly loading rod, therefore an exemplary rod, would be defined by a guide-equipped broom handle, even a two-by-four. They would be fully loaded all the time and require very short casting strokes. I consider any unloaded firearm a poor club but admit never worrying about the pre-loaded state of my fly rods. The flyfisher should load a rod as needed and seen fit, not fight a too-stiff rod.

Several years ago I suffered tendinitis in my casting arm's elbow with steelheading time rapidly approaching. I surveyed my steelhead fly rods. At 9½ plus feet they looked and felt foreboding. I needed a lighter but adequate rod. Some rummaging around, spurred by clouded recollection, uncovered a 2-piece, brown-colored 9-foot for 8-weight Fenwick HMG (High Modulus Graphite) blank. I'd had it for perhaps 15 years. I fished and felt fondly of this model in the original gray blank for many years. For an 8-weight it was powerful yet light. I took many steelhead with that old rod. It was just what I now needed.

The original rod was destroyed when my exuberant youngest son rolled a hundred-pound riverside boulder down and over the rod where it lay as I unhooked a fish—a disreputable whitefish if memory serves. I still had the salvaged reel seat from the old rod and in a fit of nostalgia glued it to the new blank. A grip identical to that of the old rod was fashioned as well. I would recapture the old days, and my elbow problems would be solved. In the building of a rod you have much occasion to fiddle with, shake and otherwise acquire clairvoyant feel of the rod to be. I had dormant knowledge as well from years of using the old, identical rod.

While building my new rod I had occasion to work vacation relief at a fly shop. The new Sage SP models had recently arrived. Like most flyfishers, I shake and fondle new rods. Wiggling the new Sage SP, 9-foot, 8-weight provoked my sensibilities. I'd felt the "feel" of this thing before. It seemed nearly identical to the Fenwick I was building at home. To verify my feelings, I carted my newly finished custom Fenwick to the shop and compared the rods, side-by-side. The Sage was only slightly lighter and barely smaller in blank diameter, but they *felt* the same. They should. Correct feel is correct feel, and the same man designed them both. So, nothing has changed as far as desirable feel and measurable fishability is concerned in over 30 years, except price.

There are other makes or models of fly rods having desired feel. I use the Shakespeare-Grizzly-Fenwick-Sage example to show the fleeting and changing leadership of companies and the interwoven thread of desirability sameness over many years. What company will be next to lead? To fall? Don and Jim Green had a lot to do with desirable rods made of differing materials and by several companies. The point is the most knowledgeable of modern rod builders built—with curious lapses—rods having the same feel. Don then found his ideas mostly ratified by countless flyfishers. *Feel* is what's most important, not appearance or maker or material or reputation or advertising distortion or price or snob-appeal.

Desirable Rod Economy

We know Fenwick remains a dirty word to the sophisticated Elite industry. It's small wonder. You can have the fishability and design qualities of one of Mr. Green's rods in a Sage SP for about $500.00 at a fly shop or you can have it in a Fenwick HMG from Cabela's at this writing for $169.95, postage paid. If you opt for the Sage what do you get for your extra $330.00? I just called Fenwick and was told they will replace, free of charge, any rod of any age that does not show abuse. So it's not extra guarantee as some would have you believe. It's not performance or better rod fittings or finish; both are top quality. You will get a nicer rod-tube, but mostly what you get is the right to pay for all the glitzy advertising, dreamy promotion, and profits of the Sage Co. and its dealers—lucky you. Of course you may feel you acquire correctness or prestige. Not to the *un*sophisticated you haven't. Or you could buy the Fenwick, securing a fine rod for years of efficient and enjoyable use *and* donate $50 or $100 to your local flyfishing conservation group. You would be doing something needed and positive for your fishing and still be lots of money ahead.

There are lots of cheaper rods on the market that sell much faster than the super expensive ones. I'm told premium rod sales are flat. People willing to pay up to $500 for a $170 fly rod must be lacking—or coming to their senses. That doesn't, however, eliminate problems. Newer, cheaper, rods generally exhibit too stiff actions copied from "big name" models. The flyfishing and casting of the buyers of such rods will still suffer, but if and when enlightenment comes, the cost of junking poor rods will not be as great or maybe as hard to do. Meanwhile avoiding poor rods remains difficult.

Broach the subject of price-fixed, rip-off prices of "quality" rods to their users and sellers and you solicit a bunch of gibberish about extra performance (what?), extra guarantee (no), and dollars needed for research and development to bring us better rods. Better, how? From WW II forward (even before with bamboo rods) we have been able to buy and enjoy *near ideal* feel, smoothness and utility in rods. The only real and provable advantages (not merely the silly mind wanderings of sophisticates) of recent bank-busting rods and lower priced clones is a small amount of less weight and diameter. Modern Elite produced rod discourse is indeed as William Shakespeare wrote, *Much Ado About Nothing*. Superficiality, deemed important by irrational or unenlightened consumers, holds sway in flyfishing as in more important societal underpinnings. In the meantime lots of flyfishers are restricted by too stiff, too expensive, too misunderstood rods. How does it happen?

Industries' modern marketing, including rod marketing, is *really* about continuing to successfully sell new, often wrong ideas and theoretical differentiations at high prices. Marketing is also, always, about making profit as large as possible. That's impossible if flyfishers are well informed. Don't be fooled by impressions of benefit or advantage nonexistent concerning rods or anything else.

Fenwick rods, or at least their blanks, are now made overseas. I'm a strong and proud proponent of buying American. I also believe in fair and free markets. "Pro-shop," price fixing programs contradict common (also personal) good and desirable free-market economics. It would be easier for me to accept exorbitant and fixed prices if I knew a *decent* share of income generated was used to benefit our fishing.

Rod Fittings

Let's take a detailed look at the parts and fittings of fly rods. Reading, you might take the position of a person critically looking at a variety of rods, blanks and fittings planning to build, or have built, the "ideal" rod. We know lightness in hand, smoothness and softer action culminating in "feel" are the most important features of a decent rod. Such attributes come mostly from a rod's blank. Rod fittings can make a big difference, amplifying or negating feel. Sometimes a rod will contain an adequate blank but be adorned with less than adequate guides, threadwork, grip, reel-seat or finish work. Let's look at the several rod fittings and rod construction steps one at a time.

Guides

Manufacturers of cheaper rods save on costs by eliminating guides. All guides are hand wrapped and create significant labor costs. A rule-of -thumb: A rod should have one guide for every foot or portion of a foot of length, plus one more. Don't count the tip. One guide more or less *may* be acceptable. Guides should be large in size. The guides on most rods are adequate if not ideal these days, but watch it on older rods.

Guide spacing is important to functionality. I like the first guide (not the tip) 4 to 4½ inches down from the blank's tip. The bottom, or first stripping, guide should be located: A slightly stretched non-rod-hand reach up the blank, when the blank is held by the grip (or where the grip will be) in a relaxed manner, at your side. The rest of the already determined correct number should then be placed in natural progression between the located top and bottom guides. An almost universal problem of factory rods is a first stripping guide located too close to the grip. Too close strippers limit line shootability, encourage tangled line and limit ability to strip line in panic situations. Forcing too many guides onto a rod always aggravates this problem and is quite common.

The earlier referenced large part of importance concerning guides is inside ring diameter. Some stripping guides are large and bulky, but have small holes for the line. Nearly everyone uses some kind of ceramic or space-age material inside a cushion ring, inside a metal ring these days. There are cheap and expensive guides that look similar. Better rods by better manufacturers will have decent, but not necessarily the best guides. I've experienced more trouble with stripping guides than the high-quality snake guides that should be used on most of the rod. Considering there are about 400% fewer stripping than snake guides on the average rod, the problem rate speaks for itself. Because strippers are large and bulky they are subject to damage. Make sure what you choose are strongly made and securely affixed to the rod blank.

I build a few fly rods now and then and custom built them commercially for several years. I can buy the described insert type stripping guides for 47 cents or $2.75 each, wholesale. I use the expensive ones with large holes and solid frames; they're worth their cost. Three stripping guides are useful on medium to heavy-weight rods with the third one up being hard plated steel rather than ceramic construction. Such a guide makes a nice transition to snake guides while aiding line shootability. I use at least two strippers on all rods except classic bamboo. Stripping guides undergo lots of line sawing motion during fishing. Rough or broken strippers will ruin fly lines quickly.

You may see a few rods with the bulk of the guides being something other than snake type. Such guides are either fragile, heavy or wear quickly. Stick with top-quality, industrial chrome plated snakes. Use a large diameter pear-shaped tiptop in the same finish. If the latest quality snake guides in a finish other than chrome will see those finishes last for more than one season's use, I'll be surprised—none of their predecessors, in gold or black, ever have for me. I used high quality, single foot, circular ring guides on the last rods I've built for myself. The jury is still out until they undergo adequate use. I strongly suspect, lacking a second foot, they will prove too fragile. At least one major rod company is using single foot guides now. It's easy for me to replace a rod's guides quickly if I desire. It may not be as easy for you to have a rod rewrapped.

Guide Wraps

Guide-wraps, first and foremost, are meant to hold the guides on the rod, solidly. Builders frequently use them for fashion statements or unplanned fish alarms. Wraps, other than those on guides, must strengthen the rod (as at ferrules), provide minimal and tasteful decoration or perhaps fish measuring marks. Suit yourself, but subtle, dark, simple, small and completely finished wraps perform and look best in this rod-builder-flyfisher's opinion. Thread must be fine size "A" or finer if the builder's eyes permit. Heavier threads look coarse and require too much heavy finish. We almost had to use nylon thread for years; now silk is readily available again, neither will rot. Silk is softer of color and adds an air of yesteryear to a rod, if it matters. Nylon stretches causing some wrapping problems, none insurmountable.

Guide Finish

Guide varnish or finish should be neat, complete and smooth to the point that no thread can be felt through the finish. Experienced finishers know how to pleasingly taper the finish of a guide wrap from bare blank to wrap-end and other clever tricks concerning finish work. I've found all epoxy finishes fracture with time and use, particularly at ferrules. Some of the finest rods made today are finished using spar-type varnishes. Varnish is time consuming and more problematical to use; epoxy finishes are more often used even if they're not the best. Spar-varnish is easy to touchup later in a rod's life: epoxies, not so easy.

Like finish carpentry, it's easy to destroy an otherwise fine building job with poor finishing. Consult a pro and do it right if it's your first rod. Finishing isn't difficult; it only requires a little care and time. Excess finish, or any weight, along a fly-fishing lever causes a dampening and softening of the action. Use no more finish than is needed unless you calculate to soften a blank. Softening attempts usually yield undesirable results. Start with a blank of correct feel, then treat it right. Blanks require no finish other than periodic waxing. Because blanks are softened in building a rod, start with a blank slightly stiffer than what's wanted in the finished rod. Test completed rods to ascertain the correct blank to use.

Reel Seats

As guide wraps are to hold guides on the blank, a reel seat's only important function is to hold your reel firmly. You see lots of fancy and expensive seats these days. Tasteful reel seats are nice, but first ensure any seat will accommodate the reels you plan to use and hold them firmly in place. Anything else regarding fancy seats is fluff and extra expense. Fine older reels, like the Pflueger Medalists, have large, thick feet that will not fit some newer seat's hoods.

Reel seats can be up or down locking. It's fashionable of late to use the up locking variety. Maybe my casting is sub-par, but my line frequently catches on the rearward protrusion of up locking seats. The extension may protect your reel when you lean the rod aside, but I've never had problems with my down locking seats, using care. It could be there is validity in moving the reel closer to the casting hand via an up locking seat. It's also likely that some sophisticates think covering the upper reel seat hood with cork is clever or handsome. It's superficial; handsome is as handsome does. The extension below the reel could help in fighting large fish. Know, however, that little reel seat extension or longer ones, added *on* the blank, detract from the overall working length of a rod. Poorly designed grips might be caused by the use of up locking seats.

Rod Grips

The importance of fly rod grips is overlooked and underrated. They should be of dense, top-quality cork and comfortably allow positioning of the hand with the thumb on top of or along side the grip. I know of no better example of correct design than a claw-hammer handle with its flatted sides and swell at the rear to hold your hand in position. Such a grip provides a place for the ball of thumb, from whence power is transferred to casts. Despite that, the last three, even two, fingers of the hand hold the rod a great deal of the time while fishing. (The thumb and first two fingers are most used in casting.) Motion used driving a nail with a hammer is not unlike the motion used in casting. Just try to find a modern factory rod with a hammer-handle grip. They were used on some well thought out older rods. Such grips are more time consuming and therefore costly to shape.

The Orvis Co. recently "discovered" damaging rod vibrations emanating from the grips of their rods and have taken semi-radical grip design steps to reduce such pesky emanations. It's marketing hocus-pocus, but might have slight basis in truth. Softening rod actions would diminish or eliminate vibrations more. Don't fall for something until it's *proven* to be fact. Most "discoveries" never will be. Some common factory grips are abominations.

If you would, close your rod-hand lightly and look into the hole created. Notice your little finger nearly touches your palm, and a sizable hole, one-inch in diameter or more, is defined by your index finger and thumb. I've tried to show my hand in the described position with the illustration. A grip, to be comfortable, through long hours of casting should accommodate that shape as well as provide a cut-out place for your thumb and a swell to keep your hand from slipping toward the reel. Lightly flatted sides make the grip even more comfortable. You will see such grips in illustrations scattered throughout this book. Many factory rod grips are backwards to natural hand grip shape, causing hand creep, strain and cramping. A grip that looks adroit in a shop may prove very wrong after use.

Grips on factory rods are too long in my opinion, often too large in diameter and occasionally too small. I suppose they're made to accommodate the ham-handed among us. Can you live with an "average" grip? Six or 6½ inches is plenty for most people, certainly if correctly designed. Too long grips encourage incorrect hand placement and contribute excess weight in a game where saving a fraction of an ounce here and there amounts to the difference between a rod light in the hand and one that isn't.

Hookkeepers

Hookkeepers aren't of much use and are more trouble than they are worth. I didn't always think so. Many years ago I designed my own—a clever one that wouldn't crush the hackles of a dry fly. I had a metal finisher friend chrome plate my creations and installed them on many custom rods. It's quite similar to several now used by big rod companies.

My chief complaint, among several, with hookkeepers is that their designed use and placement causes kinking of the butt section of any leader longer than the rod used. Such leaders are commonplace. Leader butt kinks are cast destroyers, annoying to remove and hard to avoid unless line and leader are kept lightly draped under little tension. Try to maintain a lightly draped leader while wading, walking, boating or driving to the next piece of water. A better method is to hook your fly somewhere on the frame of the first stripping guide and run the leader down and around the outside diameter of your reel. So doing still puts a kink in your fly line. A kink in the line will cast out and is not cast destroying like one in a stiff leader butt that must be repeatedly hand removed. I no longer put hookkeepers on my personal rods.

Custom Rod Builders

You have seen the fittings and design of factory rods can

be easily improved. It's quite easy to build (or have built) better rods than factory rods you can buy. Just make sure you know why you are making changes. Many custom rod builders fabricate only factory clones and are uncomfortable or incapable of improving rods. Builders often fail to understand fly rods, and many haven't flyfished enough to know what does or doesn't work or why. Custom builders, and many self-builders, seem paralyzed by thought of diverging from accepted, but improvable norms. You can buy the blank of nearly any factory rod and blanks from firms that sell no finished rods. Blanks and components have factory warranties. The labor of a custom builder will not be warranted if you break the rod. There are pamphlets, even books, dealing with rod building that will show you needed, even unneeded, technique.

Rod Recommendations

If you build or buy fly rods what lengths and line weights should they be? There are lots of recommendations floating around. Whom do you believe?

Two flyfishers, fishing for the same fish species, of similar size, with similar flies may require different lengths and weights of rod and line. One may fish smaller brush protected streams and the other larger, still or flowing water where wind is a problem. A 7½-foot, 4-weight may be ideal for the first and a 9-foot, 7-weight best for the second. You see recommending ideal rods per tippet, fly, species or length criteria is foolhardy. Fishing conditions are too variable for anyone to make valid recommendations that are not condition specific. That doesn't mean there aren't helpful considerations.

Short rods require more precise timing in casting. They require faster casting strokes than longer rods and can't keep the line as far above the ground, brush or water as a longer rod. Short rods do not permit mending line as easily and create more severe angles between rod tip and water surface. Severe angles generate more slack to manage. Short rods can be a joy to use when conditions favor them. Longer rods are the option.

Longer rods are heavier than shorter rods of the same material. Long rod use has grown steadily over the years, some in response to lighter rod materials and some because industries' marketers and controllers haven't yet decided to re-establish short rods. Long rods are far from ideal. The longer a rod, the more tiring to use and the more leverage a hooked fish, even the line, has on your aching wrist (the fulcrum). A rod is nothing but a long lever, and it works against as well as for you. That's simple physics. Remember that well if considering a two-handed rod. Two-handed rods contradict obtaining enjoyable feel, certainly lightness in hand and perhaps smoothness—*all* the attributes of an ideal rod.

Long and short are relative. A person fishing an 8½-foot rod for steelheading is on the short end of the range where 9½- to 10½-foot rods are common. But the user of the short rod may be fishing a smaller, brushy coastal river for steelhead, and his rod could be ideal. An 8½-foot rod is on the long end of the range for smaller streams supporting smaller fish, even those of 4- or 5-weight. Let's simplify.

Considering the requirements needed of rods and lines in 95% of all flyfishing, it's possible to list a scheme of rod lengths and line weights to accomplish most tasks:

- a 7½- or 8-foot, 4-weight
- an 8½- or 9-foot, 6-weight
- a 9½-foot, 8-weight
- and a 9-foot, 10-weight.

If you don't plan to pursue large and heavy freshwater or saltwater fish, a simpler but effective selection could be:

- a 7½- or 8-foot, 5-weight
- and a 9- or 9½-foot, 7-weight.

Looking at the two sets of rod and line weights and picking the middle forces you to about an 8½-foot, 6-weight. While a very useable length and weight combination, it is limited one way or another. A *correctly labeled* 6-weight will struggle, pushing bass bugs or larger steelhead and trout flies and doesn't have the muscle needed for most saltwater or large freshwater fish. It will be too long for cramped quarters and perhaps too splashy for fussy fishing. But look at what can be done. With a decent 6-weight rod and DT floating lines of 5-, 6- and 7-weight, you will *more* than double your effectiveness and preparedness without the expense of additional rods and possibly reels. You will need extra reel spools. You could also buy and spool a 6-weight fast-sinking line for still water use. A better all-around plan follows.

An 8-foot, 5-weight, and a 9-foot, 7-weight, with a couple of reels and some spare spools equipped with floating DTs of 4-, 5-, 6-, 7- and 8-weight, is an awesome battery. Add 6-weight sinking lines for the 7-weight rod if you like. So equipped you can fish for all but the largest of game fish and push all but the largest of flies. Please keep in mind that all these selections require accurately labeled rods. They are difficult to find considering the mess of mislabeled rods these days. The next chapter on rod-line balance will get into that most fetid kettle of fish.

Chapter Six:
Fly Rod-Line Balance

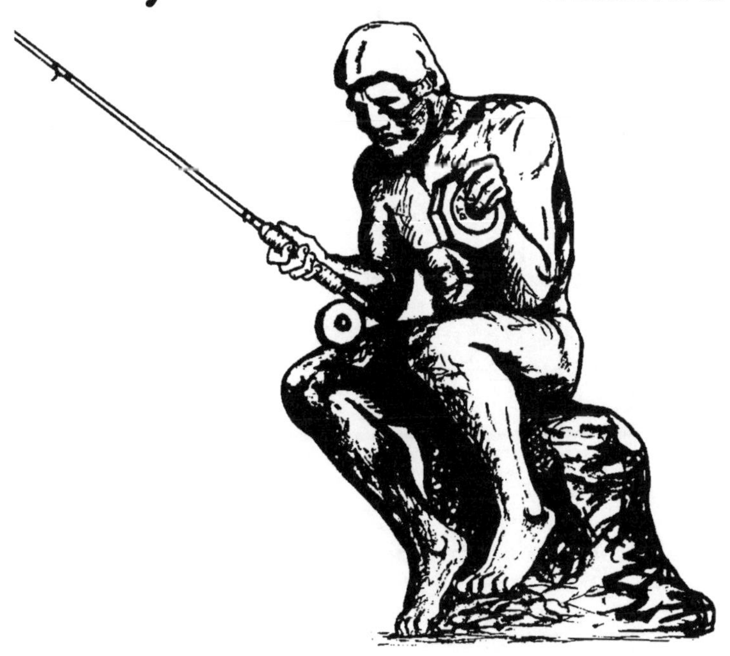

"O what a tangled web we weave, . . ."
Sir Walter Scott

This chapter is challenging to write. The subject matter isn't particularly difficult. But the real world problems of achieving rod and line balance have been allowed, even intentionally caused, to become unreasonably difficult. Industries' flyfishing damaging actions and influence are so prevalent in flyfisher thinking that overcoming them even with fact and reason is arduous. Here goes.

A fly rod and its line should be compatible for most effective and enjoyable use. *Such Rod-Line* relationship, often referred to as *balance,* has been **defined** for many years. There are *no* valid *or* definition-permitted reasons for producers to deviate from the boundaries of defined balance. But they do—extensively.

Rod-Line Balance Defined

Each factory produced fly rod of the last 30 years or more has carried a numerical designation (4, 8, 10, etc.). That single designation (often near or with other labeling) not only characterizes the rod, but also defines the weight limitations of the line said to match that rod. Again, both rod and line characteristics are defined by a single, *producer nonarbitrary,* number. A single, weight determined but dual purpose number's original purpose was to help users achieve balance and simplify rod-line selection.

Sound, basic and still valid work was done in the 1960s by the American Fishing Tackle Manufacturers Association (AFTMA then, American Sport Fishing Association [ASA] now). Action was taken to escape then significant balance problems and ease customer understanding. That good work is now disgustingly and almost uniformly ignored by manufacturers. The flyfishing industries have taken huge steps backward to flyfishing damaging turmoil. It's similar but worse than problems existent prior to 1960.

In 1960-61 major rod and line manufacturers and a few caring flyfishers—including Sunset Line Co. as a leader and Myron Gregory as an instigator—came together in a now unknown spirit of problem solving cooperation to further flyfisher understanding. The result was more uniformity and ease in obtaining rod-line balance by uniform manufacturing standards than experienced before or since. It was called the AFTMA system, and it was needed.

In the early 1960s, materials and methods of fabricating rods, but particularly lines, were rapidly changing. Fading were silk fly lines and in their place came new lines of dacron or nylon. Dacron is heavier, and nylon is lighter than silk. The existing "A to I" designation of lines, or portions of fly lines, by diameter wouldn't work for the varying weights of dacron and nylon. One maker's H diameter (now level 7-weight) line wouldn't work on a second company's H designated rod or have the same specifications as a third producer's H diameter line.

The new AFTMA system assigned fly lines numbers from 1, the lightest, to 12 the heaviest, by grain weight. A few grains plus or minus were allowed for production variations. *Furthermore, the assigned weight must be contained in the line's first*

AMERICAN FISHING TACKLE MANUFACTURERS ASSOCIATION

NEW FLY LINE STANDARDS

AFTMA
FLY LINE STANDARDS

#	Wt.	Range	#	Wt.	Range
1	60	54-66	7	185	177-193
2	80	74-86	8	210	202-218
3	100	94-106	9	240	230-250
4	120	114-126	10	280	270-290
5	140	134-146	11	330	318-342
6	160	152-168	12	380	368-392

Weight in grains—based on first 30 feet (exclusive of any taper tip). Range allows for acceptable manufacturing tolerances.

Mr. Fly Fisherman

In past years, "alphabetical" fly line markings were based on silk weight. All fly lines were produced on that premise. However, the letter system indicating diameters (H .025 — G .030, etc.) loses its importance, accuracy and efficiency when nylon or dacron or other synthetics are used. Because the specific gravity of silk is heavier than nylon, and lighter than dacron, ech material performs differently on the same rod.

- This is why a new standard had to be developed.

Identification Symbols Under New Fly Line Standardization

Level = L	Floating Line = F
Double Taper = DT	Sinking Line = S
Weight Forward = WF	Intermediate = I (Float or Sink)
Single Taper = ST	

EXAMPLES

DT9F (Double Taper 240 grain floating line)
L4I (Level 120 grain intermediate line)
WF12S (Weight forward taper 380 grain sinking line)

Basis of New Standard

The weight of fly line with rod action casts the fly. Performance is poor if the line and rod are not compatible. Recognizing this fact, American line manufacturers in cooperation with the American Casting Association and the International Casting Federation, have spent two yeears in preparing these new universal standards. They are based on the weight of the working part of the fly line—the front section. Exclusive of any tip on a taper, the first 30 feet of line is weighed to determine its category. Now, guess work in matching the line and fly rod is eliminated.

COMPARISON NEW AND OLD

NEW DT 9 S DACRON
TIP — 30 ft 240 GRAINS —
DT 9 F NYLON
TIP — 30 ft 240 GRAINS —
OLD HCH SINKING DACRON
TIP — 30 ft 265 GRAINS —
HCH FLOATING NYLON
TIP — 30 ft 205 GRAINS —
(NOT TO SCALE--DIAGRAMMATIC ONLY)

For converting your present line to the new standards, write to your fly line manufacturer stating name, type and size of line.
Printed in U.S.A. by AFTMA
20 North Wacker Drive
Chicago 6, Illinois

Original AFTMA advertisement

30 feet and disregards core structure, materials, diameter or taper of a line. In addition it was **agreed,** by **all** manufacturers, that any rod that best responded in casting to *30 feet* of a certain line, say it's 7-weight, will be designated a "7-weight" rod.

As may be seen from the original AFTMA advertisement, the first 30 feet of a 7-weight line must weigh between 177 and 193 grains; a 4-weight, 114 to 126 and a 10-weight, 270 to 290 grains, to select a few examples. The system is simple and proven to be easily useable. It provides an island of *valid, needed, defined* and *constant* ground concerning fly rod-line balance. The AFTMA system would remove confusion for everyone now, *if adhered to by producers.* The *producer accepted* (but largely ignored) AFTMA system should be required daily reading for all modern rod or line designers and producers—until it's fully understood, including the damage done by its disregard. An *abundance* of flyfishers also needs enlightenment. I dwell on AFTMA's rules, the only *bona fide* presently existing rules and definitions we have concerning rod-line balance, because it's so important to understand.

By definition, *and also by fact of actual usage in labeling,* a rod maker states its rod, labeled a 6-weight, will best handle *30 feet,* and *only* 30 feet, of correctly labeled 6-weight fly line. By using the defined and nonarbitrary AFTMA system, a producer *pledges* conformity to its rules. The system makes no allowances for real or imagined individual casting styles. So called advanced, power, aggressive or sophisticated casters are given no more consideration by AFTMA ratings than new or duffer casters. To eliminate human factors some of the old rod companies used unbiased casting machines to determine when 30 feet of a certain line worked best on a certain rod. They were doing their best to comply to AFTMA standards in a day when a company's pledge to customers was taken seriously and meant something.

AFTMA Shrugged

Given information presented in previous chapters and *if* you were provided factory rods of AFTMA correct designation, you could make easy, logical and known correct adjustments in tackle for different fishing circumstances. It's simply done by using varying leaders and different DT line weights on rods known to be correctly designated or custom built so.

You then achieve wide versatility and decrease tackle cost while obtaining optimum fishing effectiveness. If rods are incorrectly designated (as many are these days) and you believe those erroneous designations, you have little chance of achieving desired effects easily, or at all. Rod makers create more problems than line manufacturers.

I recently tested, by weighing the first 30 feet, varying lines of three major manufacturers: Cortland, Scientific Anglers and Wulff. I found the lines of all three to be within the prescribed AFTMA weight limits, with one exception. But some line makers also sell rods, and all line producers stand to profit from the rod-line balance mess whether they make rods or not. Because line producers did not stand up and decry what was happening to defined rod-line balance, line producers can't be held guiltless for damage done flyfishing understanding.

Because numerous modern rods do not balance with the 30 feet of the line weight pledged to be correct on the rod, users not wanting to modify tackle have built-in modification from the get-go. What are the chances it's what's needed, wanted or is understood? Such problems are particularly sad in effect on newer or beginning casters, but experienced flyfishers are far from exempt. Unknowing users acquire supposedly balanced tackle, but it doesn't work. They can wave line around, but cannot get the "feel" of casting. They almost uniformly feel the problem lies with them and not the stated and *pledged* balanced rod and line they were sold or ordered from a catalog. Of course industries' answer is to have anyone experiencing trouble go to a pro-shop where "expert" help can be found. That's a farce, as Question No. 66 revealed in Chapter Two.

Knowing what we have just spent so much time understanding about defined, nonarbitrary and pledged rod and line balance, read this quote from Jeffrey Cardenas, writing for *Fly Tackle Dealer (FTD),* the trade publication of the flyfishing industry:

> "As both rod and line tapers become more complex, dealers should understand that not every 6-weight line will match with every 6-weight rod."

Then why the hell are they labeled 6-weights? Arrogant manufacturers, as a matter of course, disregard AFTMA requirements and their pledges, thinking nothing of lying to our frustration and expense. Uncaring or flyfishing standard ignorant, but flyfishing "expert," columnists perpetuate their lies. AFTMA rules are to protect us from industries' irresponsible actions, but the industries won't comply. Refuse to participate in industries' deceit any time you can—for flyfishing's sake, if not your own or mine. Demand truth and change if you will.

Stiff Rods and AFTMA

Recently, fly rods from most makers have become very stiff. Such rods negate needed "feel" with the *defined* 30 feet of the line *pledged* by the maker to be the matching and ideal line. It's necessary to use lines at least one and frequently two or more line sizes larger than the one sworn to be correct to make mislabeled rods work with the defined 30 feet of line. Rod makers aren't stupid, only unethical. They know they are perverting standards and attempt to explain away their actions. You will continue to hear their nonsense about the rod needs of "modern" or "power" or "aggressive" casters. Just what are modern or aggressive casters—sophisticates who think they're special?

There are truer reasons fly rods "got stiff." Rod and blank makers bungled repeatedly in building rods from a stream of new, misunderstood and inadequately tested space-age materials. Poorly performing WF lines encourage stiff rod use; we've seen that. Rod makers also faced a market, some years back, that did not have all the flyfishers we now have, and it was a rod-saturated market. Very few flyfishers needed another 9-foot, 6-weight. Short rods had been "done" and long rods had only recently been taken to practical, even impractical, lengths. What was a starving rod company to do?

Enter a blizzard of can't-do-without specialty rods, made of *stiff* materials, including many of 1-, 2- and 3-weight. A *true* 2-weight is a near pointless thing, not to mention the absurdity of a *true* 1-weight. (The modifier "true" means AFTMA defined.) To be a decent fishing instrument any *new* 2-weight has to have more of the characteristics of a *true* 4-weight than an impotent true 2-weight. But an aggressive, modern, full-line rod company would then have something approaching *two* 4-weights. The problem is the stiff new one is mislabeled a 2-weight. Now what does the company do? Admit the foolishness of their new wonder rods and junk them for flyfishing's betterment—they are selling well to the ingenuous—or do they try to "reason" their way out of the dilemma? You know the answer.

Companies or indeed industries make mistakes or get into an occasional mess. Admitting mistakes and going on with customers', and in this case fishes', best interests at heart requires character, more than apparently possessed by rod producers and their supporters. The result—during the time new 2-weights became more like true 4-weights, and to use only that example—was stiffer rod migration on up the full range of rod weights. The "silly rod" protecting migration was complimented by the continued misuse of new materials and overuse of WF lines. Ego manipulating and camouflaging distortion about "power" casters and similar rot contributed. True 6-weights ended up being labeled 4-weights, true 8-weights as 6-weights and so on. Effects were varied and seldom desirable.

Long and over-stiff rods are capable of waving a lot of line around. Starry-eyed viewers of *A River Runs Through It* think such waving is casting. I recall a promotional poster for that movie (most fly shops had them displayed on their walls). It showed a caster, on a river bank, with large, long, complex and conflicting loops of line in the air. Anyone, having flyfished more than twice knows the whole cast came crashing down in a tangled mess seconds after the picture was snapped. Ignorant newcomers, were easy to sell expensive stiff rods to once they impressed themselves with their own magnificent line waving. I, and probably you, have seen these poor souls astream. Let's consider other stiff rod problems.

Explanation, so far, has been overly simple but germane. There are actually all kinds of rod variations, materials, mistakes and overlaps. There are 3-, 5-, and 7-weights to consider in addition to the even-numbered examples used. Among many variables were and are new rod tapers, a proliferation of multi-section rods and rods of lighter weight. All were modified with near-yearly new batches of some space-age material. The selection and prices of rods grew larger as inside industry competition plunged downhill to provide faster loading (stiffer), more powerful (stiffer), and ever lighter (fragile) rods.

Each rod company participated differently or entered the fray at different times.[1] You would expect competition and

[1]Some rod companies may not have participated or did so in minor ways. Winston Rod Co., among possible others, seemed to not participate. The biggest companies were the leaders and sucked other underthinking, gullible companies into rod building's "dark times."

oversupply to bring prices down. It didn't, the industry intensified price fixing via pro-shop programs more or less concurrent with an explosion of new, flush and flyfishing unfamiliar buyers. Both dynamics help keep prices artificially high, and rod discourse centered on the new, superficial, "special," and unimportant, even the damaging.

A recent article from FTD reviewed all the new rods of nearly every maker. The comments addressed: Finish, luster, intricate thread wraps, eye catching sparkle, specialty rods, "stealalizing" finish, rods with matching numbered paintings, lighter graphite, stronger graphite, bird's-eye maple reel seats, 3-piece rods, reintroduced fiberglass rods ($380.00) and lots of other such—most fishability ignorant drivel—sizzle but no steak. But we know sizzle sells. (Remember Confucius said an inferior man knows what sells.) The Lamiglas Co. perhaps took the damaging-drivel cake: "XM6 custom graphite rods are the result of new and *radical* technique. . .highest modulus (least elasticity) and fastest (stiff and brittle) actions *offered by anyone.*" (Emphasis and parentheticals are mine.)

Achieving balance was once, and occasionally still is, made somewhat easier by rod makers listing two or more suggested line weights on and for a given rod. The worst stiff rod making offenders, however, haven't followed such practice recently, to my knowledge. Listing several lines could be reinstated or adopted to aid flyfishers, but that *still violates* AFTMA definitions. It's still *required* and makes most sense to accurately label a rod per AFTMA rules. Any rod best balances and casts with 30 feet of *some* line weight; only *that* weight line should be listed on the rods shaft. A *few* people can otherwise cope.

Some experienced flyfishers know how to "over-line" a mislabeled and too stiff rod or to pick a rod with the desired action regardless of line designation. If over-lining is done only to make a stiff and mislabeled rod work, a person suffers a heavier line than may be wanted or needed. Many flyfishers do not know to over-line, and less experienced flyfishers can hardly be expected to know what to do. Knowledgeable flyfishers (remembering flyfishing experience, even extensive, doesn't ensure knowledge) won't be duped as often.

An Effect of Stiff Rods

Knowing the misrepresentation that goes on, truly knowledgeable flyfishers become ever more disgusted, distrusting and cynical toward the industries', including their rod "inventions." The tackle sales part of the industry, however, doesn't much care about knowledgeable flyfishers. They aren't the ones most likely to spend the big, stupid dollars. Experienced *and* knowing flyfishers are largely outfitted, don't buy at shops or aren't as easily fooled as the newcomers. But many flyfishers with "experience" are as gullible as rank newcomers. Who counters the gullible "experienced"?

What the detached industries misunderstand are the intelligent and made cynical flyfishers who advise a great many, including newcomers, not to shop at fly shops. The time should come when the industries need every customer they can get. When asked, I advise people to obtain what they need in decent tackle by spending the least with the industries that try to trick them and care little for flyfishing's welfare. I know others who do as well. My industries' exploitable "useful shop life" expired long ago. How's yours? I'd support the industries in a heartbeat—when they come back to earth concerning products, compliance and start donating heavy money to fish welfare. Let's revisit light rod-line balance.

Balance and Fish Welfare

A balanced, true 4-weight rod—by definition, one that best handles 30 feet of 4-weight line, weighing only 120 grains—remains a fine and delicate tool. A 4-weight is most capable, likely ideal, for finest leaders and smallest flies. Yet 4-weights have marginal power to subdue larger fish, should one be inadvertently hooked, without unduly stressing the tackle or, more importantly, the fish. If you know the gentle, docile feel and capabilities of an accurately labeled 4-weight rod, then you also know a true 3-weight edges toward uselessness, a 2-weight is 95% there and a 1-weight is irrational.

The Orvis Co. instituted its "One Club" some years ago for fish of "remarkable character" taken on its 1-weight rods. I don't know if they still have such a club—but hope not. "Remarkable character" almost always translates into "large" in the minds of flyfishers, particularly 1-weight users. What else could have been meant or was to be logically expected? Pictures in the Orvis News "One Club" section showed many, *large* fish taken on 1-weight rods. There is no telling how much damage and death is perpetrated on our gamefish by the arrogance and selfishness of the too light tackle crowd. But Orvis sold more tackle. *If* it takes great skill to land a fine and large fish on a 1- or 2-weight rod (questionable), that skill is *nothing* compared to skill necessary to cause a fish killed by excess stress to live again—skill possessed only by God. It doesn't matter that an overstressed fish swims away after release—it still dies. It might as well have been kept to be eaten, or left alone, or taken with less damaging tackle.

Toy rods need like lines and reels to achieve balance, and they came bubbling forth. Rod, reel and line makers work together, on purpose or not, to exploit flyfishers, while disregarding fish. To look right, reels for trifling rods must be diminutive and therefore terribly inefficient and foolish. But they are cute and cute sells, to some.

Bombastic sales promotion suggests users of light tackle are more sophisticated, accomplished or more expert. Potential customers are told they will derive extra satisfaction from the fight of small fish. What is a small fish? Who wants to exploit them? In truth, accomplished flyfishers seldom give a damn about the *fight* of any fish and certainly not that of a small fish. Serious flyfishers know that a true 4-weight will handle all light line fishing. (You know the actions of the inaccurately labeling industries are what forces me to annoyingly use the word "true.") If you honestly want to make fish more difficult to hook, use *heavier* not lighter tackle. Howard Blaisdell said that in *The Philosophical Fisherman* years ago.

Certain flyfishers fume and fuss about criticism of too light tackle and the need and efficacy of same. Such persons will swear they do not kill fish with their light tackle and offer up weak proof. The facts are: mishandling, which includes overplaying, does kill fish often as much as 30 hours after release according to controlled studies. Lactic acid builds in a hooked fish's system, blocking oxygen and possibly stopping the heart. It takes up to 12 hours to dissipate and doesn't *peak* until three or four hours *after* exertion.

No one knows for sure, absent controlled conditions, if released fish live or die. We do know for sure that stress can and does kill fish. Too light tackle that prolongs fights causes stress. If a light tackle user becomes insufferable, relate what Theodore Gordon said: "There is nothing more absurd than a fine large man being played by a fish."

Concerning very light tackle, two English authors, Curtis and Goddard, had this to say in *The Trout And The Fly:*

> "There is no sense in using a barbless hook, if the trout is condemned to die because of the way it has been played. Many fish die or suffer from oxygen starvation and brain damage, because the fight has been long drawn out."

T. C. Kingsmill Moore, writing in *A Man May Fish,* summed up many of flyfishing's root problems including light tackle use in saying:

> "There is a great deal of snobbery in over-emphasis on fine tackle. Its advocates are anxious to impress their audience with their superior skill and delicacy of handling. Perhaps they are trying to impress themselves or live up to some standard of supposed excellence to which they have erroneously subscribed."

In the survey of experienced flyfishers, we will eventually get to, the questions regarding 1-, 2- and 3-weight tackle incited more negative comment than any of the other 175 questions, even No. 66. Knowledgeable flyfishers see no need for such gear. It's recognized for what it is, gimmickry to sell more tackle to the simple and naïveté on the part of users. Such tackle is partly responsible for the awful rod-line balance problems we face. Maybe a large part.

The Media and AFTMA

The stiff, light, small and incorrectly labeled rod-line delusion could not flourish without the help of or at least ignoring by flyfishing's media. Flyfishing publications, their writers and editors rush to extol the virtues of new things especially rods and lines from the "big names." They ignore or minimize product negatives or inaccuracies including *obvious* AFTMA bastardization. (Aren't professional journalists supposed to be driven by fairness and truth?) But it isn't good business to point out the shortcomings of your advertiser's or buddy's products. Many, ignorant or deficient flyfishing astuteness, write and publish flyfishing stuff. They *perhaps* couldn't see the problems with rod-line balance or the damage being done to flyfishers. Flyfishing writers, editors, publishers, et al., should be in other lines of work if they don't understand the most basic of flyfishing basics. Others must know very well what they write is flawed and damaging. Perhaps they suffer from lack of intestinal fortitude to fight for what's right.

Witness these comments from Barry and Cathy Beck, flyfishing columnists, in an article entitled, "Selecting a Fly Rod" in *Flyfishing* magazine:

> "Today, we can not pick up a graphite rod, flex it and determine its true action. You need to put a matching line on it and cast the rod. It makes all the difference in the world."

Hogwash—the true action (soft, stiff, "tippy," uniform, ideal, parabolic, etc.) of any rod can be determined by flexing. What is the "matching" line they reference using? They *did not* say to use the AFTMA recommended line. Are the Becks avoiding AFTMA rules and being vague on purpose? As columnists, are they afraid to speak the truth about modern rod-line recommendation errors? Or are they incorrectly saying a rod's "action" is dependent on a mysterious, nearly indeterminable, but nonetheless somehow "matching" line? Are they confused? I am, by that type of writing.

As regards the Becks' recommended test casting: *Nearly any caster can cast several differing line weights on the same rod.* An experienced caster will automatically, even subconsciously, conform casting strokes to any line used in order to make the line go. You can hardly avoid doing so. That doesn't mean a given line is ideal *or* conforms to the AFTMA defined weight for the rod used. Absent *correct* AFTMA designation, it's easy to get fooled; the Becks should know that.

Producers upholding and conforming to defined standards is critically needed. Only AFTMA correct designations allow *intelligent,* measurable and simple divergences, based on *definitions concrete.* Such divergences are commonly needed to meet fisher ability or fishing circumstance. There's yet more from industries' scribes.

Here's comment from a recent *Fly Rod and Reel* magazine article referencing the combined feelings of Messers. Butler,

Leeson and Mosser. All are flyfishing luminaries and supposedly experienced casters. (As with all such references about someone's experience and prowess or knowledge, we know not extent, quality or exactitude.) Our testers were evaluating a large sampling of the industries' modern 4-weight *designated* rods and said:

> "Nearly every rod performed better, in some way or another and up to a certain point, with a DT rather than a WF line."

You know that as more of the length of a DT 4-weight is extended through the rod's tip, the weight of the line rapidly builds. Increasing length boosts the line's effective weight to that of a 5-weight and with more, a 6-weight. Extra weight made the lousy stiff rods bend and work better. I know they were very stiff and mislabeled; otherwise, the rods would have responded to extra length of extended but lighter WF line. They weren't reported as doing so; it required the heavier belly section of a DT to make the rods respond.

Despite too long line lengths needed to make the rods work, we mustn't forget it's only the first 30 feet of line that are to be used to determine a rod's designation. Remember the first 30 feet of WFs and DTs are near *identical.* The rods tested, by admission "Nearly every rod. . . .," were *mislabeled* by their makers and they tested rods from nearly *all* producers. Considering long lengths of line were needed to make the rods perform, some must have been very much mislabeled—at least one and maybe two or three line weights—meaning most of the industries' new 4-weights were actually 5- or 6-weights, perhaps 7-weights.

Why didn't the testers just say the rods were mislabeled and should be labeled 5-, 6- or 7-weights? Is it fear of exposing manufacturers to the point of not minding appearing incompetent themselves? Is it arrogance? It's also possible I give flyfishing writing experts too much credit. Maybe they actually don't understand AFTMA rules or realize the damage done flyfishers by producers ignoring and bastardizing rules. If so, they certainly wouldn't grasp damage journalists do supporting those bastardizations. Are too many guilty of writing strongly and positively—dangerously and incorrectly?

Writers, as rod makers, aren't stupid. They know who butters their bread and seldom risk offending those feeding them with advertising dollars, salary or articles-sold paychecks. What of falsehoods spread, allowed to live, or hurt done flyfishers? But a few writers, who apparently care more for truth about rod-line balance and common flyfishers will speak more as honorable writers should. Realize writers speaking whole, plain truth are ostracized by those in the industries, are largely unknown and poorer monetarily than they might be with fewer scruples. But I suspect virtuous writers are rich with caring, self respect and the respect of the people worth having respect from.

At least one person sounded the rod-line balance alarm. Frank Amato writing in his *Flyfishing* magazine, concerning a separate 4-weight rod test, said:

> "**Rod line ratings:** The biggest suprise [sic] in the testing effort was how many rod makers under-rated their rod's line casting ability. Many No. 4's, I think should have been rated 5 or even 6. This is a critical mistake because it is much easier for a new caster to cast a line that is a bit heavy for the rod opposed to one that is too light. Specialty rod makers and old-line fly rod manufacturing companies seemed to rate their rods correctly more often."

Frank even hedges some, concerning "old-line" and "specialty" builders, maybe correctly. He spoke truth in a fly rod world of falsehoods, and that's laudable. There were exceptions on the part of a few rod producers and not all stiffened and mislabeled their entire rod lines as has been noted. Frank and I probably just see things a little differently.

Fly Lines and AFTMA

We know the several fly line makers are partaking of the fruits of confusion in concert with rod companies. There is money to be made everywhere. New line tapers to supposedly fit new rods, special colored lines for special situations, lines that sink so slowly you need to set underwater stakes to see any movement or lines only for Muskies with pink spots and purple stripes. Line densities and combination floating-sinking lines of most confusing array were trotted out. All were crassly promoted with the rest of the new, "needed" stuff. And the gullible open their wallets. An absurd situation holds sway to be sorted out by unassuming flyfishers.

Late in the mislabeled, stiff rod madness progression, the belly sections of WF lines began to creep longer. It was probably response aimed at forcing "balance" or making too-stiff rods bend. Longer bellied WF lines are the most useful (remembering WFs have little use) to casters capable of casting moderate to long distances. Beginners can seldom cast to distance, and their rods are likely to be incorrectly designated and too stiff. Without ability to cast to distance, beginners' rods won't work any better with a "long-belly" than with a regular WF line. What beginners need most often is the *correct* (heavier) line for their rod regardless of how the rod is labeled or what some think. They should use a DT for economic reasons and to enjoy most effective flyfishing.

Competent casters and knowledgeable flyfishers won't get caught in the unneeded, new- or specialty-line, stiff rod nonsense as often. We've seen a beginning caster can't utilize long-belly or other specialty lines. So, are there actually enough "advanced beginners," or whatever they may be called, left to use all the specialty lines manufactured? (At last count 450 different lines from SA and 400 from Cortland.) If not, then there must be lots of easily swayed (advanced?) flyfishers. People forget what Clint Eastwood said in several of his roles, "A man's got to know his limitations." Also, his real needs. The industries must see few limitations in their ability to sell the uninformed, sophisticated and even flyfishers considering themselves knowledgeable and experienced.

Flyfisher Woes

Rod-line misbalance has been allowed to evolve into a confusing monster. The shame is in all the poor souls frustrated and caused unneeded grief and expense. Frustration caused by poorly working tackle will cause some, perhaps many, to quit. Others will continue to show up on the doorsteps of the fly shops seeking "professional" cures for misunderstood woes.

> "I'm vulnerable to graphite rod advertising and presently have representative rods of every generation from Fenwick HMG to Sage RPL. There must be something basically wrong with me because each advancement in graphite seems to take me farther

from my ideal: a rod that flexes progressively right down to the corks."

Those are the words of a fellow responding, via letter to the editor, to the same 4-weight rod test article in *Fly Rod and Reel* that we examined. Bless his heart. He knows what a fly rod should "feel" like. I'm sorry for his and others' frustration, but I'd bet many in the industries could care less or don't understand the lamentable importance of what he's saying. He's been "sold" lots of unneeded rods and recognizes the superiority of the Fenwick HMG.

There has been a movement back to softer rods of late, and we know some companies never or mildly participated in the stiff rod rash. Other company's dim corporate awareness was only jogged by customer complaints and high broken rod returns. Enlightenment came long after any authentic flyfisher knew they had bungled. Watching them market and promote "new," softer, rods is amusing.

After taking rods to ridiculous levels of mislabeled stiffness, how are the industries to justify and market the new softer rods without looking stupid or as intentionally misleading buyers with earlier stiff and AFTMA-incorrect rods? They can't, despite continuing claims certain rods were made only for "advanced" or "special" casters. If that's true why were so many sold to beginners, average or poor casters?

But myriad flyfishers, being ignorant or oblivious, will miss the significance of what's happening. They'll allow the industries to jawbone, market and weasel their way out of reprehension richly deserved. If the industries are successful—they likely will be—it will bc due to flyfisher lack of caring, innocence or forgiving nature and not industries' benevolence or business competency. Many of industries' individuals must judge competency to be large profits or inside industry esteem not the goodwill of most flyfishers or lots of good done flyfishing. A sad situation.

Specific Problems

Industry-wide, complied to, standards give an experimenter a sound base from which to start. It's easy to over or underline an *AFTMA defined* rod for some valid reason or to recommend doing so to another.

Suppose a person receiving valid recommendation from someone knowledgeable innocently buys a wrongly designated 6-weight rod of some modern make—a rod that is in actuality an AFTMA defined 8-weight. He then proceeds to underline it with a 5-weight DT (one line weight, he thinks), for far and fine fishing, as instructed. Our experimenter is then three line weights under the rod's true weight and has an unworkable muddle. If he chose another maker's rod he might be only two line weights light, and a remote chance exists he would actually find a correctly marked AFTMA 6-weight.

A wrongly designated 6-weight rod (that's actually an 8-weight), is automatically two line weights underlined if the *sworn* correct 6-weight line is used. What if an uniformed buyer doesn't want or need to be to be automatically underlined but rather prefers being one line weight overlined for close fishing or to learn casting? Following the rod's incorrect line rating he would mount a 7-weight. But he's still underlined one line weight. Success would require a 9-weight. How many know to or would do that? Who should be required to? Do you want to get caught in this mess (you are)? Trust the shops or industries that put you there to further advise you? Here's another common problem.

Many 2-weight rods of modern designation are closer to AFTMA-defined 4-weights. If we have users of new 2-weight rods using what they think are matching, and usually AFTMA weight correct, 2-weight lines, what does that mean? It seems reasonable that dinky rods are best suited for closer fishing, yet we find our user may be automatically two line weights underlined and probably using a WF to boot. A 2-weight line would only start to balance a stiff, near 4-weight, rod or bring out "feel" at cast line distances of something like 50 feet, maybe more. And that's with a DT, not a WF. Closer casting of too light lines requires unenjoyable, inefficient, stressful arm- and wrist-dominated casting. It's another crazy situation brought to you by your caring and deep thinking flyfishing industries. But underlined, dinky rods massage the ego of users. "I'm actually casting 80 feet with a 2-weight rod," thinks the sophisticate. Disgusting—let him try such a cast with more than a breath of wind.

A New System

There is currently a clamor from within the Elite industry

for a new system to determine rod-line balance. I'll bet they'd really like something to bail themselves out of the box they've built themselves. They'll screw it up worse—wait and see. At this writing the North American Fly-Tackle Trade Association (NAFTA) is working through a formal committee to review and "update" *fly line* standards. Look out. The current information I have is the Elite wants to *adjust both length and weight* of that portion of line used to designate lines or at least some lines. Given only that, it's impossible to determine the outcome. Some things we do know for sure.

There will be new variables to lines allowing more differentiation and confusion of flyfishers by the industries. Change deliberations will be dominated by a few exceedingly sophisticated, profit-dominated Elite industry insiders. A new system will be disliked by segments in and outside the industries. Changes to fly lines and the balance system will be aimed at selling more lines, justifying specialty or stiff rods and selling more tackle of all kinds via confusion and supposed need. I can see now that our old lines will be declared obsolete and not capable of "maximum performance" or failing to match "modern" rods. The "revolutionary" new lines will call forth yet more special and "needed" rods, leaders, reels, techniques and on and on and on.

Until someone can prove the average cast made today and likely to be made tomorrow is 25.7 feet or 42 feet or some distance other than the AFTMA used 30 feet, there exists no sound reason for changing anything. *What's needed is product compliance to the AFTMA system we now have.* There is no flyfishing protecting, courageous, overseeing body to govern the flyfishing industries. Absent one, you and I need assume that role and responsibility. We have the dollars the industries want. I won't give them anymore than I absolutely must. To do more is to validate their damaging, incorrect ways and lack of reality recognition. Uninformed or easily swayed flyfishers believing the industries' bogus self-centered yammering and spending heavily are another, a serious and a *causal* problem. Such flyfishers cause a never ending string of unneeded and detrimental products to be run at all of us.

Basic rod-line balance, defined by AFTMA, is mighty useful for beginning flyfishers, indeed any flyfisher, ***if*** the industries comply. Thirty feet of line to run a rod is apropos and well thought out.

A Test

Having said and examined all we have about balance, let me tell you of a test of medium to heavy rods of mine. I cast seven differing DT and level 6-, 7- and 8-weight lines of three-makes, on six different custom rods. The rods were: 9-foot, 8-weight Fenwick Boron; 9-foot, 8-weight Fenwick HMG graphite; 9½-foot, 3-piece, 7-, 8-weight Steffen graphite; 9½-foot, 8-, 9-weight Lamiglas graphite; 9½-foot, 7-weight, Fenwick Eagle graphite; and an old 10½-foot, 9-weight, Fenwick HMG, 3-piece, graphite.

For the test area, I chose a stretch of riverside gravel bank with a moderate uniform current flowing from left to right. I measured distances on the bank below me and marked them with piles of stones at waters edge. I tested each line on each rod. It took several hours to complete as I tested both conventional cast pickups and roll casts (several times each) for a total of 84 record tests.

The idea, in the pickup test, wasn't to see how far I could cast conventionally but to see how much of the floating lines length and weight I could pick from the water. That tells the lifting ability or usefulness a rod-line combination has for me. I then measured and recorded the longest length of line lifted from the water as revealed by my piles of rocks. All distances measured included the length of the rod but not the leader. With the roll cast test, I was looking for the distance I could cast each rod-line combination comfortably or just beyond comfortably.

The tests had nothing to do with overhead casting distance. Conventional casting distances are too variable and based on a caster ability, experience and, as mentioned, subconscious adaptation of casting strokes to the line used. I use lots of roll casts in my fishing. I can cast conventionally as needed or wanted by adjusting my movements or false casts. I didn't test WF lines. They can't be roll cast to distance or used effectively when long lengths of line need to be picked from water's surface, as I was doing.

In summary: Pickup distances ranged from 45 to 70 feet. Roll cast distances ranged from 50 to 85 feet. If I throw out the results of the dog of a 9-foot Fenwick Boron and the long and powerful 10½-foot Fenwick, both pickup and roll cast distances cluster between 60 and 70 feet with a few exceptions longer and shorter. Pickup distances averaged about four feet more than roll casts. The upshot is that regardless of line weight or taper shape, individual rods performed about the same. One rod picked up and roll cast all the lines better than all the other rods, again with a few exceptions. That rod was the 7-weight, Fenwick Eagle. It originally had a 9-foot blank that I had plugged at the butt to make it 9½ feet long. It was the *lightest* of the rods tested.

Conclusions

Ideal rods, those that end up being favorites, have ability to accommodate several line weights and to perform without unduly stressing casting style or enjoyment. I fish three DT line weights on several of my rods, large and small. After all the discussion of this chapter about achieving rod-line balance, am I now telling you it doesn't matter? Absolutely not, each rod handles an ideal length of a particular line weight best.

The line to be fished on a given rod, at a given time is selected based on the job to be done. That includes, but isn't limited to, distances to be cast. Notwithstanding what we know, there exists an average or "all around" best line that balances the rod at an "average" distance for average purposes. AFTMA 30-foot requirements do a credible job of defining averages. Society and commerce are full of needed standard sizes and designations of things that producers wouldn't dream of stupidly modifying or ignoring to further selfish purposes. (One foot *always* equalling 12 inches, for instance.) Why should the flyfishing industries? Why should we tolerate them doing so? But that's only part of the point.

It's quite possible we will have some "new and improved" system of supposed balance jammed down our throats in the future. It might be completely different but will most likely be a hybrid of new and old. Despite, if and when something different arrives, cling to the spirit of rod-line balance and usage. Stay informed about what the industries are doing and use what works, regardless of someone's recommendations or new system. Fight for honesty and compliance from the industries. As it now stands we have only one valid system. That's the most useable—when complied with—AFTMA system.

Rods and lines, accurately labeled *per producer agreed to AFTMA definitions* would make our flyfishing effectively so much easier. AFTMA compliance would preserve integrity, understanding and uniformity in the market. In avoiding disorder, flyfishers gain ability to learn, grow and better enjoy themselves—particularly to buy, modify or experiment protected by rod-line designations long *defined* and *uniform* regardless manufacturers' and industries' agendas or their ideas of correctness.

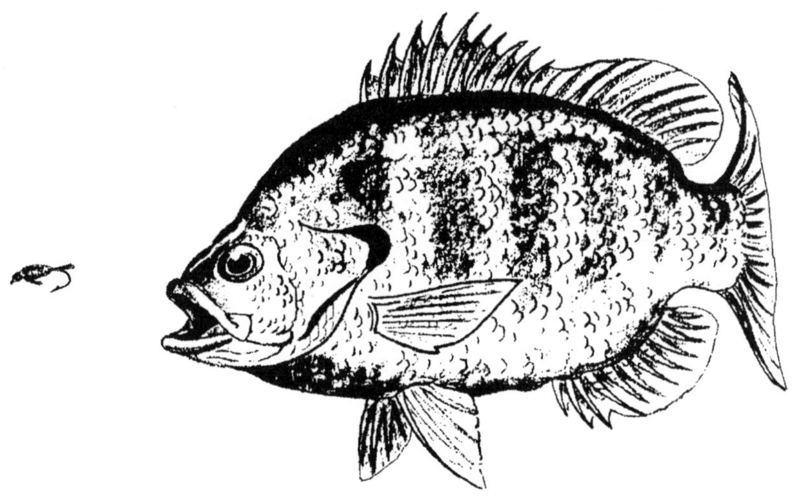

Chapter Seven:
Fly Reels

Fly reels are of minimal importance to fly fishing—most of the time. They're not minimal as mere places to store line as some say but minimal as being only decent machinery, well maintained and adequate for its tasks—tasks a reel must perform, error free, every time called upon. Fly reels, like good shoes, should fit, be simple and functional, durable and light of weight.

Many new and unneeded reels have come to the market amid significant hoopla the last few years. It's said every aerospace contractor losing a government gravy-train contract began making fly reels. Many new reels carry prices that assume as much naïveté or irrationality on the part of reel buyers as the government. Some people buy these too costly new reels. Lots more don't. Maybe it's a natural for some. Who wants to put a $50 reel on their new $500 rod?

To set the tone of this chapter and put fly reels in proper perspective, let us recall the 148-pound sailfish taken by Lee Wulff. It was done many years ago, and the feat was filmed. The sail was taken on a $12 glass fly rod—it was selected because it was blue and Lee liked blue—and a simple, click-drag, Farlow reel with 300 yards of backing.

These days it's widely believed a special, expensive and heavy disk-drag reel is needed for powerful and largish fish like steelhead and Atlantic salmon and many saltwater game fish. What about the literal millions of such fish taken easily on much simpler, click-drag reels over the past 100 years or so? Would more have been taken with disk-drag reels? Probably not. Many people selling the new high-priced reels and those believing disk-drag reels are commonly needed must be unread, inexperienced, or so profit motivated they don't mind appearing so. Newcomers, the gullible and those unthinking provide ample and easy targets for the producers and sellers of supposedly needed, fancy or "high quality" reels.

Reel Types

Of the three types of fly reels: automatic, multiplying and single action, the first listed is least used. If stripping nonrunning fish by hand rather than playing them off the reel is a person's method, an automatic could work. Automatics are always heavy, have limited line capacity and are prone to mechanical failure. They are bombs waiting to explode amidst flying levers and springs for those venturing to work on them. Despite "free stripping" features advertised, strong fish can't take adequate line even if the reel could hold it. Fighting a powerful or fast moving fish with coils of line strewn about beckons disaster. Pass them by unless you have a specialty use.

A multiplying reel, like a pet monkey, seems a nifty idea at first. They retrieve more than one spool revolution's worth of line for each turn of the reel's handle. Trouble is, if the line comes in that way, it goes out the same way, and that puts heavy demands on the reel's overrun engineering. Extra demand can be overcome with a fancier drag system and with it comes more maintenance, chance of breakdown and extra weight from the extra drag parts. Multiplying gears also add weight. The cause of extra weight makes these reels heavy in price as well. There are reels on the market that have fancy gearing, preventing reel handle revolution when a fish takes line. Sounds like more problems to me, but I've never used one.

I have owned and used several multipliers, including a nifty Cortland with a two to one retrieve ratio. It's clever to be able to gain line with rapidity as compared to grinding away with a single action. It's adroit to be able to literally winch a small fish, even across the water's surface, to be quickly released.

Years ago a better than average North Umpqua steelhead was hooked using the Cortland. It proved anything but adroit or clever. The fish ran unimpeded by an ineffectual and overpowered drag. Its downstream wanderings eventually took it, with me in tow, to a point a few yards above the waterfall at the Rock Creek flyfishing deadline. There, in typical steelhead fashion, it inched and weaseled downstream, tail-first, against my best efforts. In arriving at the falls, I squeezed the backing tight against the rod grip trying to keep the reel from giving line as I stumbled along, over and through the stream-side rip-rap and brush, alternately pausing attempting to gain line or moving, trying to keep up with the fish. Bit-by-frustrating-bit the increasing suck of pressure on the fish, now at the lip of the falls, increased. It went over. I released my hold on the backing, hoping somehow to land the fish below the mass of white water.

Besides wearing out a fair number of DT lines, I've worn out a bait casting reel or two. Never have I experienced a bait-caster backlash similar the magnitude of the one that erupted from that multiplying piece of junk when the steelhead went over the falls. I had to cut deeply into the remaining backing to extricate things and felt lucky to recover my fly line by hand-over-handing it out of the jumbled mess of rocks and water below the falls. It was badly damaged, and I know now small loss, being a WF.

Single action fly reels (one to one retrieve ratio) can backlash, usually mildly, particularly using light drag adjustment or with reels having only nonadjustable clickers (pawls). To give strong fish inferior-reel generated mechanical advantage in addition to their considerable natural abilities is fishing suicide. I sold the Cortland to a fellow enamored with that model and, I suspect, not yet cognizant its full potential. Another multiplier I own is used to quickly strip fly lines or backing from other reels. Its weight, spool slop and clanking are acceptable in my den where it can do no serious damage. Let's look at single action reels.

One turn of their handle equals one turn of their spool or drum. The basic design of single action reels remains unchanged in well over 100 years. Materials used in construction have changed, mostly for the better, while do-dads, bells, whistles and sophisticated modifications have been added. Many modifications only allow differentiation from other reel models or brands. We know the value of differentiation for primarily increased sales.

Reel Attributes

History-proven single action reels have simplicity of design. That includes click-type overrun (drag) controls of constant or adjustable pressure design. If adjustable, adjustments need to be easily accomplished and positive in setting. Drag parts must be well made of materials with correct hardness and compatible with other metals or materials inside the reel. Often they are not, and any softer parts wear far too rapidly.

Try to find parts for reels, from even the big companies, made one year and discontinued the next. It will be a growing problem; not all of the recent new reels or reel companies will survive. Do you want to own one of their modern wonders when the company goes broke or quits making your model? Long-term availability of parts, extra spools and repair service should be major considerations when contemplating reel purchase. A couple of wisely chosen, quality reels with a few matching spools will last a flyfisher's lifetime. What should you look for in a reel?

The spools or drums of reels should be deep and narrow. Narrow is defined as 7/8 to 1-1/8 inches wide. Deep should be as deep as possible. Spool depth, and consequent capacity of some reels (often multipliers), is reduced because a portion of the available space is used internally for gearing and drag mechanisms. Such reels usually attempt to compensate for minimal capacity by increasing spool width—a fatal blunder. Such reels then have excess weight and spooling problems caused by wider spools. Most damaging, however, are small diameter (often wide-spooled) reels' slow retrieval rates as compared to larger diameter, narrow spooled reels of similar or even larger capacity and much better design.

Reels with outside diameters of less than three inches are more toys than serious flyfishing tools. Small diameter reels cause lines to set in small coils. Only tediously slow retrieves are possible with small diameter reels. They are often as heavy or heavier than decently sized reels. Tiny reels may look cute or balance small rods, but those belong in the toy box as well. I recently saw an advertisement for 3/4-weight rods and reels to match; they must be toys for toddlers or toy fish. *A three-quarter weight?* P. T. Barnum was right.

Ideal Reels

Reels made of lightweight, high quality metal or alloys have withstood the tests of time. They should have small, but strong, spindle shafts allowing desired deep and narrow drums. Outside diameters of 3 to 4½ inches will handle all flyfishing I can envision. Any reel in this size range will accommodate several, more or less appropriate, line sizes comfortably with adequate room for backing. You may need to disregard line size recommendations often implied in a reel's model name or numbers.

Example: I have several English, Hardy-made, Scientific Angler (SA) System 7 reels with extra spools. This reel is my all-time favorite trout reel, and I have used several of them for over 25 years. (It is now produced by Hardy alone as their Marquis #7, and any of the new or old spools interchange.) Both are strongly made, lightweight, simple, dependable and easily repaired. They have outside diameters of just under 3-1/2 inches and an outside width of just under 1 inch. Despite SA saying, by model name, that the reel is for 7-weight lines, I have always used them for 4-, 5- and 6-weight lines, and you will remember I always use DTs. The System 7 works and feels right on the rods I use with those lines. Filled to within 3/8-inch of the spool's reinforcing cross members (pillars), maximum reel efficiency results, yet there is still the security of lots of backing with any of the lines listed.

With a DT-7 over maximum backing and a spool filled to the correct level, I am set for most of the fish I will ever hook using the System 7. The reel, being light, feels too light for most 7-weight rods, and I'm actively looking for larger fish these days and prefer more backing. I also use the next size, a System 8, for 6- and 7-weight lines. It's a decent reel, but I don't consider it the reel the System 7 is. Don't ask me why. It's now made as the Hardy Marquis #8/9.

I also use Hardy Perfect reels in 3-3/8 and 3-5/8 inch sizes for 5-, 6- and 7-weight lines. While they are fine reels featuring thick housings, good drags, ball-bearings and agate stripping rings, such embellishments add too much weight to make the reels my ideal. You will recall lightness in hand was the first criteria for an ideal rod, and a reel mustn't destroy that lightness. I'm aware popular opinion says weight below the casting hand on a fly rod is unimportant. Use a heavy reel for 10 hours of casting one day and a light reel the next. You will notice difference.

My most used large fish reel, a Hardy St. Aidan, is about 3¾ inches in diameter and, being in the Hardy Light-Weight series, is indeed light. This reel handles up to a DT-9 with plenty of backing capacity. Hardy reels are paragons of dependability. Parts are dove-tailed and riveted together; very few screws are used and those in relatively unimportant places. Over 100 years of Hardy's reel making know-how, reputation and parts availability protect users.

Quality made, well maintained and balanced reels with a minimum of problematic screws and excess weight will serve you well for many years. Hardy reels remain relatively inexpensive, particularly used ones, if you can find them. As this is written Hardy reels are less expensive from some outlets in Canada. If you know someone going to London, have him buy direct to save. I've done that several times.

Pflueger fly reels with 60 or more years of history are also time and angler-tested. They are reasonably priced and available in correct sizes. Pfluegers are a little heavy and have some other minor problems, none insurmountable, which we will discuss in a minute.

Nice Features and Problems

Any fly reel should have a handle you can both quickly grip and let go. It should be large enough to provide a comfortable grip. I own an older (1940s) English-made J. W. Young reel. Its handle is cupped on three sides; it's very comfortable and efficient to use. This reel also has a tiny screw in the very center of the outside of the spool, on the handle side. I wondered about its purpose for years, then discovered it adjusts away annoying, wear accumulated slack that allows sideways play of the drum within the frame. Try to find features like these on the newest and "best" $400-plus wonders.

Of screws, a reel should have a minimum. I'm puzzled when I examine the innards of most of today's high priced reels and find dinky screws holding important things together. Anyone who has owned and used the fine Pflueger Medalist reels, or their copies, for any length of time, knows about loose or lost screws. Screws that need "Loctiting" or lacquering in place are one thing on a $35 reel and quite another on a reel selling for $350 or more.

Vibration shakes reel screws loose. It can come from prolonged use, vehicles, airplanes and fish. I recently tested a 3-3/8 inch diameter reel of mine. It retrieves (or gives) 10 inches of line per spool revolution when correctly filled, half-full 4-3/4 inches. Just for fun, let's say a fish is taking line from this reel at 25 mph (many have the ability). The full reel will spin at over 2,600 rpm, half-full—all the line and some of the backing out—the spool will revolve at nearly 5,600 rpm. Increase the fish speed to 50 mph—saltwater game fish speed—and the spool revolves at nearly 5,300 and over 11,000 rpm, respectively. Small vibrations at 2,600 rpm can become violent at 6,000 rpm or more.

One make of super-expensive reel, advertised as being for the strongest of saltwater fish and containing small internal screws, is smaller in diameter than the Hardy used in the above test; it would revolve even faster. Will it endure prolonged 6,000 to 8,000 plus rpm usage? Some blue-printed, fiddled-and-fussed-with race-car engines will, but they aren't held together with diminutive screws. Maybe there's something new with the way screws are made or work that I don't understand, but I've got to go with my experience. I don't want tiny screws holding my reels together.

Some fly reels have revolving, exposed, exterior rims (spool rim fits over frame); they're useful, I'm told. The System reels I've described have them. What little trouble I've had over many years with those reels is mostly attributable to those rims. I occasionally take a bad spill in the tangled, bankside jumble of rocks of the miserable water I prefer to fish (not many others fish there). Clearance between the revolving rim and the frame below is very tight, and it is possible to bend it—in a fall for instance—to a point where the spool will not turn. Out come my pliers and a file to bend and then refine the rim to a point where it will clear the frame. My light weight St. Aidan is of enclosed-rim design, and it would be nice if my favorite System 7s were. If so, they would be called Hardy Princesses. If I didn't already own the 7s, they're the reels I'd use. I can do without revolving rims.

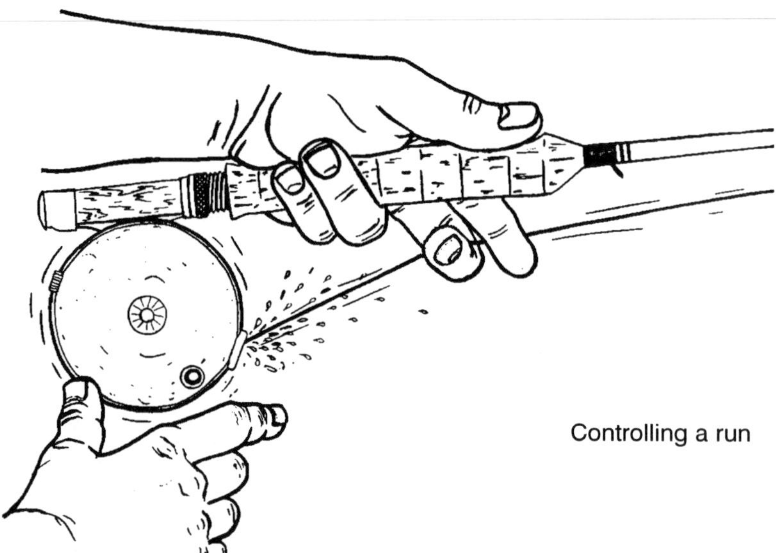

Controlling a run

Theoretically you are supposed to "palm" or finger the exposed revolving rim for additional control over a hooked fish if the click pressure control won't do the job. I think such procedure too sophisticated. There are better methods. A favorite method is shown in the illustration. Use the first two fingers of the hand that holds the rod at the moment. Pick the line up with those two fingers running the line over the middle finger and under the index finger. That causes the line to travel a modified "S," variable by changing the alignment of the two fingers. By altering your fingers' positions you can hold the line tight, drop it free or apply any amount of drag pressure between those extremes—instantly—even with anticipation or sixth-sensing of a hooked fish's next reaction. Nothing beats this method. If and when you need another method of applying drag, insert a finger, of your nonrod hand, into the reel's spool and apply pressure to the *inside* of the spool, line or backing.

Aircraft aluminum, that's the magic stuff of reels, according to the anointed or sell-siders. But just what are they jabbering about? I live in a town where Kaiser Aluminum makes aluminum, and it makes *many kinds* destined for use in aircraft. Perhaps a salesman will change his tune when you question his knowledge of aluminum and he tells you his reel is machined, not cast. Modern casting processes are so precise you can see the tool marks left on the original die in the finished product. Sturm, Ruger and Co. makes receivers for very high pressure rifle cartridges from cast metal. They also make golf club heads by similar process. Such metals and technique should work for a reel. Adequate reels are made in several ways.

What about a reel's finish? It should prevent corrosion, be *subdued* in color and last for a reasonable number of years. Few of my Hardys have held up as well as I would like, but it's been 25 years of hard use for some of them, and I view their muted battle scars fondly. I have a friend who recently purchased a very expensive Abel reel. It's dazzling gold in coloration. I watched him fish a run while using it under bright sun on Idaho's St. Joe River. Each casting stroke sent rays of reflected light stabbing in all directions. The St. Joe's cutthroats aren't the brightest of trout, certainly not the 10- to 12-inchers he caught. He doesn't fish badly and was using the right fly in the right place. A week earlier the run yielded several fish of 16 inches or so, and I caught the 10- to 12-inchers as well, releasing them all. Was it the flashy reel? Maybe.

It's acceptable, but not critical, for a reel to be adjustable for left or right hand retrieve, and most are today. Such reversibility will accommodate left-handed people but *should not* be used to select preferred-hand winding. That selection is often wrong nowadays and will work against you. Many wind with the wrong hand. We'll get into that in the chapter on fly-fishing.

Many inexpensive (under perhaps $75) reels are poorly made but so are some very expensive ones. New SA System reels, some Orvis reels and a host of others are probably adequate but tend to be heavier than I like. SA abandoned one of its recent reels after only a year or two of production, and so did Sage. I know several people trying to now find extra spools for those reels. When considering fly reels, look for the features we've discussed: Simplicity, durability, parts availability, light weight, correct size, narrow and deep drum and a builder with a proven history. Don't fall for meaningless, potentially expensive or false sales spiels.

Chapter Eight: Knots

Roderick Haig-Brown said: "Fear of casting keeps most people trolling or using other clumsy tackle." If casting is the first fear in flyfishing, knot-tying might be second. People permit bamboozling, fear knot-tying or discount correctly tied, necessary knots and try to "get by." They will inevitably suffer. Why would anyone travel to far destinations, spend $400 for a rod or reel or presume to talk as if knowledgeable of flyfishing, when, in their heart of hearts, they know they can't tie simple, needed and correct knots?

Some flyfishers say they simply can't tie knots. I don't believe. Such people lace shoes, thread needles, tie flies or pick up dimes. Most who can't tie knots simply refuse to practice. Tie a knot correctly ten times in a row and, like using a new word, it's yours for life. Knot books show extensive confusing knots; most are variations of basic ties. Learn the basic knots needed. Practice tying knots with small diameter rope or cord to see how the knots go together. The results are easily untied for further practice. Do final practice, however, in the material you will be using.

Any knot used should be inherently strong (testing a high percentage of the straight breaking strength of material used), unless you have a good reason to use another. Tests show knots always slip before they fail. Tighten knots fully and correctly. Correctly means with uniform and sufficient tension. Tightening knots creates heat through friction; therefore, use material that withstands heat and abrasion (discussed in Chapter 3). Minimize what does arise by lubricating knots with saliva before tightening. Glue or knot preparations are unneeded and capitalize on ignorance or failure to learn to tie knots correctly.

Ruling out specialized knots used primarily by saltwater flyfishers, knot requirements are simple. You *need* to be able to tie leader butts and backing to fly line, join pieces of leader material, affix backing to reel spool and tie flies to tippets. Six knots will suffice.

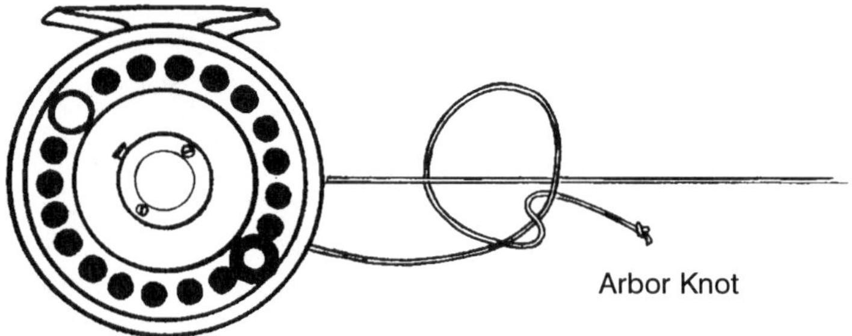
Arbor Knot

Let's start with the Arbor knot, used to attach backing to reel. Consult the diagram. First tie a simple Overhand or Granny knot in the backing's very end and pull tight. Run the backing around the spool and tie another Overhand knot *around* the standing (longest) part of the backing (the standing backing runs through the middle of the knot). Pull that knot tight. Then pull hard on the standing line above the knot. The second knot will slide down to the arbor and slip until it comes up tight against the first knot. A piece of cake.

Fly to Leader

Tie flies to a leader using a Clinch knot for straight eyed flies and a Turle or Turle Replacement knot (not *Turtle,* as spelled in Cortland's current fly line information booklet) for all others. First the Clinch: Please study the diagram if you're trying to learn this knot.

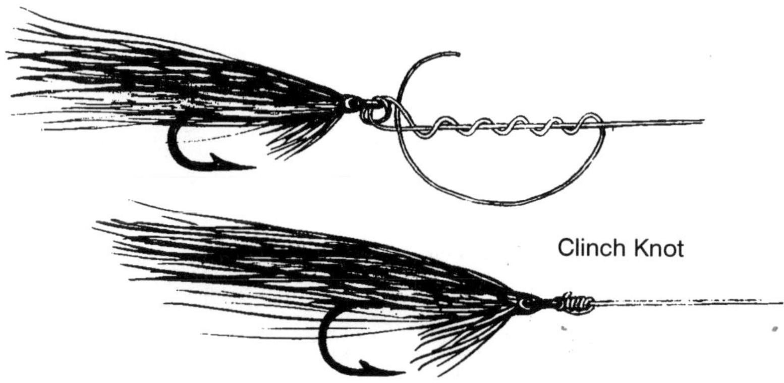

Tests prove five wraps of the tag (loose) end around the standing portion hold best in the middle diameters of leader, say 6- to 12-pound test. Under 6 pound, take 6 or 7 wraps; over 12 pounds, 4 will do; over 20 pounds, 3 are adequate. Do remember to go through straight eyed flies—the *only* type eye where a clinch is used—*twice* with the tag end before tying the knot.

I don't recommend the Improved Clinch, having had few problems with correctly tied basic Clinch knots. The "improved" part takes time, complicating tying and especially tightening, particularly in near darkness. Other knots will work on straight eyed hooks; however, the Clinch is easier to tie and the only one allowing stripping the knot loose with thumb nail and finger tip when you wish to remove a fly. Consequently the basic Clinch is fastest and cannibalizes the least tippet material subjected to frequent fly changes.

The Turle Replacement knot is similar to the Arbor knot. It may be known as the George Harvey knot; the result is similar to the Double Turle. But not having to poke the fly back through loops as is required with the Double Turle simplifies and avoids problems of the leader invariably catching on rearward, or upward, fly material projections. Either knot keeps flies tied on up or down eyes correctly in line with the tippet. That's important.

To tie the Turle Replacement consult the diagram and proceed as follows. Hold the fly behind the eye with one hand after folding materials back, out of the way. Complete the knot's wraps as shown. Pull on the standing end with the other hand. As the knot tightens the constricting loop will crawl

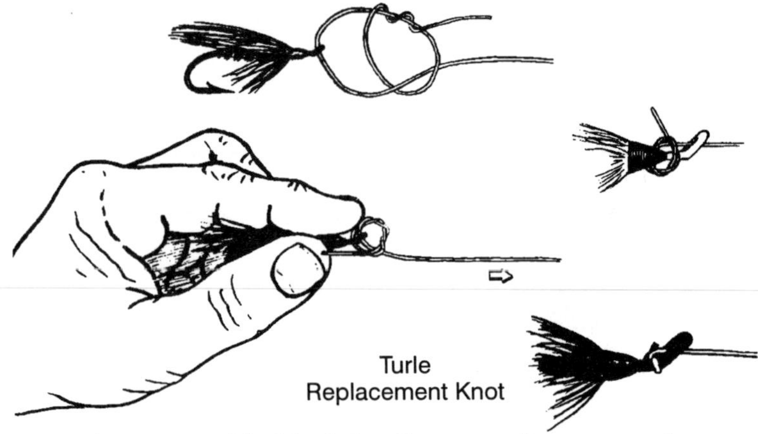

cleverly over and behind the fly eye and set securely around the hook's shank. Practice on larger hooks at first. Hints: Hold the constricting loop against the shank, close behind the eye, with one finger of the hand holding the fly while pulling on the standing end. Three wraps are necessary to prevent slippage of small diameter material or on large diameter shanks like those of double hooks—or with too large fly heads.

Besides being problematical to tie, there is confusion about just what a regular Double Turle knot is. Roderick Haig-Brown in his *A Primer of Fly-Fishing* illustrated a Double Turle differently from the description of A. J. McClane in *McClane's Standard Fishing Encyclopedia.* Remember I'm showing the simpler alternative (Turle Replacement) of George Harvey and Lee Wulff to achieve the same highly desirable knot performance. Practice. This knot is important.

If you absolutely cannot tie the Turle Replacement (doubtful), *do not* revert to tying Clinch knots *on* up or down turned eyes. A substitute is to use the Clinch but *only in this way:* First, insert the tag end of the leader through the hook eye from the front; second, wrap the tippet completely around the *hook shank behind* the eye; third, thread the leader back *out* through the eye from behind; fourth, tie the Clinch knot. The knot will tighten *into,* not on, the fly eye keeping the fly more, but not exactly, in line with the leader. I'm unaware of a formal name for this knot; I guess it's my "invention."

An admirable attribute of the Turle Replacement knot, over others and in low light, is its ease of tying without having to poke leader ends or flies through tight places. It's an easy knot to tie by feel alone. Only concentration keeping materials clear as the knot sets around the shank is required. Practice at home, not on the water. I restate the importance of using a knot that will keep the fly in line with the leader. Don't be one of the many losing fish by failure to conform to proven wisdom.

Joining Leader

Only if you're content using endless quantities of purchased tapered leaders at $2 to $5 each and wishing to limit your effectiveness can you avoid joining pieces of leader. Learn the Blood knot (named for a Mr. Blood) or as a *poor* substitute, the Surgeon's knot. Surgeon's knots are bulky, but worse, leave tag ends protruding at odd angles inviting wedging in rocks, limbs, weeds or brush while accumulating debris from the water. Blood knots are tight, compact and have

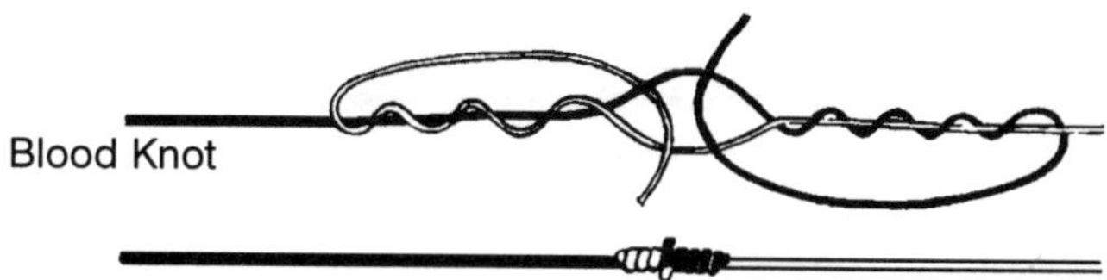

clever built-in tapers to avoid wedging, accumulation of unwanted material and excess water disturbance.

Rather than give confusing and boring, step-by-step instructions on tying Blood knots, I'll give some hints. If my method doesn't work for you, remember it doesn't matter how you tie a knot as long as you tie it *correctly*. Study the diagram. My tying method uses the thumbs and first two fingers of both hands to tie the knot while ring and little fingers of both hands hold standing ends and maintain tension on the forming knot. I place the heaviest material in my left (weaker) hand.

Ensure at least 4-inch long tag ends of each material being joined. Create an "X" by crossing the two tag ends. Grasp this X with the weak hand thumb and index finger. Wrap the heaviest material around the lighter first, using the thumb and index finger of your master hand *and* the second finger of your weak hand. Now insert the tag end of the heavy material just wrapped, back through, the original X created. Fold the tag end back to now be held, along with the X point, by the thumb and index finger of the *master* hand. Note holding hand was switched. Now complete the required wraps of the lighter material using whatever fingers, of either or both hands, that work best for you. Also insert the lighter material's loose tag end through the original X point. Pull the knot mostly tight using a hand on each standing part, then tug on each tag end protrusion, before final tightening. Simple. Lubrication helps the knot tighten. Trim tag ends close when you're sure the knot is tight. If that was step-by-step, excuse me.

When tying a Blood knot, take one less wrap with the heavier than with the lighter material. (Recommended number of turns appears in the earlier Clinch knot discussion.) Doing so makes a neater knot that tightens easily. Completed knots should reveal the two tag ends sticking out opposite sides of the knot. If they do not, work on your final tying step to ensure they do. Realign the X opening by slightly rolling the material between the holding thumbs and index fingers. My knots tend to come out correct, naturally. I hope yours do as well. If not, you know how to correct the problem.

The Blood knot may also be tied, mostly by feel, in near darkness. You need only hold the nearly completed knot up to available light (the sky) to complete the final tag end "stick through." Pushed, most flyfishers admit favoring the inferior Surgeon's knot because they can't tie Blood knots. You can, with a little practice. Just decide you will.

Use Blood knots to join materials of similar stiffness and not more than .003 inch diameter difference. That includes dacron backing splices. Experiment if joining differing material brands. Smaller, stiffer and tougher material like Maxima Chameleon will cut softer, even larger, materials like Orvis, Umpqua, Climax or even softer Maxima.

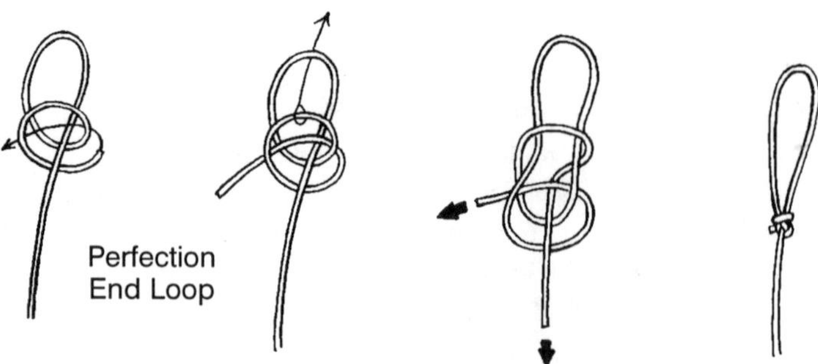

The only loop knot most know how to tie is created by doubling the line and tying an Overhand (Granny) knot. It's a serious mistake; this knot tests, at best, only 60% of straight breaking strength. Use the Perfection End Loop.

Again, study the diagram. A simple explanation of the knot is: Create a *loop* you look straight through (with tag end *behind);* go completely *around that loop* with a second loop of the tag end; take the tag end *between the two loops* and poke downward; pull the second loop *backwards* through the first. Done.

Tied correctly the knot will not slip, and the tag end will protrude at right angles from the knot body. Hints: In tying, don't let go of anything with your holding hand while pulling backward on the second loop to tighten the knot. Let go only when the knot is almost tight. The size of finished loop is *variable* and *determined* by size of the second loop taken in tying.

Use pairs of interlocking Perfection End Loops to join materials, particularly tippet to leader. Loops allow joining materials of larger diameter difference than Blood knots and facilitate quick, easy changing of tippet. Sets of loops don't cannibalize the leader section just above tippet shortening it to the point Blood knots are impossible to tie unless time is taken to replace that section and eventually the one above that, then the one above that. If such needed repairs aren't made, leader function is compromised. Interlocking loops avoid such repair problems. The flyfisher survey revealed the more experienced a person is the more use is made of loops in rigging. Loops are efficient. Joining of two loops was diagrammed in Chapter Three about leaders.

The Perfection End Loop is not as strong as other knots commonly used but strong enough. Its handiness and multiplicity of uses forgives it that one transgression. It's still the best, quick and simple loop available and the *only* simple loop that runs directly *in-line* with the leader's axis. That's important. Uses, in addition to attaching tippets, are attaching full leaders to permanent butt sections and adding long sections to leaders or tippets when time to build or affix a correct leader is unavailable. Sometimes speed in getting the fly into the water is preferred over absolute correctness.

Fly Line Connections

A fly line needs a leader attached to one end and usually backing to the other. Securely attaching a leader to a line requires a trustworthy, correctly functioning connection. That rules out the braided, gripping, glue-on or heat shrink things, little metal pins shoved up the fly line and nearly everything else other than a Nail knot or one of its variations. Wright and McGill Co. markets a connector called a Leader Link that *might* be acceptable to some. I have used them to splice lines, but their excess diameter annoyingly bumps through rod guides, occasionally fouling. They look strange and could fail if used for line-leader connections under large fish stress. The same is true for glue-on connections.

I hear a growing number of horror stories about braided glue-on or heat sensitive connections, and little prognostication was needed to foresee problems. Problems are created and fish lost by indolence and failure to learn to tie a basic flyfishing knot. Most glue weakens with continual wetting. Heating ends of fly line or leader is prescription for subsequent disaster. It's too easy to do it wrong.

Persons with most of the fingers on both hands can't consider themselves flyfishers unless they can tie correct Nail knots, anytime, any place. Yet I know many who do, who can't. Flyfishers look for shortcuts and then stumble on the short-

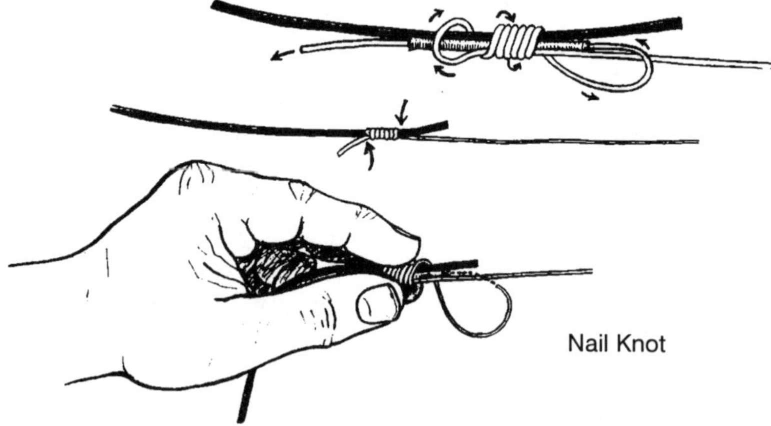

Nail Knot

cut's rough spots: Practice. There are other knots to attach leaders to lines, all inferior and obsolete, included are sundry Figure-Eights, Sheet Bends and half-hitches. Such knots may slip under pressure. More problematic, they are bulky.

Bulkiness affects casting and fishing and will not allow such a knot to easily and quickly traverse guides when needed.

You may see from the diagram what needs to be done to tie a Nail knot. I'll eliminate the blow by blow instructions since what's needed is too obvious from the diagram. Again, there are hints which may help. Start with plenty (six inches) of tag end leader. Carry a small tube on-stream and have several spares at home. Hobby shops sell small diameter tubing in 14-inch lengths of brass, aluminum and plastic. Cut it into three-inch lengths with scissors or file. A large needle will work in lieu of a hollow tube for tying Nail knots and so will a nail (hence the name), if you carefully insert the leader tag where the nail was withdrawn after completing the knot's wraps.

Make the wraps of Nail knots with moderate pressure and slip each successive one under finger and thumb holding the knot as shown. After poking the tag end of the leader through the tube and removing the tube, don't let go the wraps until you alternately pull on standing *and* tag ends of the leader with the free hand. Feel the wraps constrict before letting go. Tease errant wraps into place with thumb nails then tighten the knot—hard—with strong pulls on standing and tag ends. Trim everything close and test again. The knot won't slip if tied correctly. Acquire the habit of examining Nail knots frequently.

Needle Nail Knot

Nail knot constriction eventually breaks the finish of the fly line, creating a cast-destroying hinge in your casting loop. Retie, on the spot, when you find a hinge condition. Prolong the life of Nail knots by coating them with rubber cement. Use the Nail knot to attach backing to a fly line and do coat this junction with cement to ease the knots lightning-like passages (we hope) through the guides.

An apt variation of the Nail knot is the Needle Nail knot. For leader to line attachment use a needle to open the center of a fly line's end to a distance of about 1/4 inch; then force the needle out the side of the line. Insert the leader butt—after trimming its end to an angled point—up the line's center and out through the side opening created. Then tie the Nail knot as usual. Backing requires pulling through the line openings with the needle. Needle knots look nice and traverse guides easily. They're particularly useful for backing to line connections.

I've been critical of some—failing to understand anyone negligent, by vice of practice neglect—unable to tie needed knots, when and where needed. It takes so little time to learn what is so important to a lifetime of flyfishing; *knots are potential fishing destroying weak links.* Know how to tie the ones needed, correctly and quickly. If needed, use glasses, and carry them on the water. Forget knot tying gizmos. We all need practice in some flyfishing endeavor or another—often it's with knots. It's not demeaning or time wasting, unimportant or indicative of mumbled makeup—*quite the opposite.* Are you going to be a competent, successful flyfisher or not?

Everyone ties bad knots—it just happens—retie and keep going. Valuable practice is found tying all steps of a knot possible by feel alone. It will pay dividends when darkness encroaches or you need to keep your eyes on something else, like a cruising fish. I can more fully appreciate knot tying problems as my vision changes with age. I never missed the final "poke through" of a Blood knot in 25 years (exaggeration) but now miss about half without my specs. I haven't taken to carrying a pin-on light yet. It's just another piece of junk to carry, or lose, or worry about extra batteries. Fishing mechanics, including knots, should be uncomplicated, fast, effective and efficient. That allows concentration on finding and hooking fish, enjoying oneself and others.

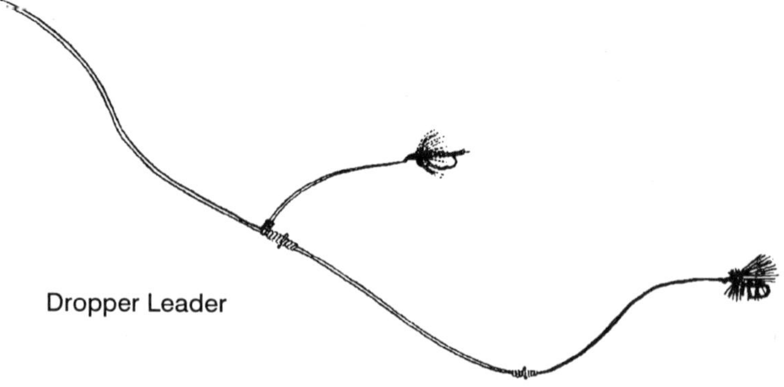
Dropper Leader

Other Knots to Use or Not

Suppose you want to fish a second fly via a dropper leader. Using a Clinch knot, simply tie a piece of material *around* the main leader an appropriate distance up the leader and just above one of your leader's Blood knots.

The dropper will protrude from the main leader at right angles, minimizing tangling while the main leader's Blood knot prevents the dropper sliding down. Keep droppers under six inches in length and of material stiffer than the main leader near the tie-in point. Doing so also helps avoid tangles. The dropper described is easily removed by stripping the knot loose to be added later if desired. A Blood knot's tag-end extensions used as droppers are not so flexible. To tie a dropper to a knot-less leader, cut the leader where you wish the dropper and then tie it back together with a Blood knot. Tie your dropper in above that knot.

Hubbub is perpetual concerning the superiority of certain knots. What is superior? Palomar and Uni-knots, often portrayed as superior or cure-alls, are bulky compared to a Clinch, no stronger or faster to tie and can't be quickly stripped free; you have to cut them. Neither of those knots can be *correctly* used on anything other than straight eyed hooks. They were designed for fishing other than flyfishing where swivels, rings and straight eyes on things are common. That doesn't, however, keep lots of flyfishers from using them and suffering the consequences.

Introduction of leaders made of new materials or with supposed new processes is constant. Test your bevy of knots in marvel stuff before using. I've tested quite a few new materials over the years. Some are bad jokes or worse, and others are questionable in their ability to out-perform Maxima Chameleon. The very newest ones cost way too much, and ridiculous price makes them even less suitable. If electing to use something new and wonderful, it may necessitate knot modifications or changes.

Understanding and mastery of knots described grants ability to build leaders or use only one or two commercial tapered leaders for an entire year of flyfishing, modifying them for immediate need. You may make leader, line, or backing repairs and complete installations of same without relying on "professional" help. A little practice eliminates needless expense, bumbling knot "simplifying" do-dads and knot replacement or tying devices. Practice also eliminates reliance on someone else to do for you or doing things in slipshod manner, something you *will* regret.

An acquaintance of mine has done a great deal of saltwater flyfishing for the toughest and fastest of fish. He often fishes with the biggest of big names. Besides seeing the "best"(expensive and hyperbolized) rods blow up and the "best"(expensive and hyperbolized) reels freeze up, he tells me the greatest fault of even the "best" flyfishers and flyfishing writers is their inability to tie correct knots.

Saltwater knots—occasionally needed for freshwater—such as required to attach heavy shock tippet (pike and musky fishing) seem a bit specialized for average flyfishing. When you need a knot, however, you need it. There are decent knot books available to teach special knots.

Chapter Nine: Fly Hooks

It's important users of flies understand fly hooks. How else will you know if flies are tied on hooks appropriate for efficiency and success? Teaching fly tying classes, operating a tackle shop, tying custom flies, guiding and talking to lots of flyfishers has revealed that most understand hooks poorly. Understanding hooks is difficult partly because the industries have made it so through ignorance and on purpose. Uninformed or confused customers are easily swayed to purchase a certain hook (or other tackle) even if it isn't what's *needed.*

There is an old, but still valid, if poorly used, standard for hook classification and nomenclature. It may have been born in Renaissance Great Britain where a number of early hook makers were located, supplying hooks to the then known world. It's interesting, however, that the very old Scandinavian hook manufacturing firm, O. Mustad and Sons, conformed to the same standard, more or less. I don't know for sure why or even who was first to use the standard. In any event, there exists a "standard hook" from which variations of shank length, wire diameter, bend style, gape (gap) and other characteristics are usually *implied* to always be derived. Please see the diagram; it shows "a" standard hook and labels its parts.

Standard Hook

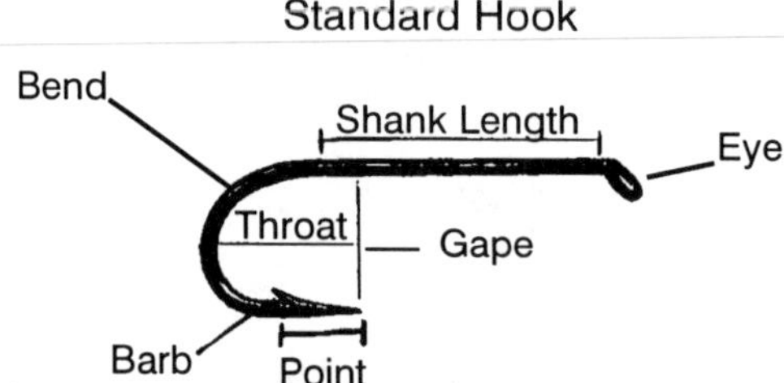

Roderick Haig-Brown in his *A Primer of Fly-fishing* (an excellent book for beginners and others) defines the old English hook system very well. Datus Proper says original explanations are clearer than somebody's rendition; let Mr. Haig-Brown explain hook measurements and hook standards himself:

> "Standard hook sizes represent the length of the shank (without the eye) to a point level with the outside of the bend of the hook, measured in fractions of an inch. A No. 20 standard hook is 5/32" and sizes increase from 20 to 14 by thirty-seconds; from size 14 to size 4 they increase by sixteenths; from there on they increase by eighths of an inch. Hook sizes larger than No.1, which is 1¼ (inch, {sic}), are shown as 1/0, 2/0, etc., in an ascending scale. There is also a standard wire diameter for each size of hook, and less precisely, a standard gap between shank and point."

Modern usage sees hooks measured more by a "standard gape" than shank length. There is a mathematical relationship between hook shank length and gape width. The "standard" hook of most producers has 1½ to 2 times more shank length than gape. Hooks having such ratios both hook and hold fish well, arguably better than those having other ratios—certainly those with longer shanks. Now that we understand a standard hook, deviations may be considered.

Shank and Wire Deviations

Hooks with either longer or shorter shanks than the standard hook are denoted as so many "Xs" long or short. Each "X" is equal to the shank length of one size hook larger (X long) or smaller (X short). A hook with a standard size-6 gape but the shank length of a size-4 would be called a size-6 2XLong or more commonly, size-6 2XL. If our hook had the shank length of a size-8 hook, it would then be denoted a size-6 2XShort or size-6 2XS or No. 6 2XS or #6 2XS. Note that size-5 and -7, not commonly seen, are still sizes considered.

The same method is used for wire diameter deviations, the letters used are "X," again for the appropriate number of size differences, "S" for stout or strong and "F" for fine wire. It gets a little confusing and ambiguous. Does an S you are reading mean short or stout and strong? I believe it customary to state differences in shank length before differences in wire diameter. So Size-6 2XS, 2XS would be a size-6 gape hook with a shank the same length as a standard size-8 hook and wire diameter of a size-4 standard hook. Such a hook might be used for small but strong egg patterns.

Knowing all that, what good is it? It means a good deal and would be even more useful if producers honored the system and labeled hooks correctly. You know the problem well from our discussion of rod-line balance; they often don't. Hook makers want you referencing their model numbers. You still need to know hook model specifications if you expect your dry flies to float and the rest to sink or perform acceptably.

Many flies are tied on inappropriate hooks. You can add weight to a hook or leader to make it sink, but using a correct hook is preferable. There is, however, nothing doable to make a dry fly tied on a too heavy hook float better or one of too fine wire hold large fish. Dry flies are most often tied on hooks that are standard to 3XF in wire diameter. I have too heavy a hand to use 3XF wire hooks of smaller size and break them, even in tying a fly. I could train myself to use them; then innocent fish would suffer from senselessly prolonged fights.

If you want a fly to sink, use heavier wire even to 4XS (S equals stout or strong in this case). Hooks of heavy wire diameter are harder to set, being slower to penetrate due to extra wire diameter. They need sticky-sharpness with low or nonexistent barbs. Flyfishers who tie their own flies most often make mistakes of hook choice, but commercial tiers aren't exempt.

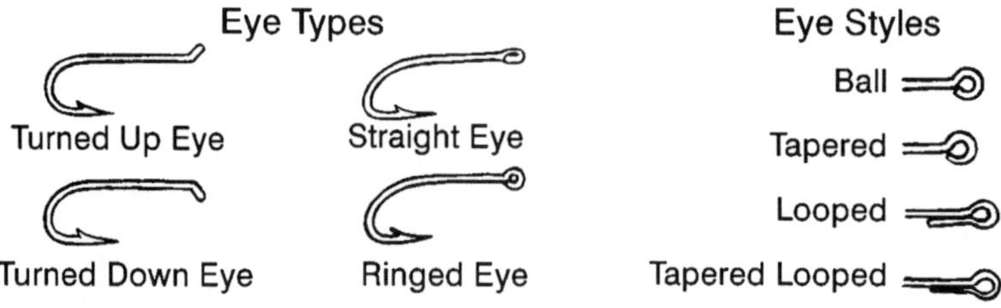

Hook Eyes

Early hooks didn't have eyes; now we have several types. Straight eyes are in the same plane and straight extensions of the hook's shank. Turned-up and turned-down eyes (TUE or TDE) tip up or down from the shank. Basic eyes are of variable inside diameter and many have small openings and sharp edges where the hook wire bends back to meet the hook shank. Those openings and edges must be filled or covered with thread in the fly-tying process. Eyes can be made of quickly tapering wire (tapered eyes) resulting in smaller eyes and neater fly heads but causing leader knotting problems if correct knots aren't used.

Bending shank wire into a pear-shaped eye and causing the wire to extend back, along the shank, for a short distance results in a returned-loop eye (RLE). If the backward protruding wire is tapered to a neat point, we have a returned-loop, tapered eye (RLTE). Tapered wire, return eyes permit neater and smaller fly heads without causing problems, if the wire returns far enough. Most do. Return eyes can be straight, turned-up or turned-down. They leave no gap at hook eye as do basic eyes.

It's critical to have the shank of a fly's hook continue the line and be an extension of the tippet. Doing so ensures the fly will fish "in-line" without tipping up, down or to one side as happens when you tie directly to the eye of TUE or TDE hooks, even to a tapered wire basic eye. A fly will fish, and most importantly, hook and then hold best when kept in line with the leader.

To ensure a fly fishing correctly in line with the leader, *you must* use a knot that allows it to do so and correct for the fly eye being used. Herein lies an ignorance- or laziness-borne mistake of lots of fishers. Failure to conform to this simple, long known fact causes *countless* fish to be missed or lost after short struggles. The failure to use correct knots on varying hook eyes ranks as an all time, primary error of flyfishers.

Use a Turle Replacement knot on TUE or TDE hooks. Correctly tied flies, by knowing tiers, reserve space *behind* the eyes of TUE and TDE hooks to allow a knot to be properly and easily seated. Many flies fail miserably on this important point.

Straight-eyed flies leave little choice but to tie directly to the eye. Knots tied directly to basic eyes of hooks commonly slip around to one side of the eye during casting and cause the fly to fish out of line. Tapered wire in a fly's eye accentuates side slipping problems while the pear-shape of a straight, looped eye almost eliminates side slipping. Special, but easy, precautions need to be taken with some hooks. When using *straight eyed* hooks take two wraps *through* the eye before tying a Clinch knot. Doing so doubles the contact area of leader to steel minimizing sideways leader movement and, as a bonus, increases chafing resistance where relatively soft leader material meets hard, perhaps rough, steel.

Hook Bends

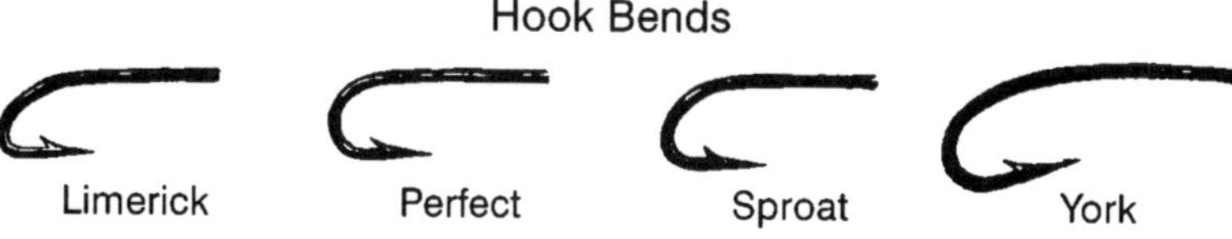

Hook Bends and Gapes

Long ago, makers and users of hooks realized a hook with a Limerick bend best holds large fish. It's still so, but few are made today. I don't know why. Limerick bends have a long and gently sloping rear bend necessitating a severe, and fish holding, angle to bring the point and entire throat back parallel the shank. O'Shaughnessy bends and the currently popular York bends are similar Limerick bends. The former is commonly used for "standard" hooks of several hook companies and is much used for saltwater flies. The York is a very good bend; its slightly turned-in point still hooks and holds well.

Model Perfect bends (U shaped) are popular for dry flies and work well enough if the depth of throat is sufficiently deep. Many popular hooks are too shallow in this crucial measurement, and fish can escape them easily. I find most Partridge hooks to be deficient of throat depth, even their Limerick bends. Mustad Model Perfect bends have adequate depth as do the Japanese hooks I'm familiar. There are other bends and shank shapes. Some are specialized, new or improved. You know about such qualifications.

We know hooks are modified by manufacturers regardless of standards, ease of angler understanding or tradition, and it's done purposefully. You see "wide gap" hooks advertised. The gape is so wide in say a 1/0 hook of this wrongful designation to actually be a true 4/0 with a 1/0 shank length. The hook, by correct terminology, should be called a size-4/0, 3 extra-short shank (size-4/0-3XS). Is it ignorance or senseless differentiation that causes companies to do such things? Do you know what "wide gap" means? How much more gape?

A Hook Example

Buyers of flies will most often find them tied for average consumer and use. Such flies fill many needs. You could wear trousers too large or small, but I bet you best like ones that fit the way you prefer. Perhaps you need a hook with a different bend, finish or weight. If you know you need, or want, flies with specifications other than average, you will have to tie them or have them custom tied. In either case you need to understand hooks in order to buy or request the right ones. If you travel to fish far destinations, you may or may not find needed flies at local stores. It's a good idea to examine and perhaps buy a few recommended destination flies. It's a better idea to already have most of what you will need, including hook specifications, based on sound research and the basic fly selection discussed in the next chapter. Let's go fishing to see.

Assume you are a mid-Western flyfisher of five years' experience who fishes at every opportunity, mostly for trout, on limited local waters. You know the effectiveness of sparse, smaller Elk Hair Caddis patterns on local streams and tie or buy them locally tied on light wire hooks. You hatch a plan with a buddy to fish Montana's Beaverhead River; it's something you've heard and read about and wanted to do for several years. You plan a late June departure and will drive west to Montana in your van. Research revealed a rubber-raft, or jon-boat, set up to row easily, will be needed and that Elk Hair Caddis are favorites on the Beaverhead.

You tie a bunch of caddis and load the jon-boat atop your van. The first evening in Montana you float the Beaverhead just below Clark Canyon Dam, amidst an armada. You find the banks brush- and willow-lined like you've never seen. There are few places to wade; the water is too fast or deep where it isn't brush-lined. The fish that begin to rise, as evening approaches are often large and, sure enough, taking caddis flies but only under the protection of the overhanging willows or right next to cutbanks. These fish are daily pounded by fishermen, lots of them. You and friend cast, in turns away from oars, as best you can from a moving boat. It's something you've never done before. You're trying to hit the tiny openings or within two inches of the edges, striving to obtain some smidgen of decent fly drift. It's hard, very hard.

You've broken three flies off on brush during your turns at fishing. The one fish either of you hooked smashed your "fly size balanced and correct" 3X tippet like a cobweb. The heavier tippet you then employed did nothing for avoiding the willows, and now you start breaking the hooks of your flies. Then you wrap your leader butt around a branch; it holds, and the Chinese-finger leader-butt-thing strips right off your fly line. Rapidly approaching darkness, thunder and lightning with rain squall, ever larger clouds of mean mosquitoes and the no-bull warning of rattlesnakes at the take out—wherever that is—all add to your enjoyment. Famous Western rivers, flyfishing, flowers, birds and the great outdoors are just wonderful—don't you think?

After hitching a ride back to the put-in to shuttle your van, you ride luckily not snake-bitten, but much bug-bitten, toward your motel pondering the evening's events. You dwell on the talk with the locals at the take out. A 6-pound rainbow, a 4-pound brown and lots of lesser fish fell to their Elk Hair Caddis. It was, by *their* consensus, the best evening of flyfishing in many days. What's the matter? The new rod, the reel and spools you bought for this trip—that cost you a bundle—didn't help. The new Cortland WF line you used was recommended as "just the thing" for your new 6-weight Sage RPL. But rod, line, or the combination didn't seem to work right. The guy at the big and famous fly shop back home—who has flyfished six years, even in Alaska—couldn't or wouldn't have sold you wrong, could he? Would he?

You remember inquiring of that fly shop wizard concerning the trustworthiness of the glue-on leader butt and were assured they, "never fail." The highly touted, strong and supple tippet you were sold seemed to break so easily after even slight abrasion from the Beaverhead's willows. It's all confusing and discouraging, and you wonder if you're the world's worst flyfisher, or biggest sucker. Your friend, sullen and quiet so far, suggests you hire a guide for the morrow, if you can.

You contact a highly recommended guide in Dillon the next morning. You're in luck; he can take you due to a cancellation. You're told to meet him at 4:00 p.m. at the same put-in you started from yesterday. He's heard the fishing was, "very good up there last evening. . . ." You repair tackle, catch-up on sleep, tour the town and then meet Eric, your guide. He's already launched the boat, seen to shuttle arrangements and now wants to inspect your tackle.

You earlier replaced your rudely brush-stripped leader with another, gluing it very carefully to line end this time. Eric says nothing but cuts it off along with about 12 inches of your new line's front taper. From his kit comes a knotted and tapered, reddish-brown leader. It resembles rope. After nail knotting it to your line, he performs the same operations to your friend's line while you examine the leader tied to yours. Eric tells you to stretch the loose coils; as if magic, the leader stretches perfectly straight. You notice an 8-inch long tag end from a Blood knot and are about to trim it when Eric says— "don't." He opens a box of flies, all Elk Hair Caddis about size-12, and affixes one to your new leader's tippet. To the dropper you were about to sacrifice, Eric ties a size-12, Soft Hackle wet-fly. Your friend's new leader gets the same treatment.

As the boat pulls away you quiz Eric regarding flies and leader. You've noticed the flies look different from yours. You're told the leader is about 9 feet long, of Maxima Chameleon, with an 8-pound tippet and 10-pound dropper. The flies you noticed to be different are standard patterns, of standard size, but tied on extra-stout (2XS) Mustad model 7957BX, or maybe slightly lighter model 7957B or 7948A hooks. The wire diameter of the hooks is much larger than that in your flies, and you don't need to ask why such terminal rigging is used.

Your stiff rod and sticky new line still won't work right for the short casts needed—you notice Eric carries a soft-action traditional Powell—but you don't lose flies, or break hooks with Eric's rigging. "There's nothing like a competent professional," you think. You're really sure when Eric nets your first ever 5-pound rainbow. Maybe the sensationalized tapered leaders and wimpy tippet you've heard so much about, and were sold, aren't the cat's meow. Who ever told you to carry flies of varying hook strength? Few recommend an 8-pound (0X) tippet for a size-12 fly at the Elite shops or in the expert magazine articles.

Average flies are just that, average. The preceding example is indicative of many situations. Perhaps the size-3/0 tarpon flies shown in the catalogs are better tied on lighter size-1/0 hooks for easier setting in tough jaws not to mention easier casting to distance or in wind. Atlantic salmon and steelhead flies tied on obligatory turned-up eye black hooks may work better if tied on bronze or with straight or turned-down eyes. Different points and barbs, shank lengths, wire diameters, finishes and hook bends are often called for and influence a fly's, therefore your, effectiveness. Following are points that will help you select hooks.

Hook Producers

Older, primary manufacturers of hooks: Wright and McGill in the USA, Mustad of Norway, VMC of France and the several English producers, of which Partridge is best known, have never enjoyed complete agreement regarding hook sizes. (A late note, Mustad recently purchased Partridge.) One company's size-1/0 is comparable to another maker's size-3/0 in terms of measured gape although shank lengths may be similar. Wright and McGill, with its Eagle Claw hooks, is perhaps the worst offender compared to others. In larger sizes, over about size-4, Eagle Claw hooks have gapes about two sizes larger than those of other makers.

The Japanese producers of late have more closely followed Mustad in size-gape relationships. In some hook models, however, they are the worst offenders of understanding and tradition. A recent catalog of the Gamakatsu Co. is brimming with mistakes regarding fly hook terminology, sizes and general fly hook understanding. It's barely understandable. Perhaps something is lost in translation from Japanese; it shouldn't be.

Japanese hooks share a common trait from pre-WW II to date. Their hooks are brittle. Nearly any flyfisher prefers a hook that will bend, under severe stress, before it breaks. Flies are often salvaged by forcing bent hooks back to original shape, but nothing can be done with a broken hook. I don't suggest pliable hooks, the key is under *severe* stress. Partridge made hooks too brittle while Mustad's and particularly Eagle Claw's hooks usually can be bent back into shape.

Eagle Claw makes few fly hooks that are decent in design at this writing. Their hooks never quite look or perform correctly, and they are often poorly made. That's a shame. Many of us would like to buy American made hooks. Be advised that paying a premium price for fancy imported and embellished hooks does not guarantee you will receive premium hooks. Some of the oldest models, made by Mustad, are still the proven best.

Sharpening, Points and Barbs

There has arisen clamor about chemically sharpened hooks the last few years. Any flyfisher who doesn't know how, take the time and have with him the tools needed to keep hooks sharp isn't worth his salt. What happens if a chemically sharpened hook is dulled on the first cast? Use them if you like, but they are aimed at exploiting laziness, as are lots of unneeded fly tackle items. Do you want to abdicate your success to someone's wonder-junk? It's our responsibility to take control of our fishing.

Hook points, that portion from the top of the barb (or where the barb should be) forward to the very tip, should be short for fast and easy penetration. If you fish for tough-mouthed species, and maybe if you don't, a point of triangular cross section that's sharp on three edges works well. Use a fine-toothed file on larger hooks and a fine stone on smaller ones. It's wise, but more difficult, to do your honing from tip toward barb.

I don't care for hooks made without a barb, but rather prefer to modify barbs to my liking—that's usually to completely flatten a barb leaving a small hump; however, there are times when I want a slight barb. If you land fish quickly and know how to handle, unhook and release fish, small barbs do little, if any, damage. Of course many, having landed 30 or 40 fish, and thus becoming consecrated experts, look down their long noses at persons using barbed hooks. After releasing thousands you learn to do it without damaging the fish. The new mini-barbs on hooks are nice, but some hooks with them have too long points.

Someone said: "The barb on a hook is to hold the hook *in* the fish, not hold the fish *on* the hook." The *bend* holds a fish *on* the hook. If the angler makes no, or few, fish fighting mistakes, barbs are irrelevant. Absent or small barb thinking was offset by Wright & McGill recently with their introduction of a double-barbed bass hook—two large barbs in line. Lots of bass guys fish for money and acclaim. Ego and greed, not fish welfare, prevail in fishing for cash, notoriety and endorsement income. Let it continue to largely escape flyfishing. Flyfishers face enough problems of greed genesis. As a side note: Size of barb, or its existence, was found to be the most important variable in allowing broken-off fish to rid themselves of hooks and live, according to a recent study of, I believe, one of the Northeastern coastal state's conservation departments.

Hook Strength and Finishes

Wire diameter is indicative of hook strength; however, chemical composition and tempering affect steel's resistance to bending, hardness and corrosion resistance as well. Over tempering leads to steel brittleness and hook breakage as does incorrect amount or wrong alloys. Stainless steel hooks resist rust, but hooks made of it are weak compared to hooks made of steel with more, but rust prone, carbon content. Metallurgy is complicated, and I make no claim to know much about it. I see little need for stainless steel hooks. "Carbon steel gets sharper and holds an edge better than stainless," so says one knowledgeable user, and it "never flexes open like some stainless hooks."

Stainless steel hooks give a broken-off fish the worst chance to live. In my area lots of flies are tied on stainless hooks for use in freshwater. Some big-name outdoor writers even recommend stainless hooks for freshwater use. Lefty, are you listening? Many fine game fish have doubtless died because of stainless hooks when another finish may have allowed them to live. I recently heard of a new hook for saltwater use. It will completely dissolve after 48 hours immersion in saltwater. If found to be useable it should save fine game fish.

Common argument says the stainless hook of an expensive fly can't rust. Any flyfisher who fails to dry his flies is guilty of sloth. Many are the times my open fly boxes have ridden home under the heater of my vehicle after a rainy or deep wading day. Other times, my boxes sit open near the heater in a motel room or in the back of my vehicle if the weather is warm. I've had to replace valuable flies rusted beyond safe use. Perhaps my errors will help you avoid costly mistakes.

Some carbon hooks are coated or made with substances to inhibit rusting. Cadmium plating, involving zinc in an arsenic process, among other processes may not be desirable for environs. Such hooks sound dangerous left in a fish's mouth.

Nickel plating gives hooks a very shiny silver color but trivial rust protection. I believe very shiny hooks detract from a fly's effectiveness; examined underwater, their metallic flash and shine is overpowering and phony to my eye. A good many flyfishers can't tell a nickel plated hook from one of stainless steel. That accounts for some inexcusable use of stainless hooks. Both are shiny; stainless is less so and exhibits a *distinctive gray* color. Cadmium plated hooks are gray but not shiny.

Shiny, nickel plated, hooks of small size might work well for dry flies or wet-flies fished near surface. Such hooks will blend with surface disturbance as chop from riffled water or against light backgrounds above the water's surface. They might help suggest gas bubbles from hatching insects imitated by decent body dubbing on a fly.

Black "japanned" hooks are of carbon steel and coated with black lacquer. Bronze hooks are also carbon steel and coated with clear or bronze finish. Any finish, once damaged or altered to expose high carbon steel beneath allows rusting. Carbon steel hooks in bronze finish are extremely useful. They are strong and blend well with the dressing of many fly patterns. Black hooks are traditional for some flies. I don't care for them if I can obtain appropriate hooks in dark-bronze finish, unless the fly pattern is predominantly black.

Black hooks stem back to the days when lamp-black was used to coat and protect hooks. We have advanced to better finishes now, particularly bronze. Gold, blue, red and green hooks are available. Some might be useful, but they exist mostly to sell more hooks. Some bronze finishes, particularly on Japanese hooks, have too much gold in them for my taste. Note: I'm recently told by a knowledgeable flyfisher that gold-colored hooks work very well for chinook salmon in freshwater.

Flies and their hooks are not as important in flyfishing's success formula as some would have you believe. Neither are they unimportant, unless we can reckon some other way to hang onto fish. Flies tied on inferior hooks, correctly used by good flyfishing hands, will catch fish. The opposite is not so true. Most of us need all the help we can get. Paying attention to seemingly unimportant and forgotten or ignored history proven details, including those about hooks and knots, will yield many more fish than all the new rods, lines and fly patterns we might buy.

Chapter Ten:
Flies

"Exceptional fishing results in a glow of benevolence which causes a man to see everything in the best possible light, and particularly the fly he happens to be using."

Harold F. Blaisdell

I suspect that in the subconscious of every flyfisher, despite knowledge and experience, common sense, reason or denial lies some belief in sure-fire flies. Such irrational rationalization plus unjustified preoccupation with flies in general may account for more wasted time and effort, money, ink and paper than all of flyfishing's other failures of logic. Egotism and ignorance, quests for immortality by "fly invention" and profit motivation lead to flagrant excesses in fly discourse. The notion we will somehow catch more fish with a super fly or one more new pattern is exploited by others or rises from ourselves only because we allow it to happen.

Fly Theories

Exploring the universe of catching fish with flies, you encounter differing schools of thought. Two predominate concerning flies and balance one another somewhat. On the one hand you have the "presentation is paramount" bunch, on the other the "supremacy of precise imitation" zealots. Turf delineations aren't always clear, and the antagonists freely wander in each other's territory. The idea that you can imitate a fish's food with flies has spawned a good share of the world's flies and writing of them. Of course you can, but ideas accounting for much writing, particularly that of close, exact or precise imitation, should require their proponents, early on, to provide satisfactory explanations.

First among them would be explaining the presence of a hook in an *exact* imitation. Is the hook ignored by the fish? If fish ignore hooks and can see leaders, as many believe, yet still strike, then what else will they ignore? Can a certain size or shape or color or combination be as critical to success as many would have us believe? I think not; neither reason nor experience support such conclusions.

Fly selection, by tying or purchase, remains negatively influenced by old world ideas and writing that spoke, to great extent, of specific patterns. Specific pattern thinking leaves little room for flies of similar, even different, style that may prove equally or even more effective. That's changing as more flyfishers come to better understand fish behavior, vision and foods. Many flyfishers, however, remain slaves to specific patterns or specific materials called for in fly patterns—it's silliness, mostly.

The "correct" fly poorly presented will catch fewer fish than a "wrong" fly correctly presented. Lee Wulff and Charles Waterman, decent fly presenters both, wrote of spurning "correct," "right" or "hatch matching" flies in favor of flies quite different from accepted norms and suffering no decrease in share of fish hooked. How, not what, thinking naturally fits the more advanced. Less informed flyfishers are more likely to seek magic patterns or put too much emphasis on flies. They probably don't believe in magic but hope the "right" fly will

make up for poor presentations or other fishing shortcomings. It very seldom will. Rather than accumulating more flies, people are better advised to practice casting and watermanship along with study of some of the older and better books on fish vision and behavior.

Everyone wants decent flies, and the best flies are generally suggestions of things, not exact imitations. Using diverse materials, time and creativity some tiers produce flies appearing almost exact imitations of things, save the hook. I've held grasshopper patterns and stonefly nymphs tied by Al Troth feeling I should close my hand lest they hop or crawl away. Polly Roseborough summed things up this way:

> "All my flies were tied on the theory of simulation. The exact imitation you can only get by molding plastic and once in the water, everything stops moving. They look dead."

Exact imitations are also tied of materials other than plastic; they remain as stiff and often more fragile. Exact imitations customarily imitate body parts precisely with sharpness and definition while insects taken by fish, particularly hatching ones, are quite disheveled. Good flies have built-in motion, exact imitation or not, particularly those fished below the surface.

Designing exact imitations fills a creative need in tiers and is not without its economic side, for some. Flyfishers have always been more likely than fish to tumble to fancy flies. Many flies are tied primarily to catch fishermen since a fly must first intrigue a buyer or spend its life forever in some little bin. Scant consideration is given to how flies produce or endure by some "inventors" or commercial tiers of lifelike flies.

The first reason for selling or publishing flies is the quest for profit, and that's acceptable. Participate or contribute as you may. The second reason is rampant quest for notoriety, oblivious or ignorant the foolishness of new contributions. There is an insufferable, confusing, excess of published patterns given the few actually needed. It's fun to "invent" or "improve" flies if you tie—have a ball—but *know* it's next to impossible to come up with something undone. Most who think they have, simply haven't read enough or far enough back into flyfishing's history.

Newer flyfishers, or those too believing of tedious embellishment from the industries, can be swept off their feet. Sellers hope so. Flyfishers' wallets often then fall from their pockets. You can't expect a neophyte to be astute, but neither should you expect the more-knowing to take advantage of them. Most fly selling is purely profit motivated, some incorrect recommendations are innocent and lots plain ignorant. The "knowing," doing the tying or selling, often aren't. It's all too common in flyfishing, certainly regarding flies. Decent flies, however, share common characteristics.

Simple design, multiple use, and durability are virtues in flies. Flies that suggest several food items to us or are thought to provoke strikes for other reasons, then seeing our opinions ratified by lots of fish, deserve the most room in our fly boxes. Multiple use means less cost if buying flies and ease if you tie your own. There are a great many life forms the Muddler Minnow, Gold-Ribbed Hare's Ear or Bucktail Caddis suggest. But food suggestion isn't always paramount.

Flies are taken by fish for lots of reasons other than hunger, more often than people think. The more I fish the more certain I become. Good and proven food suggesting flies, for all we know, may be taken because a fish could see our offering easily, was curious, or just didn't want the thing in its face or space, not out of hunger. Some reasons imply belligerence or territoriality. Reasons are variable according to fishing type, species and time of year to mention only a few possibilities. An outstanding example of a fly that elicits fish attention for lots of reasons, hunger and otherwise, is the Woolly Bugger.

On The Henry's Fork

Long before the Woolly Bugger's current popularity, I stumbled into Pat Barnes down from West Yellowstone to fish a favorite stretch of the Henry's Fork near my home. Pat was then a near-famous guide in that part of the country. It was early spring with high and discolored water. Blue-winged olive mayflies were due but not hatching. As I fished, I watched Pat catch a couple of nice fish from the riffle below an irrigation diversion. When our fishing brought us together we talked, and at my request he showed me the fly he was using.

It was a head-weighted, size-6, pure black Marabou Muddler type fly with a smallish head. He said he was using and fishing it to suggest the Henry's Fork's abundant giant stonefly nymphs. The fly had a black chenille body, no rib or tail and a black marabou wing. Except for material arrangement it has all the attributes plus some advantages over modern Woolly Buggers. Pat's fly, absent a tail and with a short wing, doesn't miss or encourage short strikes. The sculpin-like, spun, black deer hair head is an advantage in suggesting several fish foods.

Woolly Buggers were doubtless influenced by Woolly Worms being no more than the latter with a marabou tail and more uniform spelling. The original purpose of the Woolly Bugger was probably as a leech suggestion, and I suspect some of the old Canadian leech patterns with flowing mohair wings also influenced its design. A fly could have worse parentage. I have trouble calling the Woolly Bugger a streamer as most do and do not use it as a streamer. "Streamer" implies minnow or a small fish, and Woolly Buggers don't look much like minnows. Perhaps they do to fish. The Woolly Bugger is a fine pattern; it's most useful if lightly weighted, in the head area only, to give a jigging action. It probably triggers strikes due to beguiling motion more than strict food imitating power, color, shape or size.

High Lakes

I used to fish lots of high mountain lakes in late summer when lower valley temperatures were high, the temperature of rivers also high and fishing success low. Upon approaching a strange lake and not knowing what to expect, if anything (Idaho's high lake stocking program was random and haphazard despite supposed three-year rotation stocking schedules), I almost always started with a dark brown, dubbed body (mohair or polar bear), head-weighted, Woolly Bugger type fly in size-6 or -8. I fished them on a floating DT and a longer leader. If trout of any species were present they usually followed the fly even if they wouldn't take. At least I would know if fish were present; most often they would take. I often used no other fly unless surface feeding was evident enough to draw me to the extra fun of catching fish on dry flies.

In Iceland

I recall a final afternoon of fishing Iceland's Grimsa River. My friend Oskar, with whom I shared the fishing time, and I were finally rotated to the lowest of the lodge's beats. We were anticipatory, primed by several evenings' lodge talk, about the large salmon holding in several pools below the waterfalls of the water we were about to fish. These fish had proven mostly uncatchable to members of our party.

As we fished upstream through the assigned water, we eventually came to a long and deep pool below a chute of fast water. The chute had been formed by bull-dozing a bank of gravel toward a bed-rock point on the far bank causing the flow of water to be compressed and run along the rocky protrusion. We immediately saw salmon rolling in the pool, several large, at least one was dark showing lots of red and a hooked-jaw. This must be the place of the lodge talk. We each took a turn, to no good end, casting the tiny size-12 and -14 double-hooked flies that had proven by far the most productive during our stay. It had been slow fishing with less than 20 fish taken by the 18 members of Reykjavik's flyfishing club and me. I was, however, learning a little of the language.

It was Oskar's turn to fish and the incessant rain and wind were gaining strength after a lull. The vehicle was nearby, so I decided to coffee up and watch Oskar cast and the salmon roll. Everyone fished this run from the drive-in, dozed-gravel side. Ease of approach, back cast room and wind direction favored that position. I decided to try the other side, if I could wade the river. Heading upstream, I got the angle and crossed more easily than anticipated. Maybe a fly presented from a different angle would work. It hadn't on fish in other pools earlier in the week, but I'm a slow learner I guess. Oskar saw me approach the rolling fish, reeled in and waved for me to have at them as he headed upwind for the car and hot coffee.

Earlier in the day I had fought hard at the Strengir runs (Icelandic for riffles and once described by Ernest Schwiebert as the finest set of Atlantic salmon riffles in the world) to keep from being blown into the river, no kidding. Casting, even standing was as near impossible as I've experienced, and I grew up on the Snake River plains of Idaho where the wind lives—I thought. But how could you not fish such a place when your turn comes?

The wind lay down some again, and my DT-8 floater bucked it tolerably. Nothing responded to the double-hooked size-12 White Wing or a similar Green Highlander. There was nothing to be lost in trying something radical even on one of the world's most tradition-bound rivers. In one of my boxes were two size-4, black, slightly weighted, scraggly, polar bear bodied and marabou tailed Woolly Bugger type flies tied on Partridge down-eyed steelhead hooks. I found them and knotted one to my 8-pound Chameleon tippet adding two Twist-Ons (small strips of lead), spaced along the leader, just as I would if fishing a deep stonefly nymph on Montana's Big Hole.

Casting almost straight upstream—after wading into the flow as far as I could and abreast of several of the rolling salmon—I allowed the Bugger to drift through—nothing. I cast again, the same way, but this time I stacked slack with roll cast mends on top of the sinking leader to allow the fly to gain greater depth. The whole mess was drifting down to me rapidly, and I stripped the accumulating slack, also rapidly, while pivoting my body to allow the low-held, thus partially wind defeating, rod tip to lead the line.

The rod tip was jerked underwater followed immediately by a cock salmon jumping. Winding slack tight to the reel while backing out of the river, I waved at Oskar and tried to keep an eye on the salmon. It ran to the tail of the pool's shallow riffle break jumping twice and, not wanting to leave the pool, turned back toward me. Control was now attainable. Oskar was running, raincoat blowing in the wind, carrying a huge net and preparing to wade the river. The fish tried it upstream through the chute a couple of times, but the rod stopped it. On a short line it panicked again, jumped and wallowed but everything held.

During the fight I had planned to release the fish. Dead fish don't mean much to me, and taking one home, halfway around the world, was impractical and silly when I seldom take one home from 50 or 5 miles. Nobody can stop you from releasing a fish if you're really committed. Oskar encouraged me to keep it for several good reasons and didn't have to encourage much. It weighed 12 pounds, a decent Grimsa salmon, but not the 20 pounds some fish in the pool were reputed to weigh. I have a picture Oskar took of me holding the salmon on the rock point where it was landed. Schwiebert's Lodge shows in the background. The picture is mounted with the Woolly Bugger fly that killed the salmon. It stimulates fond memories. I gave the matching Woolly Bugger to Oskar.

Fly Color

Since exact imitation is nearly impossible to obtain, likely ineffective if achieved and if flies suggesting several life forms and possessing the power to provoke strikes for other than feeding reasons are best, then where do color, size and shape of flies enter the mix? Let's look at perhaps the most discussed variable, color, first.

In many types of fishing, West Coast steelheading and all streamer flyfishing as examples, the general size and shape of most flies are defined by tradition (steelhead flies) or the basic characteristics of the creature being suggested (small fish). Fish are known to partake of flies similar in size and shape that differ in color, sometimes wildly. Fly tiers, somewhat limited in two of three variables, size and shape, remain highly motivated to create "new" or modify existing patterns by experimentations in color. Playing with color is fun, if little understood.

Color awareness and experimentation are sometimes taken to ridiculous levels. I tie large commercial streamer flies of polar bear hair for the world's largest rainbows found in several of northern Idaho's and British Columbia's lakes. Their basic food is uniform-colored kokanee (sock-eye) salmon of two to eight inches in length. The fishing method for these large rainbows, which run to over 30 pounds, is largely defined. It's a troll fishery and in spring and fall, an on-surface fishery. With size, shape and now method of fishing largely defined, color receives even more attention, certainly more than it deserves. But people just *have* to experiment, looking for that magic color combination. I'm not totally exempt either.

I also tie commercial steelhead and Atlantic salmon flies of polar bear. The swinging damp or wet-fly technique used in most steelheading and Atlantic salmon fishing is as nonarbitrary as the troll fishery just discussed. Examination of the flyboxes of fishers or the pages of often needless books of fly patterns for steelhead and Atlantic salmon reveals flies to be similar in shape with minimal variation in size found. Though general color of flies varies, there is naturally a certain sameness. Most of the steelhead wet-flies in any book of patterns are some combination of homogeneous materials in red, orange and white. Of the remainder a few will be neutral in coloration, but most will be dark with lots of black and purple, often in conjunction with some white.

The pattern books of steelhead flies need fill lots of pages. A book showing only a Skunk or one of its variations, a Muddler and a Thor wouldn't sell well despite being as useful as one showing 150 equivalent patterns. Flyfishers who strive to fish as well as they can study, to understand their quarry, then fish hard and smart. They will be well served by a relatively few wisely selected flies. Books or catalogs showing gobs of similarly sized and shaped patterns for trout, saltwater species, bass or other fish are as unnecessary as those of steelhead or Atlantic salmon patterns.

Similarly colored flies of similar style are a waste of money if you buy them and a waste of ink or space depending on whether you're talking about books or fly boxes. Myriad fly patterns are aimed at getting your money or satisfying somebody's ego or both. What one red-orange-white steelhead fly will do, another, similar fly of same color scheme, size, weight and materials will do about as well. The same goes for darker patterns. Flyfishers of all types hold themselves captive to strange ideas, overemphasis of fly color is one.

With over 30 years of steelhead flyfishing under my belt, I consider it a long suit. Many years ago a well known steelheader told me, in response to my inquiry about best fly colors: "I have a red fly and a black fly. I crawl in the water at daylight and get out after full dark. I catch my share or more." Now after my years of sloshing about steelhead rivers, I pretty much agree, but I'm not sure you need the red fly. This is also an appropriate place to consider what Joe Bates, author of many books particularly about streamer flies, thought of the "bright day, bright fly; dark day, dark fly" creed—"It's rot."

My familiarization with steelhead and streamer flies served as example of the silliness surrounding fly coloration. Learning-impairing thinking encompasses fly selection; it's often color oriented but certainly isn't limited to that. As a custom tier I receive unusual requests. A customer often wants very specific colors even to the point of wanting a specific shade of say, lavender. I never considered lavender as having shades. Do I see or understand pale lavender to be the same as my customer? Probably not. Color is very complicated, hence much misunderstood.

If I asked a customer wanting a particular color of polar bear hair or dubbing what the specific value, hue, intensity, translucence and shine of the requested color should be, I would most likely get a blank stare or silence on the telephone. If we could somehow agree on all the components of a color, by what leap of thinking do we presume the fish will then see it as desired? Under what light conditions? In what water clarity? I make no claims to understanding color as fully as I'd like.

There are some good older books that address fly color scientifically and how fish perceive color. Reading them provides valuable insight while opening Pandora's box. If you judiciously try to allow for and correctly use the many aspects and variables of color, you may go insane. It's easier to admit that color is little understood, can't be understood from a fish's viewpoint and just isn't very important despite what you hear or read to the contrary.

Don't fool yourself by thinking you are achieving near perfection using a "hatch matching" fly with a particular shade of yellow body. Another angler may catch more, bigger or more difficult fish under same circumstances using a fly with a bright red body and better or even equal technique. Keep color in its proper place. It's third of the trio: shape, size and color. Remember fly tiers, other flyfishers or fly salesmen may not understand color as well as you. One thing certain is a never ending parade of "new or better" flies. Many will lean heavily on some specific color, and most will be the product of someone's imperfect understanding, research or testing. Burden your mind with more profitable worries.

Size or Shape

With color in its proper place we are left with fly size and shape—always remembering a fly must act, or be made to act, suitably. Which is most important? Most writing and prevailing opinion says size is most important and often critical to success. Perhaps, but I can't recall many cases where size was more important to me than proper shape, and silhouette, within reason.

Within populations of insects, at all life stages, forage fish and other fish prey, there exist tremendous percentage differences in the size of individual members. Size differentials are due age, sex, species and simple individuality. Water often contains species of fish food that are similar in shape and lifestyle but quite different in size. Fish gobble them all with little regard to size, most of the time.

In a hatch of mayflies, caddis or stoneflies, males and females can vary in size by as much as 60%. Adult stonefly males of one species may average 1-1/4 inches in length and females well over two inches. That equates to at least five hook sizes (size-2 to size-6 for giant stone flies). I've witnessed many hatches of mayflies and caddis flies where individuals appeared to vary just as much in size "percentagewise."

It's common to encounter situations where you have differently sized (but similarly shaped) species of the same insect hatching and certainly present in their immature stages beneath the water. Some terrestrial insects, of similar species and therefore shape, will vary even more in size than aquatic insects. Nymphs of many species of aquatic insects have multi-year life cycles. Nymphs of differing year classes vary greatly in size but not in shape. They will also vary in color depending on their surroundings and stage of molting. Studies have shown meat eating fish have preferred sizes of the baitfish, but like all predators they are opportunists and will take minnows, other food or our flies much smaller or larger than they prefer if the thing looks vulnerable or they *want* it. No, shape is more important than size most of the time.

On The Henry's Fork Again

Situations you may have heard or read about, even experienced, when fish would only take a certain sized fly (usually color or specific pattern is thrown in as well) are oftentimes exaggerated and nearly always unscientific. How do you know the tale-teller gave adequate effort to testing lots of other flies during the hot bite? It probably wasn't done. I happened to grow up on Idaho's Henry's Fork where much of the precise size, complex hatch, "you-gotta-have" an exact fly research and writing was done and was even involved in some. I don't much believe. Maybe I don't irrigate my gray

Continued on page 161

About The Fly Plates

Flies shown are mostly the ones listed in the upcoming "Flies Not To Be Without" list. Variations and suggestions are given there and exact dressings of displayed flies are given in the Appendix starting on page 273. All save one fly utilizes polar bear hair or dubbing and most are tied completely from polar bear. Additional information on tying with polar bear hair is found in the Appendix starting on page 267.

Streamer flies should run straight up to be most effective, or effective at all. The "Round Boy" patterns are tied to look exactly the same to fish regardless of viewing angle. They have no horizontal reference points and might fish as well upside down, canted or right-side up. In addition, the hook is adjustable for position, and the fly is very light accommodating easy casting. Round Boys are nearly weedless and can be adapted to any streamer pattern.

The articulated "Adjust-O-Leech" is an adaptation of Lee Wulff's jointed tube flies. I use this add-on tube leech not only to permit quick and easy size alterations, but also to obtain undulating leech-like motion. Segments are tied with dubbed polar bear bodies and rabbit fur wings; mink fur on the hide sparkles more, if you want that effect.

See dressings for flies of plates in Appendix II, page 273.

Polar Bitch Creek
Golden Stone Nymph
Bomber
Block-Headed Muddler
Claret and Black
Thor
Polar Leech (Mink Tail)
Polar Bi-Buck
Polar Leech
Marabou Muddler

Fall Favorite

Rainbow Fry Tandem

Jacob's Coat

Black Ghost

Kam Killer Supreme

Polar Round Boy

Jacob's Coat Blonde

Polar/Marabou Round Boy

Adjust-O-Leech

Dorado (8-inch)

Billfish (11-inch)

Bonefish

Cockroach

Deceiver

Clouser Minnow

matter with enough Scotch whiskey—single-malt of course—to understand.

Late June of one year found the green drake mayflies sporadically hatching in the Railroad Ranch stretch of the Henry's Fork. A bunch of local young bucks, myself included, were fishing as possessed. On a Saturday afternoon there was a sparse emergence. No one hooked much despite a few big fish consistently rising in their complex-current protected lies.

We were all back Sunday hoping for a larger emergence and better success. We considered ourselves skilled, well-read and current, even sophisticated. We had the latest of Swisher's and Richard's unbeatable patterns including the one with elk hair extended body, specially dyed greenish-yellow, mixed with brown hackles and slate elk hair wings. They were precisely colored green drake imitations of correct size and shape. How could we miss?

The flies hatched, a little heavier than the day before, the fish rose, and as they say, the casting did commence. There were some very large and cagey rainbows in the ranch waters in those days. Those tough old veterans ignored the best of our imitations and efforts. We were frustrated. Watching several large rainbows occasionally take natural flies, leaving large boils and wind-blown spray, poured salt on raw young egos. We sat and watched. In our defense, the fish had been fished to a good deal that day and other days, even by the "best" of famous flyfishers.

Tired of reclining in the grass and watching the irritating display, I tied a size-6 marabou Mickey Finn streamer to my tippet and placed a small split-shot just above the eye. Fishing downstream I took two of those big rainbows as a gallery watched.

Large trout of every species come equipped with anger fuses of varying lengths. I knew exactly where the fish were holding from watching them take drakes. Using repeated casts and slow teasing with the floppy streamer, I ignited the fuses of a couple. The match-the-hatch guys didn't say much. One notable did, the late Joe Brooks fishing the ranch with wife, Mary. He thought it amusing. It was just before his death and Joe was ill; Mary did most of the fishing for them. Joe was a gentleman, a most knowledgeable flyfisher and a writer of great books. You should read some if you haven't.

Perhaps what I did will be judged as incorrect or not in keeping with flyfishing's unwritten rules of conduct. I fight those feelings some myself. Looking back it seemed like fun—still does.

My example might not shed much light on the size versus shape argument at first glance. Complete divergence from the fly expected to produce in terms of size, shape, color, and presentation shows two things. One, fish can be undone by methods other than imitating their food *even* when they're actively feeding on something important and specific; and two, even when all the variables concerning flies are as correct as can be attained certain fish and conditions are most influenced by things unrelated to "correct" flies or even near perfect presentation. In the case related, perhaps it was unseen drag in the difficult currents that was our undoing. I've often wondered. People recurrently fail to recognize or acknowledge all pertinent factors in writing or tale telling of flies and flyfishing. It's easier and less humbling to tell only when a revolutionary, brain-child fly, or clever idea, slew them and ignore when and why it didn't. It's quite possible nearly any fly may have worked when "the great one" did.

Flies should most often be selected by considering, in order, shape, then size, then color. But any variable could become most important at certain times, and you should always be cognizant of how the natural food being suggested acts and strive to fish your suggestion accordingly. Basic thinking can be overridden by fishing conditions or certain fish. In selecting or tying flies lean on basic, sound knowledge and your own understanding. It may be better than you think. I'll throw out a few things that may help.

Fly Selection Hints

Most Western free-stone rivers and larger creeks—also some in other locales—have heavy early-season caddis hatches of smaller insect size followed quickly by, or in some cases concurrent with, stonefly hatches. There are often recurring caddis hatches of lesser intensity all summer. The stoneflies will most often be of the golden variety, but giant stoneflies or "salmon" flies may be present if the water is unpolluted and has numerous rocky and fast stretches. Giant stoneflies almost always hatch before golden stoneflies sometimes by more than a month. One exception I've fished the last couple of years is Oregon's Deschutes River; both species of flies hatch simultaneously. There are likely other such rivers. Following stonefly time will come the intermittent caddis hatches, grasshoppers and sometimes hatches of large fall caddis.

If water flows through standing timber, sundry moths and ants will be present in summer and fall (as they will around mountain lakes). Knowing about dominant insects and the progression of hatches, more or less, you can equip yourself with a variety of down-wing Hair Caddis patterns in size-4 through -14 with bodies of yellow, orange, tan and black (black in smaller sizes). This selection will allow you to dry fly fish triumphantly from early spring through fall.

Listed flies will work when you miss the heaviest emergence times of particular insects. Fish seem to maintain a memory of favorite, or at least abundant, foods. Hair Caddis type flies suggest so many common fish foods they will be accepted for one reason or another if you miss the major hatch periods. Since you have shape properly identified it's a matter of trying differing sizes and a few colors until you find what works. The key, spring to fall, is flies with mostly downwings, in varying sizes and of overall tan and brown wings coloration with varying body colors, often yellow-orange or tan.

Trimming a few lower wing fibers from smaller Hair Caddis flies, close to the body, and then pulling the remaining wing fibers upward creates a passable suggestion of a hatching mayfly. I seldom use any hackle on a Hair Caddis anymore. A tight but scraggly body of dubbed polar bear underfur and a wing of elk or deer hair, well cemented, provides the most durable, easily tied, long floating and most useful of dry flies. They can be trimmed a little and fished wet if you wish. A small one with some of the wing removed makes a good emerging caddis imitation or suggests a drowned insect.

I'm not ignoring the presence of mayflies or other insects of streams and rivers. But flies tied to suggest moths, caddis and stoneflies along with grasshoppers, ants and beetles provide most of the action, most of the time, on many rivers. Carry either Adams and Light Cahills or Gray Wulff and Yellow Goofus Bug (Humpy) patterns to suggest mayflies and other upright winged things (crane flies for instance). Select the former patterns for slower water and the latter for bouncy, rough water. If your smaller caddis patterns won't work these upright, divided wing flies may. I suggest size-10 to -16. A short-shank size-12 is my work horse. Thorax-type flies are simple and work well enough in calmer water. Royal Wulff or Royal Trude patterns, in several sizes, are decent attractor flies to carry.

A few sparsely tied streamer flies in several sizes will serve you well. Always have pure white ones and certainly brown over white. Splashes of red at the throat and eyes on the head boost streamer effectiveness. A chartreuse over white streamer is another good choice. Chartreuse is a difficult color to describe; some see it as more yellow and some as more green. However you see it, lots of different fish species like or perhaps can well see colors near that wave length.

I like streamers tied sparsely of polar bear hair. If a bulky or active fly is desired choose marabou for the wing. The various marabou muddlers are tough to beat. Streamers need a fish shaped silhouette that tapers to a thin tail. Too many look like blunt paint brushes and may continue to when wet. I don't care for tinsel in streamers. Metallic flash, viewed from underwater, is unlike the natural flash of a minnow.

Basic nymphs should be carried. Gold-Ribbed Hare's Ear (GRHE) nymphs in size-4 to -16 suggest many life forms. Some should be tied on long-shank hooks. A few smaller Pheasant Tail (PT) nymphs are useful for the skinny creatures and weighted Bitch Creek type nymphs for the mobile and large things. The Bitch Creek is normally tied in black with orange and is a great nymph. I particularly like it in combined shades of tan, yellow and brown. Smaller ones are productive on panfish.

Carry a selection of Woolly Buggers, large and small, in black and brown. My survey of flyfishers found the Woolly Bugger to be the only fly a favorite of trout, bass and saltwater flyfishers.

Soft-Hackle, wet-flies suggestive of emerging caddis and mayflies or drowned insects, are super flies that are easy and effective for beginners to use. In current, use them with wet-fly swings. I use size-8 to -16 in shades of tan, gray, orange, pink and olive. My all-time favorite wet-fly, a Wet Coachman, has a wire reinforced body of peacock herl, sparse brown hackle and a white wing of hackle fibers or soft polar bear fur.

It's a great early season fly and often produces when nothing else seems to. The color scheme of this fly works as is witnessed by the famous Idaho Renegade (even Royal Coachman) tied in dry and wet forms. I prefer the arrangement of the colors and the shape of the Wet Coachman over the Renegade wet-fly.

Midges provide the bulk of the food in some waters, particularly lakes. If you care to fish the larval forms, or wish to learn, obtain standard midge larva and pupa imitations in natural colors. Fish often take adult midges sitting on the water following hatching or when later mating or laying eggs. Dry flies are then apropos. Some midges attain relative large size. Smaller standard dry flies (#12 to #18) in lighter colors of dun and gray or similar thorax type flies might do. Bivisible flies can imitate two midges together (common) and allow larger hook sizes to be used.

Lake Fly Suggestions

If you fish lakes or lots of slow water, you likely need special flies. Lakes usually contain dragon and damsel flies, and many contain scuds (freshwater shrimp) as well as baitfish, crawfishes and hellgrammites (larval stage of Dobson flies, not stoneflies). All lakes probably contain midges, sometimes of large size. Size and coloration of lake insects vary widely, and I do not understand them well enough to suggest a few patterns that encompass most variations, yet remain extremely effective, as I feel I do with flowing water Western insects. I'm always working on it and some of my findings to date may help.

Lakes, lacking current to help activate flies (or cover mistakes), require effective flies be tied of mobile materials. I've used many well known and oft recommended lake nymph patterns with poor success. Most are too darn stiff. As important to motion is the way the fly is stripped, twitched and jiggled. The locomotion of lake creatures is most varied. I've been doing some recent lake fishing seeking a "wall size" brook trout. Damsel nymphs have been swimming up to me then crawling onto my float-tube to rest, reconnoiter or do metamorphosis. They're intriguing, analogous in motion to marginally slow, big-headed, little fish. How do you achieve that motion in a fly? One can't shake a fly rod that fast for long, and you can't impart quivering swimming with line strips.

Another thing, the damsel nymphs I've lately seen were not any shade of green as the books always show, rather, decidedly brown. While we're at it, how does such a large adult insect (size-6) come from such a small nymph (size-10)? Dry flies suggesting adult damsels are useful and common published ones are fine, with one caveat. Freshly hatched damsels, the ones most available to fish, are not the well known bright blue, but muted blue-gray, at least the ones I see. They turn blue sometime after hatching.

The upshot is I now have damsel nymphs tied on very short shank hooks with dubbed bodies of varying colors of blended polar bear hair *and* with extended bodies of thin strips of very mobile mink hide with hair. Legs are simulated with barred partridge. They work. Nymph color is often determined by that of vegetation or rubble nymphs inhabit, and many are probably green particularly later in the season.

Dragon fly nymphs are flattened in shape, usually greenish-brown in color, camouflaged and move in darting pulses. I haven't studied enough to adequately comprehend dragon fly nymph lifestyles and how to best imitate them. I won't fish them much until I learn (but did recently fool a 22-inch brookie on a polar bear dragon fly nymph). I should spend more time savaging dragon fly's rotten and sunken log homes to learn more but tend to fish when around water. I've tied a few correctly sized dragon fly dries. Fishing them is similar casting a canary.

Oppositely, scuds often contrast their surroundings by colors of white or orange. It's probably connected to molting or sexual in nature. Nearly all popular scud imitations are curved back, curved hook things. I know that's wrong. Swimming scuds (the way we fish them) stretch their bodies to full length; captured scuds curl. Ted Trueblood knew that when he tied his straight shanked Otter Shrimp. It's an ideal scud suggestion readily adaptable to requisite colors by blending body dubbing.

Fly Selection

Most of the flies discussed have been tested and refined over the years and will serve many needs. They simplify selection and minimize duplication. Avoid getting hung-up on one or two patterns that have provided past success. It's easy to do. Favorite flies may not have all the desirable attributes of another fly you could use. Ask if past successes could have been greater and derive ways to avoid repeating failures.

I've said flies can't be invented or improved, then proceed to modify with improvement in mind. Yes and no. If I looked in the right places, what I've done will probably be found to have already been done, despite any independent "discovery" of mine. I wish more "experts" realized or admitted that. Much to help us was discovered and clearly explained long ago—give the rightful inventors credit. Reading good books will help your endeavors. We need avoid all the confusing modernistic rubbish possible. Some flies die away only to be resurrected. A case in modern point is the tube fly. Some resurrections are inspired by profit potential or some writer needing something "new" to write about or to "introduce."

Fly Bulk and Weight

In buying or tying flies consider bulk. How heavily or sparsely a fly is dressed is important. There are few times when a bulky fly is preferred over a sparse, lithe or streamlined fly. Commercial tiers often tie flies heavily dressed thinking the end user will trim them to proportions best suited for circumstances, to give you your money's worth or sometimes out of ignorance. Lots of flyfishers don't trim them or don't think it expected or necessary. If you trim, cut materials off as close to their tie-in points as possible. Some folks like to cut the ends of wings or hackles, but it makes a fly look awful. Despite what I say, end-trimmed hackles do float better.

Overdressed flies wanted to sink can dry out during false casting and float, be inherently too buoyant or provide too large a silhouette to the fish. Don't doubt the vision, or sensory abilities, of most fish, it's exemplary. Fish vision can be hampered by cloudy water, bright light or bouncy, rough water in the case of flies being fished on or near the surface. I believe fish can see what we are offering in most cases—perhaps too well. Carry mostly sparsely dressed flies, tied correctly, particularly concerning hook style and weight.

Should flies be weighted? We have seen a small amount of weight in the head of a Woolly Bugger may enhance its effectiveness. Lee Wulff considered weighted flies to be, "feathered sinkers." Bill McMillan, perhaps the most knowledgeable, researched and documented steelheader of modern times, was paraphrased by Les Johnson (himself a most accomplished catcher of steelhead) saying, "Adding lead to a fly, while improving the sinking rate, negated the graceful swimming characteristics he sought." McMillan considers weighted flies to be "plummeting, gay-colored rocks."

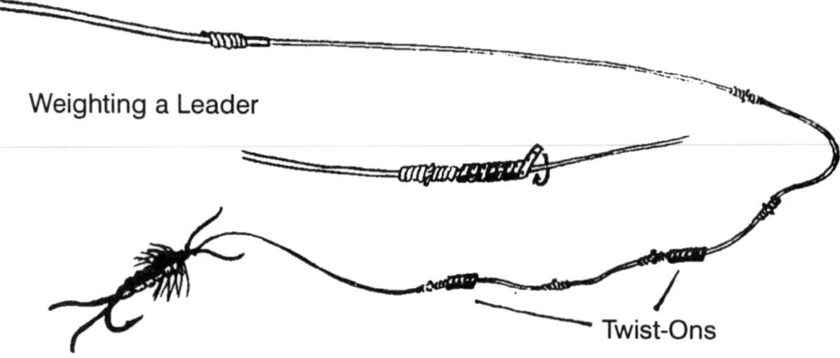

It may sound like hair-splitting, but I consider adding weight along a leader and leaving the unweighted fly to do its best seductive work a valid method when it's really *needed.* It's too bad snagging by some "anglers" has resulted in banning weight added to a leader in some waters.

Weighted leaders do not cast well but neither do weighted flies, too heavy hooks, sinking or wet-tip lines. Sinking lines and perhaps heavily weighted flies do have legitimacy in still waters if needing to fish a fly deeper than perhaps six feet. You relinquish some control of your fishing to the water when you use any sinking line or too long weighted leader. You destroy part of a fly's allure by weighting or tying on too heavy a hook. Weighted flies have damaged, even broken, many fly rods.

There are places to use weighted flies. *Very* deep or *heavy* flowing water might qualify. Flies tied of mobile materials or flies manipulated a good deal may offset the deadening effect of weight in a fly. Bead-heads or lead-eyes are popular of late with some flyfishers. You see those things added to all kinds of flies. The result is nothing more than a lead-headed jig, the tackle of spin or bait casting tackle users. Perhaps it's not surprising.

A Fly Connected Discussion

Too many newer, impressionable, or sophisticated "flyfishers" were sold or use stiff tip action rods (like spinning rods), and wind their reels with the weak hand (like spinning reels).

Why shouldn't they then use jigs like spin fisherman? Many fish their jigs under bobbers as if worms. Of course the bobbers are conveniently called "strike indicators," perhaps to hide shame. A faithful flyfisher's strike indicator is located between his ears, hot-wired to eye and hand. No other is needed if you know how to fish.

Authentic flyfishers readily accept a self-imposed mantle of tackle and method limitation. Protecting long standing fairness of play ethic and exercising skill over illegitimate technology (albeit simple) is more important to them and, in actuality, all flyfishers. Too bad more don't see that. I wonder why some people go through the grief of trying to fly cast tackle they use, or flyfish at all. It would certainly be easier to use light spin tackle. Is it so they can feel or look modern and correct, have no understanding of what flyfishing is, want fish at any price or to fish in "flyfishing" only water?

People can fish the way they want; it's none of my business, usually. It becomes my business when *avant-garde* "flyfishers" largely devoid of flyfishing's history or tradition and lacking basic knowledge and skills damage flyfishing's future as they sully age-old, gentlemanly, respectful and honorable traditions of the sport by claiming what they are doing is flyfishing. Too often the actions of the weighted fly and bobber crowd are damaging to vulnerable fish. I recently witnessed such damage on Oregon's North Umpqua and its summer steelhead stranded in hot water. Caring flyfishers will reap the negative public sentiment harvest they had no part of sowing. But most do nothing to stop the sowing.

It's a sad direction too many are going. Members of the bead-head and bobber, stiff rod, heritage ignorant bunch, who lean on low technique, have no idea of the self satisfaction and effectiveness attainable by fishing an unweighted fly deep through *skill.* The quick-fix of weighted flies or lines made heavier than water by simple technology are their self-limiting tools. The industries love contemporary sophisticates. They buy the inane tackle the industries dream up, read the magazines and frivolous books, watch the videos and listen to fly shop oracles or other "experts." There's need for human elucidation regarding ethical flyfishing and minimization of vulnerable fish exploitation.

If it weren't for tradition supporting and ethical work

done by Trout Unlimited, the Federation of Flyfishers and other such groups, things would be worse. These organizations *aren't flawless;* their memberships reflect new permissiveness, but they're the best we have. Join a club in your area, or if you aren't a joiner, donate some money to their projects. You will help yourself as well as others. Caring individuals, scattered everywhere and teaching as they may, probably do as much good. Give one a compliment if you can.

Fly Materials

Factors outside the realm of presentation influence a fly's effectiveness; tying materials are certainly one. Translucence, mobility, durability, water absorption rate and ease of tying are variables of materials. We also find ourselves back, forced to dabble again, in the quagmire of color. How sparkling and transparent, drab or opaque a fly appears when wet are important and affected by its materials. Materials that suggest life, provide movement and do not appear phony are needed. The flyfisher survey revealed 95% of flyfishers tie flies. I'll use that saturation as license to discuss some common materials. If you don't tie it may help you in selecting flies to buy.

There are some great materials and there are lots of poor ones. Marabou is highly mobile, maintains bulk in the water but is fragile. Fur and guard hair from water animals is most useful to obtain shine, translucency and water repellency. Depending on fly type and purpose fur can be used in tails, bodies, wings and collars or throat hackles. Beaver, otter, mink, muskrat, seal and polar bear are tops. Warning note: As I understand the laws (which isn't perfectly) it is very difficult if not impossible to legally deal in seal fur or products. Twelve species of seals are currently endangered, threatened or under worldwide protection. Can you tell one seal's hair from another's? Polar bear isn't so hampered, and polar bear underfur is a near equal of seal dubbing.

Polar bear is the only fur mentioned with guard hairs long enough to tie wings over one inch and up to nine or more inches long. Dyed polar bear maintains its natural shine, sparkle, translucence and durability and provides seal-like underfur for dubbing bodies or for use as tails or throat hackle. It's great stuff, ethical to use and legal from several sources despite what the know-it-alls, writers or editors say or purposefully don't say.

Polar bear is commonly ignored in fly dressings, even for those original patterns calling for polar bear. No magazine, to my knowledge, has published an article on polar bear flies or tying with polar bear in the last 20 years. Yet many fly tiers use it extensively. I'm told editors fear leading fly tiers astray. Why do they publish flies using questionable feathers?

Water animal fur is reasoned to be water repellent, and it is. But most tying fur comes from tanned hides. Tanning processes take some, but not all, of the water repelling characteristics from the fur. Tanning does not take away a most important characteristic. That's fur density on the hide and in some cases density of individual hairs. Water animal hair and fur protects its owner in cold water with characteristics that favor tying excellent flies. Throw a rabbit, an African goat or even an Arctic fox in cold water, and they will die quickly. Their hair and fur is much different from that of water animals. Despite that, the fur of these land animals is frequently recommended as substitutable for superior water animal fur, particularly polar bear.

Land animal fur lacks density requiring the tier to use more, and it's almost always too soft. If used in wing or throat hackle, it will not stand out, slightly away, from a fly's body, but collapses against water pressure exerted during fishing. Land animal fur is opaque and quite dull compared to water animal fur. If you think there is no substitute for the stripped-rabbit fur used in streamer or leech flies, you should see how thin strips of mink, otter or muskrat look and work. Their stiff guard hairs are useful for feelers, tails or to make "scraggly" bodies.

Many modern fly tiers want fly body dubbing material that is *easy* to use, soft and pliable. Any dubbing that's easy to use is hardly worth using. Gone is the spiky look, perhaps translucence and sparkle obtainable from water animals. You might as well use wool yarn or chenille. Many tiers don't know to use only a little dubbing at a time and a waxed thread if needed. Correctly done, nearly any material may be dubbed.

Peacock herl is a most useful material for fly bodies if you don't wish to dub a fur body. Peacock herl is attractive to many fish, but it's fragile; reinforce herl bodies with counter wraps of fine wire—copper is good.

Flyfishers are heaven blessed with the hollow hair of the several North American wild deer and sheep. It's extremely useful and adaptable. Hair from certain animals, like pronghorn (a goat), caribou and the several mountain sheep is very brittle but is still useable for spinning (heads and bodies), if not winging. Hair from differing parts of the hides of moose, elk and deer, both mule and whitetail, is ideal for many kinds of flies. These hairs are durable enough and dye well but come in a large variety of natural shades with markings so beautiful only nature could have designed them. There are varying textures of hollow hair; most are useful. But the shysters are always underfoot.

The industries want to sell you cow elk, bull elk, yearling elk, calf elk, elk hock, elk mane, bleached elk and dyed elk. They offer similar choices in deer hair. I'll bet most of the people selling flies or materials can't tell a yearling cow elk from a mature cow elk on the hoof, let alone from a scrap of hide. Is a yearling bull elk's (a spike's) hide sold as yearling or bull elk? I'm a serious hunter and grew up around deer and elk. I've killed many of each for meat then used their hides for tying flies. I can tell sex and age of an animal on the hoof and probably from a full hide. I doubt if anyone can distinguish such things from pieces of hide, or if citified, from full hides.

What do you or the fly shop's buyer receive when you buy or order calf elk? Not many calves are legally harvested, and few of those find their way into the hide trade. There is texture and color difference of animal hair depending on sex or age of its original owner. There is more difference, however, depending on time of year an animal is killed, which portion of the hide it comes from, or where, geographically, the animal lived and died regardless of sex or age. Classifications of hair by age or sex of animal are offered to sell more hair or out of ignorance displayed by sophisticates. Select hair by characteristics needed, not by the sex or age of an animal it *supposedly* comes from.

Stiff chicken hackles are useful, but overrated, particularly in ability to float flies. Research, even decent observation, reveals hackle works well only when it stays above the water's surface. That requires using light hooks. Since hooks are the heaviest component of flies, that means hooks of small size or light wire and light wire or small hooks cause grief. They break easily or take small bites of jaw. Fear of breakage or pull-out causes the babying of a hooked fish prolonging the fight. Prolonged fights are hard on fish, and you can't fool and hook another (maybe larger) while you are fussing with one. Hackles on large or heavy dry flies do not add as much to floatability as a lesser amount of hollow hair. Hackles may simulate legs on a fly, as can hair, if used properly. Many large, even small dries work better without chicken hackle. Price of top quality hackle these days is too high for questionable benefit. But tradition will keep hackle around.

Lesser quality wet-fly or streamer hackle is decent material. Sparse wraps may suggest moving legs or gills, provide action or bulk to a variety of fly types. In many applications flared hackle works better. The Soft Hackle wet-fly, a very useful pattern, will frequently work better with hackle that doesn't collapse against the body by pressure of current or retrieve. Since partridge, not chicken hackle, is most often used on soft-hackles, it should be wrapped to stand out more from the hook shank. Consider how flies will look and fish in the water, not how they look dry, in your hand.

There are sound reasons master flyfishers of old chose the fly materials they did when a wide array of natural materials was available to them. Why would anyone try to "improve" that perfected? Let's see. Promotion of new or different materials, natural and especially synthetic, is done to sell more product and not because new materials are needed or superior. Sometimes it's because well known and recommending tiers or authors are too sophisticated. New materials *seldom* represent meaningful improvements over the older and proven. New material seekers are similar inventors of silly new flies, often the same persons; they seek profit or fleeting notoriety over need or utility. Their tests of new materials likely aren't extensive or blind enough to be trustworthy.

Synthetic Materials

There are crowds of synthetic materials. They come with glowing recommendations and supposed benefits, then go, found to be of little use, so fast few may keep abreast. It's simpler and more rewarding to learn to use natural materials with understanding. What you need is available in natural material. Most synthetics have minimal stiffness and collapse in the water. They almost never have the exquisite tapering fiber ends of natural materials. Nature's fibers just make better flies.

Some recent fly patterns are loaded with synthetic trash. Synthetic materials are often intensely flashy and bright. If used in clear water or on heavily pressured fish, the latter becoming more common, a little goes a long way. Some tiers apparently reason that if a little is good more is better. Flies with lots of bright synthetic materials are often found on the tippets of novice and less than accomplished flyfishers. Combined, they can sure make fish spooky. Few understand that.

Beware of synthetic ribbing and body materials. Few are needed and then light and unobtrusive to reinforce the fly or suggest segmentation not to add flash. Fancy metal tinsels, some fuzzy, may look nice to you, but metallic flash, as previously mentioned, is not at all like natural flash from a bait fish or insect. I like to use three or four twisted polar bear hairs for ribbing. Sophomoric fish, many saltwater species as the several Pacific salmons in remote rivers and on spawning journeys, often fall for garish flies of synthetic materials. Next thing you know, people use such flies to seriously spook pressured fish. The ignorant, unthinking or uncaring, as always, make things needlessly difficult for others. Don't they know or sense the differences in a dull-witted Chinook or a brash Coho of an Alaskan river compared to a pressured lower 48 state's steelhead in low clear water?

My commercial streamers seldom contain flashy tinsel bodies, or any body. Heavy flash is wrong, even counterproductive for most conditions. A streamer's hook, being heavy, wants to hang below buoyant wing materials when the fly is fished unless steps are taken to minimize the problem. Most tiers don't take such steps and most use tinsel bodies. The resultant impression—created by a detached, hanging and shiny hook—hardly resembles a bait fish as the illustration reveals.

A bright, flashy, but phony body, even in the right place, seldom improves a streamer. Wings, not bodies, are most important to effective streamers. Tying part of a streamer's wing below the hook's shank helps hide the hook. I suggest and prefer short-shanked hooks. If you like, coat the hook's shank with white or a blending color thread or use nothing at all. I am aware some fish and fisheries still find heavy tinsel bodies acceptable. I wonder if the

A Poorly-Designed Streamer

users of such flies ever tried flies with polar bear wings and without flashy bodies?

Material Legality

There is widespread confusion and misunderstanding regarding legality of certain natural materials. Laws (federal, state and international) are confusing, being bird and animal species as well as date specific. Writers, editors and fly shop proprietors, rather than do simple research or consult bona fide experts, adopt negative or stick your head in the sand attitudes. Fly shop proprietors may have illegal materials on hand, *perhaps* innocently, and do not want US Fish and Wildlife officials snooping about for any reason.

There are many questionable materials and most come from fancy birds. I know something of one, polar bear hair. Hair, hides, dubbing, *parts or products* (flies) of polar bear cannot, with few and very restricted exceptions, be imported into the USA. Nor can any in country be exported legally without an export permit. According to my understanding, *and not to practice law*, state laws forbidding use of certain materials are null and void when federal law permits use. Such is the case concerning the several states and polar bear. Polar bear hides, parts or products may be imported or exported *if documented* the bear of origin was killed before 21 December 1972 (effective date of the Marine Mammal Protection Act) **and** *the appropriate permits and necessary supporting documents are obtained and used.*

I deal in polar bear hair and have the first and—as far as I know—only multiple export permit (USF&W #764657) for polar bear tying materials and products issued. An appendix concerning polar bear is found at page 267.

There may be ways to legally deal in other protected, misunderstood or rare materials besides polar bear. Don't believe or spread rumors and don't fall for less than full proof of legality. Legal dealers won't mind showing proof. Save your receipts. More despicable than unenlightened experts and resigned editors are the smugglers, sellers and users of illegal materials. They damage all of us and our sport. Flyfishing is experiencing attack from various "anti" groups. Why provide them ammunition?

Material Summary

There are a great many fly tying materials. We have only looked at some of the more important and some that present particular, perhaps unforeseen, problems or benefits. New materials arrive on the scene constantly. Look at anything that's new, improved or possibly illegal with a suspicious eye. Perhaps it or its promoter are too sophisticated. Suppliers introduce new materials knowing the stuff brought out last year has done its job of fleecing flyfishing's flock, as will the new. The cycle continues and continues. Result: flyfishers end up with chests full of junk and poorly performing flies.

In the melee of marketing, some useful materials do arrive, once in a while. New threads, glues, head cements and hooks for example. Some viable materials don't survive competing with the junk. Many tiers have solidly cemented cynicism due rubbish previously proffered by the sell-side. Decent new materials or tackle, well-tested (assuming qualified, bias-controlling testers are used) would benefit us. Expecting the industries to operate based on need with wisdom is probably beyond its greed dominated abilities. We must be our own protectors. Accurate knowledge is protection.

Additional Fly Considerations

Have you contemplated what constitutes a fly? Can it have a bead head? Then how about a wobbling disk or bill attached? Can it be made mostly of cork or plastic or have a rattle inside? How about adding smell, taste impregnation, plastic tails? Traditional flyfishers wouldn't be caught dead using such things. Others don't care if more fish are thus exploited. I can't say what does or doesn't constitute a fly. You have your opinion and I have mine. Unsound or "wrong" technological advances have a way of sorting themselves out for the best in the long run. Trouble is, harm is done and misinformation spread while we wait for the long run to expire. We're constantly confronted with new and questionable goods, including flies, having brand new and perverting long run potential. I refuse to buy goods judged to have harmful potential or disregard for true flyfishing precepts—precepts defined by the overprotection of fish and severe limitations on personal tackle and technique.

What about foreign tied flies? Their quality nowadays is generally good regarding hooks and construction, and there are lots of importers and many, too many, patterns. Foreign flies put American tiers out of work. Every dollar that goes to a foreign country further damages our balance-of-payments deficit. Apparently few care if a fly was tied by semislave labor or its country of origin.

I owned a fly shop for ten years and over the fly display, in red, white and blue, was the sign: ALL FLIES TIED IN USA. I was, and am, proud of that. Self-serving industry moguls, many fly importers, successfully scuttled recent proposed federal legislation requiring labeling of foreign tied flies. In fact, that's why the North American Fly-Tackle Trade Association (NAFTA) was formed. NAFTA paved the way for greater profits for a select few. I believe many American flyfishers would rather buy flies tied in the USA if they had a choice or were made aware of which flies were foreign and which domestic. You might ask before you buy flies. I read that NAFTA is now fighting for its organizational life and that there is an oversupply of foreign flies.

Carry flies in boxes correct for them. Appropriate boxes are strong, light in weight, dependable, and it's advisable they float. I've witnessed flyfishers crush and damage the floatability of fine dry flies carrying them in other than a deep box or by jamming them too closely together. It was many years before I could afford a shiny, held to be the epitome, silver, Wheatley fly box. I now have several, and they are used for display flies or storage. They're too heavy to carry. There are lots of good fly boxes these days. Fly boxes should be vented in case you forget to fully dry flies after use. Even then you will probably ruin some flies; try to always dry your flies after use, before storage. I remember losing nice fish to flies with rust in the eye, even flies I'd tried to remove rust from. A wet fly or two can rust a whole box full.

Summary And Fly List

To sum up, remember fish are caught for reasons other than hunger. When you select a fly to fish, first consider shape, then approximate size and finally color variables. Any fly should be tied on a correct hook with the best, usually natural, materials for the fly's intended purpose. If you don't subscribe to hatch-matching, close imitations or don't know what to use, then select basic and proven flies by style and not always by some supposed superior *specific* pattern. In any case, worry more about correct presentation than flies. There are no magic flies, only good flyfishers who try to keep the traditions of flyfishing alive and well.

Lists of flies generally duplicate or leave something out. Nonetheless I'm going to give one, a "Flies Not To Be Without" list. These flies have served me well, most for many years; some we've discussed. Many commercial flies are tied too neatly. Datus Proper noted hatching flies in particular are quite rumpled. Lee Wulff's own Wulff patterns were rough compared to modern copies. Don't feel bad if flies you tie, aimed at catching fish not impressing someone, don't look the prettiest. Rough flies seldom sell well at shops, and you will see mostly prissy neat flies for sale in the little bins.

Flies Not To Be Without

Dry Hair Caddis: #4 to #16; standard and 2XL; in yellow-orange, tan, yellow (black and olive in smaller sizes); dubbed bodies, most without hackle; heavy and standard wire hooks.

Woolly Bugger Type: #4 to #10; 2XL; mostly solid colors in black, brown, muddy-gray, a few claret and white; dubbed, heavily picked-out-bodies of fur (seal, polar bear, mohair); tails of marabou or fur strips of otter, mink, muskrat or rabbit.

Streamers: #2 to #6; standard length hooks; polar bear wings of white, black over white, brown over white, chartreuse over white, and red over yellow; red throats and two-color eyes. Marabou Muddlers of same size in white, black, and brown over yellow. Standard Muddlers in #1/0, #2 and #4. Both Muddlers on 2-3XL hooks. Hair caddis fished wet are very Muddler-like.

Wet-Flies: Soft Hackles; Few #4, but mostly #10 to #16, standard wet-fly hooks; lots in tan and olive, few in pink and orange; brown and gray partridge hackles. Wet Coachman; #8 to #12, wet-fly hooks; peacock herl bodies reinforced with fine wire; brown partridge hackle; white, soft, polar bear wings, body length. Miscellaneous: Black Ant, #8 to #12 on standard hooks; and Gray Midge, #14 to #18 on short hooks. These last two can be tied on appropriate hooks to be fished wet or dry.

Nymphs: Gold-Ribbed Hare's Ear; #4 to #16. Pheasant Tail nymph; #10 to #16. Both on standard and 2XL hooks. Bitch Creek type nymphs, #2 to #10, 2XL; yellow-brown and black-brown, some weighted, all with black or brown rubber feelers and tails. For lakes, carry basic damsel and dragon fly nymphs, also scuds. Trueblood's Otter Shrimp is a classic scud. Require mobile materials for still water flies.

Dry Flies: Adams and Light Cahill, #10 to #16; or Gray Wulff and Yellow Goofus Bug (Humpy), #8 to #16; Royal Wulff or Royal Trude, #8 to #14, on standard or short shank hooks (1XS) of regular weight wire. Thorax type flies, #12 to #18 in basic colors on short shank, regular wire hooks. John's Hopper, #4 to #8, 2XL; pale dubbed polar bear body, red polar bear tail, elk wing, spun deer hair collar trimmed to a block-head. For lakes; damsels, #8 or #10, long shank, regular wire.

Steelhead Dry Flies: Muddler Minnow, *block-headed* and gold-bodied on #2 Mustad model 9671. White-winged Bomber, #2 to #6 long, bronze steelhead hook. Hair Caddis, yellow-brown coloration, red hair tail, same hooks as Bomber.

Steelhead Wet-Flies: Claret and Black #1/0 to #6, on a variety of black hooks, mostly heavy, including doubles in #4 and #6. Tail and throat are claret polar bear; body, dubbed of black polar bear ribbed with three twisted white polar bear hairs; wing of polar bear, white under, overlaid with black, 2/3 length of the white. Jungle cock cheeks optional. Thor, hook sizes as Claret and Black but in bronze finish, tied per standard pattern, but use polar bear for all parts. I also use similarly tied Blue Charms of all polar bear construction; its yellow and blue colors show fish something different. Flies to be tied in low-water style.

Large Flies: #4/0, 6-7 inch, blue over green over white polar bear streamer with or without silver body (your choice), red throat and prominent eyes. Same fly on #2/0, 3 to 4 inches long. Size #1/0 flies, 3 to 4 inches long, of pure white, chartreuse over white, brown over white and red over yellow polar bear. Use shorter hooks to avoid fouling in casting and rust resistant hooks for saltwater. Deceiver style ties of polar bear work well.

Saltwater Flies: Clouser Minnow and Crazy Charlie types; #2/0 and #1/0 and #2 to #8, standard rust resistant hooks, colors to be solid or two-tone in white, tan, pink, rust, yellow and chartreuse; use dubbed polar bear bodies (Charlies) and single or bicolored wings of polar bear. If bicolored, use lighter color below. These flies often call for bead-chain or lead eyes, suggest some with and without. Use in fresh water *without* stainless hooks.

I believe I could fish quite effectively nearly anywhere for nearly anything with these flies, tied as recommended, on a variety of hook weights, sizes and types. If I'm wrong, they still constitute a relatively simple and effective basic selection you may add to as need dictates or you wish—and you will.

Chapter Eleven: Fly Casting

Successful flyfishing requires decent fly casting skill, but skilled casters may be poor flyfishers. Proficient flyfishers cast well as a means to an end, not as an end. Competent flyfishers learn, mostly through trial and error, to do what's necessary in casting to present flies to catch fish. Some in flyfishing construe fly casting as cryptic, perhaps as a form of self aggrandizement—or to sell "solutions."

Notwithstanding personal instruction, classes, books, videos or combinations, all casters ultimately teach themselves. Many fine casters are wholly self-taught. Some may have watched and listened to others and read about fly casting, picking up odds and ends, here and there, using what worked and discarding the rest. Principles of fly casting are simple to grasp. You're throwing a string with a stick, and it's as Ted Trueblood stated, ". . . hardly worth all the solemn words written about it." He goes on to ask if anyone ever really thought it was the bushy, near weightless fly that is cast and not the line?

Most casting instructors and instruction start with the "line not the fly," nonsense; however, a good many casting instructors ought not be teaching or should be taking not giving instruction. Truly expert casters often have trouble teaching what is automatic. Other instructors are motivated by money, tackle they hope to sell, ego or the need to show off. I'll give suggestions on picking an instructor, if one is thought needed, later.

A person looking for shortcuts to casting proficiency won't find many. Practice, before going fishing, is required but not as much or as often as perhaps thought. Short sessions, frequently spaced, are best. Practice and memorization of simple basic moves needed to toss a line with a stick, until automatic, are all required. It isn't difficult. It's a lot like learning to play a musical instrument where many give up on the verge of reward.

Steve Rajeff, many times world champion caster, says success comes in spurts after about ten hours of practice. Mr. Haig-Brown says it takes less than that: "A few minutes a day for a week will give you basic proficiency and once you attain basic proficiency you will want more." Lee Wulff says to remember fly casting is the only sport where force is applied in both directions.

As with knot tying, I have little sympathy for a person failing to practice casting then complaining or making excuses, deceitfully blaming conditions or tackle. Fly casting can be practiced in an alley, in New York's Central Park or in your yard. Just do it—as they say. The best of casters still practice to hone timing or retune time-rusted muscles. Never plan on learning basics while fishing—too many other things then demand attention. Here I recall someone telling me I underestimate the fear of looking silly that lives within many people. What? I have poor understanding of such feelings.

What's the matter with looking a little silly (therefore human), compared to being stupid, then revealing it by an inability to make simple presentations to vulnerable fish because of lack of practice? It's incomprehensible when ineffective casters travel far, at great expensc, solely to flyfish, yet it happens all the time. Joan Wulff, a terrific caster, said: "If you can cast but don't understand fish you have a chance. If you can't cast you're not even in the game." Poor casters damage others as much or more as themselves. Follow a sloppy, incompetent caster through a run and you will see how and why. Lots of "experienced" flyfishers can't cast competently. Lack of correct practice but also poorly selected and assembled tackle regularly defeat them.

I guided trout and steelhead flyfishers for about ten years. Decent guides work hard for patrons and self-respect. People I guided often couldn't cast at the required level, yet most really wanted to catch fish. They were not hiring me "just to get away." Most guides will bat their heads against a wall only so long putting clients on fish they spook or can't cast well enough to hook. What's the matter with people? A head full of romance or fantasies and "desire," a "correct" hat and all the expensive gear in the world won't cut the mustard on the water. You can either cast capably or you can't. If you can't—learn—practice. You learned the multiplication tables, to drive a car, perhaps a tennis or golf swing. Basic fly casting is probably easier than any of those. Help improving or even teaching yourself follows in a minute. First some background on teaching and learning to cast.

The Federation of Fly Fishers (FFF) instigated a program several years ago to certify industries' personnel to casting competency and, therefore, ability to help or teach others. It had written and physical casting parts. The casting test was simple; even so, many fly shop owners, managers and employees *failed*—the very people daily giving advice, teaching and criticizing fly casting. Such history is more, even if unneeded, verification for the results of Question No. 66. It's difficult for most flyfishers to ascertain if fly shop personnel have either the knowledge or ability to help them. Too many would-be casters assume fly shop "pros" have needed abilities. That's often false and dangerous.

You won't be surprised to hear the FFF program to certify the industries was put to death. It was way too illuminating and far too embarrassing for the industries to allow. It takes courage to admit ignorance and open the door to improvement for self, others and flyfishing. The FFF test was very basic with nothing specifically aimed at teaching. It's fair to say, however, that if would-be instructors can't perform minimum, basic casting moves, they sure can't teach the same.

Note: There has been a resurrection. The FFF program lives again. A friend recently taking and passing the new test tells me it's aimed at *teaching* flycasting. Perhaps to allow those who can't cast to teach.

Self-Help Casting

There are differing styles of casting and theories of teaching and learning casting. They often disagree, yet all share certain aspects. We'll take advantage of those similarities. I don't propose to give a complete course on fly casting, I couldn't. I'm a poor teacher. Before you lose faith, I am a reasonably effective caster, fairly researched, and able to discuss common mistakes and cures to help your casting, if you need help. I'll write as if I were helping a newcomer; don't take offense if you are a decent caster.

We know human adaptability permits nearly anyone casting several line weights on the same rod. It might not look pretty or be easy with badly mismatched tackle. The same principle applies to experienced casters faced with unfamiliar rod weights, lengths, or actions—they will adapt. Balanced tackle is nice; but as discussed in the chapter on rod-line balance, it's difficult for many to achieve. That's particularly true if you believe the line recommendations on rods are accurate these days. Bad advice is extensive and communicable. The point: listen to few, rely on self and your God-given abilities.

Fly casting has a physics, laws-of-nature controlled side, but also, and probably more importantly, an intuitive side. Datus Proper said something like that and equated the latter to using and learning to rely on our all-seeing, automatic, intuitive and sometimes hard to use "right" brain. Or, just do what you somehow know has to be done and also have the indefinable ability to do. Too many casters and instructors get hung up in the physics stuff too early. Most aerodynamic loop size or shape, a rod's resistance to bending or ability to "load" due space age technology *may* have pertinence later on. Learning to cast, the line either goes as you know it should and want or it doesn't. If it doesn't, change what you're doing until it does. Don't allow confusion by knaves or faddish terms and ideas. Casting jargon coming from the industries, concerned with product differentiation, correct and trendy ideas is often wrong, misstated or too theoretical. Keep things uncomplicated.

If you have read this book completely to here you know what tackle you should be using. In case you haven't, a quick review follows. Use a rod properly appointed that you like, that feels light in your hand and is neither stiff nor very soft. It should yield smoothness of feel with felt flex down into the cork grip. You need a floating double taper (DT) line in good shape to *match* your rod (very possibly not the line weight listed on the rod) with a correct leader attached. To your tippet, tie a small fly with the hook cut off at the bend. Use what reel you have for now or see Chapter Seven on reels. If serious about learning to cast and fish, use decent, not necessarily expensive, equipment. Help obtaining reasonable and workable tackle is found in Chapters Two through Seven. Specifically see Chapter Six to assure rod and line balance understanding.

Charles Ritz, a tremendous caster and teacher of casting, said being relaxed is *one-half* the secret of learning to fly cast. Could you relax with some instructor haranguing you about loops, numbers on a clock, a too stiff wrist, a too limp wrist, failure to stop and on and on? Probably not. "Most people can be explained to several times but have to learn on their own," Ted Trueblood said that, and, "Learn to cast before going fishing. I can't be too emphatic about this."

Before beginning casting practice *envision* what needs to happen. Concentration, like a relaxed attitude is important. In your mind's eye, see the line being swept upward and back by your arm and rod, straighten, hesitate, then roll out in front of you in a forward cast. Think of the movements you need impart to the rod to achieve your vision. Consider each one separately then put them together. Ritz, and Joan Wulff, both recommend pre-visualization. It works. Do things first in thought then with physical practice.

Start practice with at least 30 feet of line, lying on the ground, stretched out in front of you. If you have a stiff rod and too light line (a distinct possibility these days) you may find 40 feet of line will be easier to use. Just assure enough line length, with its corresponding weight, to *feel* the rod bending. Determine that with a few firm back cast attempts looking for

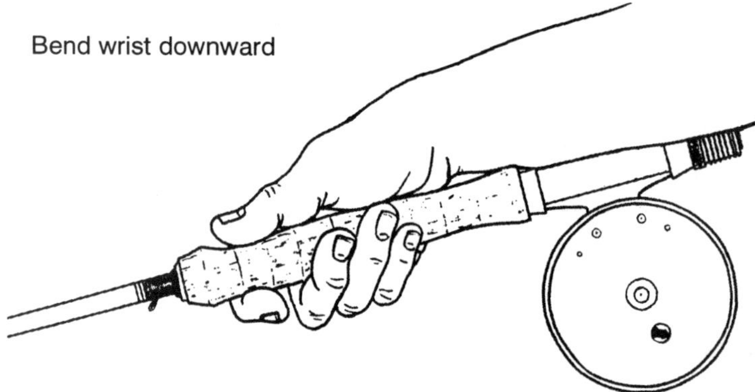

feel. Adjust line length as needed. Trust your instincts. Now, with the determined correct amount of line stretched in front, hold the rod horizontally, waist high. Bend your wrist *down* (see illustration). Higher rods and straight wrists create slack.

Slack line kills casts; eliminate slack from advent of casting. Use your left (or nonrod hand) to grip and control slack at all times. That requires it move. Start thinking, right now, how your line hand has to move to eliminate slack while casting. It needs to move more or less the same distances and the same directions as your casting hand and as Haig-Brown said, "is rarely at rest." If you don't move your nonrod hand it will tighten back casts and give slack to forward casts, killing them.

Back to casting: Squeeze the rod grip, tightening your muscles, just before *any* power application. Make all casting movements by *starting slowly, accelerating rapidly* and *stopping suddenly.* Steve Rajeff says the failure to do so is the most common mistake made. Do not apply power too soon, but when you do, do so with gusto. Remember: Sudden acceleration to an immediate stop.

Keep casting strokes short; it's normal for people to use too long strokes. False casting strokes should reveal your casting hand traveling a course parallel the ground or water's surface. There is a pronounced push-pull motion, *not* a whipping action, applied to the rod when casting correctly. Remember that also.

Gripping the rod with the thumb on top is preferred, but such a grip has the drawback of allowing natural overbending of an untrained wrist on back casts. Such overbending is also common and detrimental. While learning, place your thumb alongside the grip. So doing will eliminate cast destroying excess bending of the wrist that allows the rod to tip, too far back, on back casts. Switch back to the thumb-on-top grip as soon as you learn the stiff-to-limp wrist action needed and without damaging casting strokes. Prolonged thumb alongside grip casting stresses the elbow, defeats maximum power application and always causes the rod to twist during casting. The last effect, in turn, causes your line to travel a less than ideal path. The thumb and first two fingers provide most of the grip and power in casting. That's different from the grip of bat, club, racquet or the tools of other sports.

Concentrate on making all back casts **up,** not back. Turn your body and head to watch and assure it happens. These actions are most important until you learn the sense and feel of the line and rod. Whenever you have problems or cast strange tackle, turn and watch your back casts, observe what's happening, change if needed and continue. Throw high straight back casts consistently and you will have few problems. On the final, forward, presentation cast *do not* bend or "break" your wrist until the line has straightened in front of you. Breaking the wrist last will avoid tailing loops or tying knots in your leader—so called wind knots.

Quit casting practice after a short time; think about what you have learned, relax mind and muscles and then practice some more. Do the same the next day or even several hours later. Consider practice casting with your nonmaster hand while you rest the other. Developing casting ambidexterity is desirable. Continue master arm practice until you can throw high, straight back casts and straight, pleasing forward false and final delivery casts. You'll be well on your way and will find casting increasingly enjoyable. Avoid complex and technical advice givers. Voltaire said to be happy, "Cultivate your own garden." Bad advice is abundant and casting just isn't that difficult to learn.

Roll Casting

Before too long, some say first, learn to roll cast. It's important and requires water to learn thoroughly. Water provides necessary tension on the line to allow the cast to work. You can practice on grass and get the general idea of what happens and what's needed. Roll casting is also best accomplished with a softer rod. That's part of the reason I recommend softer rods. Envision the middle and butt parts of the rod being used more than in overhead casting. Learning to be a competent roll caster *geometrically* increases your ability to fish effectively under a large variety of circumstances.

Start roll casting practice with as much or a little more line than you used in overhead casting and *do* go back to the thumb-on-top grip. Start on still water if at all possible and cast the line onto the water to lie straight out in front. Keep your hand in the normal precast position (waist high, wrist bent down). Raise your rod hand and arm, dragging line behind, to a point where it is very near and slightly higher than your casting arm's shoulder. You will get more snap into your cast if your hand is also slightly behind your shoulder. Keep the rod pointed up. Then tilt it *slightly* back by relaxing and tipping your wrist back—but just a little.

Motion you have used to accomplish correct hand position will draw the line toward you. Let it come, and wait, until the line bellies well behind you suspended from the rod tip. Not waiting long enough is the most common fault. Snap the rod down sharply (as swatting a mosquito) to below horizontal, using shoulder and forearm with a stiff wrist. Think about and use the middle, not the tip, of the rod.

In snapping the rod down, point the tip in the direction you wish the line to go. Don't cause the bellied, and cast, line to cross over the line lying on the water by rod tip pointing or it will tangle. You can't change the direction of this cast too drastically at one time. These points will become clear with practice. You will learn to adjust line or rod, pivot your body or casting plane to allow greater changes in direction or angle of line presentation.

Using the roll cast you have license to fish from under overhanging trees, tight against steep backdrops and other difficult places the duffers and lazy can't. You will naturally learn to use a roll cast to pick line deftly from the surface in preparation for an overhead cast—a roll cast pickup. Learn the roll cast and its variations well. The roll cast is a much underused cast, and learning prepares the way to the most important of line handling techniques: mending. Mending is certainly related to, but it is not casting. We'll cover mending in the next chapter.

All other casts are variations of overhead and roll casts and sometimes mending strokes. Basic casts can be completed in any plane needed to get the job done. Many so-called casts are sophisticated foolishness (Belgian, steeple, dump, tower, etc.). A competent flyfisher with skills evolved in a vacuum would know how to use supposed difficult or specialty moves (casts). Our self-taught flyfisher would also know the shortcomings of fancy moves—something seldom heard—and would have learned to assume correct position and to use simple casts to correctly present flies according to situation.

Pointless discussions of special "casts" or techniques are usually just more bull-flop. I'd wager, giving long odds, that one of those right-handed casting experts can't make five, or even three, flawless right hand curve casts in a row. Lots of gibberish circulates. Nonsense isn't helpful to someone honestly trying to advance or learn and perhaps wondering if he will ever be able to do "reach" casts. If he can extend his arm in some desired direction near the conclusion of a cast he can and has. A newer flyfisher may find he can single or even double haul; it's naturally learned. Hauls aren't true casts either. They're extensions of using the nonrod hand to control slack line; something you've been studying and practicing since starting to cast. Right?

Instruction

Once you have developed basic skills you may find professional instruction helpful or you can continue to learn on your own. Beware of schools taught or sponsored by outfits that sell tackle. Question any instructor you consider. You might find you know more than he. Keep looking. There are competent instructors if you've decided you need one. Charles Ritz said only one in ten golf instructors can teach a person without confusing. Could fly casting instructors be different? You essentially have to teach yourself, and will, if you want to learn or improve badly enough. Fine game fish don't respond to fantasies, line waving, certificates from lame casting schools or "desire"—only capabilities.

Casting instructors and casting methods most often stress making your rod tip travel in a straight line. Lee Wulff used an elliptical rod tip path. That makes the most sense and works best for me. Back and forth casting strokes in the same plane too easily cause the line to hit the rod or itself if *all* casts aren't perfect. Whose are?

Casting Considerations

The power of any casting stroke begins with hand and arm and moves up the rod. Stiff rods transmit power too quickly. They cause jerky, hard to control, rod and line motions for most casters. The problem is amplified if a stiff rod is underlined—naturally or intentionally. As we have discussed, stiff rods can be softened somewhat with a correct, heavier, line. Even then the result is stressful, rough and tense casting with unwanted side effects. The rod industries sure haven't done flyfishing or fly casters any favors with their stiff rods. The average stiff rod proponent can't cast almost continually, for 10 or 12 hours straight, then do it again the next day, the next and the next *and* the next. Their arms would fail, or they couldn't keep up the non-stop pace without extra rest. I've had to cast those hours and days for the Idaho Fish and Game Department on fish census float trips.

The goal was to catch, measure and release all the fish possible, day after day. It's not all that much fun after five or six days; catching fish becomes somewhat boring work. Nothing aids casting, making it enjoyable (or bearable) like using a rod with a moderate and restful action—one equipped with a floating DT to match conditions and a correctly functioning leader. As a side note, I found it possible to destroy a set of quality snake guides in a few days. A worn, then cracking fly line carried fine grains of sand from the bottom of the boat converting the line into a saw.

Wind, even moderate, stops some people from attempting to flyfish. I can't understand that; wind is a near constant in flyfishing. If you can't cast in wind, you can't cast. Learn to use

the wind by keeping casts into it low and powerful. Casts with it are easy. Don't let wind blow your line into you. Position yourself differently or turn 180 degrees from the water and make your back casts forward casts. If you have developed adequate weak hand casting ability, use it as needed when winds blow. DT lines buck wind best at moderate to long casting distances. There are lots of ways to handle wind problems if you use originality and don't cop-out and quit.

Long distance in casts and special techniques are possible with time. Time is variable based on practice, dedication and desire. Some experienced flyfishers never learn long distance casting. Maybe they don't need distance; maybe they won't practice or use self-defeating but "correct" tackle. Distance casting requires modification or unlearning of some basics. Don't fret if you're just learning. Fly casting is only a part, albeit an important part, of catching fish. Learn the basics well.

As you cast and fish you will learn a great deal. I beseech you, don't try to learn casting haphazardly or over a period of years. Commit yourself and learn the basics quickly, before going fishing, then you may concentrate on fishing. As you cast and fish individual style will evolve. Don't worry about what you don't know or think you can't do. Most mistakes in a discipline, sport, or indeed most things, stem from failure to learn, know and use sound basic principles.

If you should meet an exceptional caster, you might inquire if he or she would help with something problematical. Few will decline and you may receive competent and useful help. When it comes to casting the best and truthful are still learning, at their own speed, mostly on their own. It's a good way.

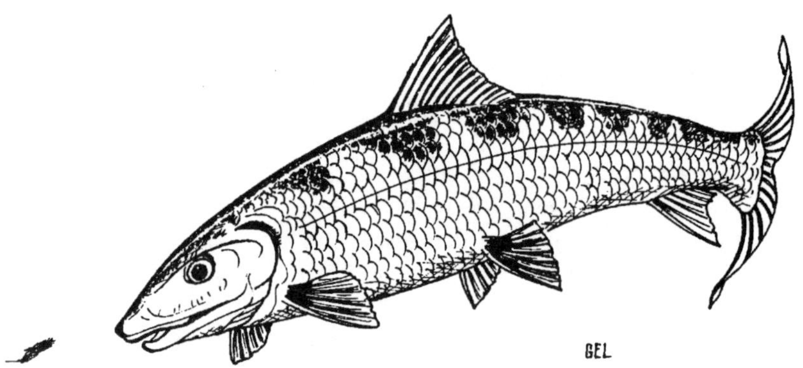
GEL

Chapter Twelve: Flyfishing

Finally, after studying why certain tackle works best and examining casting, we've reached the crux. Flyfishing is a broad and deep topic, being water and fly type, condition, weather and fish species specific mentioning only a few of *many* variables. Despite that, there are a number of things common to most flyfishing we might learn from. Flyfishing is a grand life sport, brimming with heritage, challenges and rewards. Everyone is learning, and no one knows everything.

Relax, and if you're serious about becoming competent, do so in nonhaphazard ways while having lots of fun.

Better Flyfisher Characteristics

Better flyfishers share certain characteristics. Some are inherited, but most are cultivated with conscious effort to improve. Alfred Miller (alias, Sparse Gray Hackle), noted in his writings that the best flyfishers he knew all shared keen vision. Roderick Haig-Brown believed focused power of concentration very important. Charles Brooks, in his writings of Western flyfishing, said the best flyfishers were constantly striving to learn. They study and test things remaining leery of the "new" until it proves itself, as a great deal of it flops. Dedication and true desire to learn and become ever better are attributes often mentioned by flyfishing's best writers and are related to concentration. I believe sincerity for and honor of flyfishing traditions plus driving curiosity, particularly concerning fish, to be characteristics of better flyfishers.

Authentic, lasting desire and a mind set to learn and become better counter physical limitations and buttress anemic skills and knowledge. Excelling or just becoming very good at something requires effort and dedication. Some flyfishers, however, are hopeless mind image junkies with invalid or weak motivation. Misinformation and fantasy visions are created or arise from many sources including the media and account for weak-spirited, ductile entrants. Since flyfishing is differing things to different people; perhaps no reason, virtuous and legal, is bad. Make no mistake, however, the purpose of flyfishing is to catch fish. Ted Trueblood correctly stated that years ago also saying people don't stay with flyfishing if they don't catch fish. The more, the faster, the bigger you could catch, supposedly the better. (Notice it's *could,* not *do,* catch.)

Better flyfishers often quit when the flyfishing is too easy. Challenge is gone. They might attempt to catch fish with demanding technique or with "wrong" flies. Perhaps they pursue or cast to only the biggest or most difficult fish, anything, to keep boredom from setting and to keep learning. There is no right place in flyfishing for boasting of large bags or large numbers of fish caught and released. Large catches mean nothing. A better fisher may have taken twice as many as a braggart if not bored or devoting time to experimentation and learning or maybe helping a newcomer catch a few. Yet boasting is common.

Flyfishing Maturation

Edward Hewitt first noted flyfishers go through stages of development, and you've probably heard them before. None are bad in and of themselves, and all stages should be enjoyed. A flyfisher first wants to catch a fish. Progressing, a person then wants to catch lots of fish, and many flyfishers seem to get hung up there, playing the numbers game. There is beckoning allure to the most advanced of flyfishers to regress and occasionally participate in catching large numbers of fish. Little harm is done; dalliances are short lived. Perhaps there are people who enjoy catching fish one after another, every time out, day after day, year after year. I hope I don't have to fish with any of them.

Hewitt's third stage finds the flyfisher pursuing large or difficult fish. There is disgusting misunderstanding here. Large may not be at all difficult. Large is purely relative as well. There is more accomplishment in taking an old and cagey 14-inch brown trout in a stream where the average is 9 inches than in landing a dozen 15-pound salmon in an atmosphere of Alaskan extravagance where a chimpanzee with a fly rod could catch them. Lots of flyfishers participate in such easy fishing then want you and I to think they have done something meritorious.

Every year numbers of rainbow trout in the 10- to 20-pound range are senselessly killed on Idaho's Lake Pend'Oreille and a few other Canadian lakes that support the giant strain of Gerrard rainbow. Murdered fish are often proclaimed, "The largest trout (or fish) I've ever caught; I'm going to have it mounted." Confronted with taxidermy costs of $10 to $12 an inch of length, discovered *after* killing the fish and failing to properly care for the proposed mount, few people have fish mounted. The fact that a 10-pound rainbow is the largest a person has caught means absolutely nothing in light of the maximum size of this rainbow strain. It's over 50 pounds. Sport caught Gerrards near 30 pounds are taken most years. Ten-pound specimens are ordinary—teenagers, if you will. A quick picture, followed by immediate release would allow many fish to live, perhaps to true trophy size. The killing of average fish, carrying great potential, in a trophy fishing situation is disgusting and due to ignorance, vanity or even fear. Charter operations that define their businesses, success and future bookings in terms of providing customers dead fish rather than fond memories and *education* contribute to misunderstanding and perhaps fishery damage.

Many places accommodate killing to eat fish. It's arguable *authentic* trophy fish, carrying desirable genes to soon be passed on, should be released in favor of killing lesser fish, if we kill at all. There are also places where caring and informed flyfishers will kill a limit of fish whenever possible. Populations of overpopulated or perhaps planted fish need thinning. A flyfisher needs know when to do what and can't rely on fish and game laws for correctness, only justification. Because something is legal doesn't necessarily make it fair, ethical, in flyfishing's or a fishery's best interest. Fishery conditions can change rapidly, laws seldom keep pace. Game and fish laws cater to the masses. Laws are political as many voters define success as killing fish or game and managers cater to their votes and caterwauling. Guidance is available.

State, national and world-wide sport hunting and fishing organizations have long established criteria for defining trophy specimens. While arbitrary to individual definitions, sound criteria have saved the lives of countless game animals and fish. Regarding game animals, the minimum point score for what, with sound reasoning, is defined a true trophy falls near 80% of the existing world record for the species. If a person fishes or hunts he ought to know what constitutes a truly exceptional specimen of any species pursued. Sadly, most do not. That is not to say one should only trophy hunt or fish. But don't cause fine, with potential to be finer, game or fish to die through vain "trophy" pretense or ignorance.

Released fish may live. Those gill cover hoisted, netted or kept out of water too long or otherwise mishandled (often for photos) probably suffer much higher mortality after release than most think. An animal shot dies; but discipline based on knowledge and caring to not shoot an inappropriate animal or to never harass, knowingly or *otherwise,* a tired and beaten game fish for ego's sake is certainly a high virtue.

Difficult fish are trophies of different sort, usually released, but much remembered. Smart old trout, shy permit, tough jawed and aerobatic tarpon, rare Montana grayling all may or may not qualify. It depends on the angler and his experience. Method and tackle used are trophy defining criteria *always* selected so fish aren't damaged any more than absolutely necessary—no ultra-light exploitation, please. Quality and memory of experience will always outrank quantity or size of fish caught in the minds of flyfishers worthy the name. I don't know how to feel about a mediocre mounted fish stimulating and helping the angler recall fond memories. A quickly taken picture or a custom plastic mount might work as well.

Hewitt recognized a final maturation step after large or difficult fish—bird and flower enjoyment. Hugh Falkus, British author: "If a person exists who can give a damn about the birds and flowers after a fishless week, I never met him." Flyfishing is always about catching fish, but "the fun is in the trying," as Trueblood said. A trip with fly gear in tow to enjoy nature, unwind or escape even though it involves going through some flyfishing motions, is correctly defined as a "drive (or walk) in the country" not flyfishing. Apt flyfishers may take such drives, but when they fish it's nearly always with serious intent, time devoted and thought aimed at catching fish the way they want to catch them.

If you don't understand your quarry or can't handle tackle as circumstance requires, you will have to settle for drives in the country, birds and flowers. People who profess abnormal enjoyment of nature's side shows frequently can't use the tackle or don't understand their fish. Nature enjoyment is a fine thing but shouldn't be used as a handy and known acceptable, built-in excuse for flyfishing incompetency or failure. I commonly see people use such excuses. They even convince themselves.

Line Control

Fly casting receives an excess of ink and breath and is almost synonymous with "flyfishing" in the minds of some. Fly casting concerns airborne fly lines; it's more important to control line while *on* or *in* water. If you can't or don't, a fly fishes at the mercy of the water, seldom correctly. Controlling your line on the water and to some extent in the water is called mending. Mending is best done if minimized, made easy or both. That's done by selecting the best casting position, casting correctly and using appropriate tackle. Cast from places putting line in a minimum of conflicting currents or current speeds. If fishing ocean or still water be aware of subtle currents caused by tide or wind. Position yourself so any current or wind will serve, not hinder, your purposes. Newcomers will find positions with current coming from the same side as their casting arm easiest. Fishing shorter lines, by first achieving best casting position, is important for beginners, or anyone.

A moment of explanation: I have used "beginner" or similar words a good deal. Beginning flyfishers can range from those with no fishing knowledge, flyfishing or otherwise, to accomplished anglers switching to greater rewards and challenges of flyfishing or any level of fishing understanding between. Advantages enjoyed by those understanding fish are considerable, but they can be negated by attendant attitudes of arrogance or cavalier flyfishing ignorance. "What's so great about flyfishing?" "I know all about fish, fishing, knots, casting, etc." Willing to learn flyfishers have tremendous advantage over attitude carriers. Don't worry if you don't or think you don't know much; that's much better than thinking you know more than you do.

Back to mending: It's most often done in sideways direction to reposition line. Mends are made to allow and ensure your fly will fish as *you* desire. That may be drag free, cross-current, very deeply or combinations. Any type of sinking line severely limits angler control of a fly by hindering ability to reposition line. That can be acceptable in still or very slow water but seldom in current. *As the line goes: so goes the fly.* Mends in current are usually to the upstream side of the fly, but downstream mends could be required as when fishing across an eddy or backwater. Line mends easiest if it's clean and floats high and is mended immediately after the cast hits the water before water may gain purchase on the line.

Lots of flyfishers mend anemically with counterproductive results. They flip and swish line hanging from rod tip about, building slack and doing nothing positive for fly travel. Viable mends involve lifting and rolling line much more than flipping, particularly when the preceding cast was moderate to long in distance. Flipping and swishing *might* work for short casts, and short casts are always preferable. Many circumstances, however, require long casts and accompanying long mends. Long and controlled casts cover more water much more effectively. Long mends, involving lifting and moving lots of line, might easily be called and are often accomplished as modified roll casts. No matter name, long mends are super effective at increasing flyfishing success. Full or long and most effective mends can't be accomplished with WF design lines. Fly line is easily and effectively mended in the air, just before the cast settles—aerial mends. Importance of correct mending can't be overemphasized, but always seek correct casting position.

Excellent mending practice comes, or required moves understood, from mowing lawns with an electric lawn mower. The cord must be fought and repositioned by flipping and rolling around shrubs, sprinkler heads and such to avoid walking to undo snarls. The same can be said for flipping a kink out of a garden hose. Everyone's done that. If you can roll cord or hose over the pfitzers and around the chrysanthemums think what you can do with a DT fly line and a long lever. Think rolling and lifting—no flipping or swishing.

Picking Your Expert

Scholarship regarding quarry is mandatory and will grow with experience. It's *Catch 22,* but a great deal about fish or given species may be learned reading and asking questions while proficiency catching and learning firsthand evolves. Distrust advice until collaborated by someone you trust, like yourself. Other trustworthy persons should have depth of understanding and reasoning based on experience that's both valid and extensive. Use common sense to discern decent advice, remembering lots have "experience." If it isn't valid, it's largely useless.

Ask polite but leading questions of persons tendering advice or willing to help you. How long and where have they flyfished? For what? Look for wide and varied over narrow and deep experience. "Many years," professed experience, is often heard and is always questionable; we know neither quality or true extent of reputed experience. There are more persons than recognized with "many" years of experience under their belts showing surprisingly little understanding of fish or flyfishing.

To learn and also to learn to trust self-obtained knowledge, read. Read older books anytime you can; wintertime is ideal, aiding the passage of usually slow fishing months. Public libraries have flyfishing books (often older ones), and fly clubs customarily have extensive selections to be borrowed by members. I recommend mostly older books because, as Datus Proper said, the newer ones are mostly rehashes, and original ideas are always clearer. Older books by Ted Trueblood, Ray Bergman, Lee Wulff, Joe Bates, R. Haig-Brown, A. J. McClane, Mark Sosin, Charles Waterman, Datus Proper, Howard Blaisdell and Dave Hughes (a recent author) *among others,* are worth reading.

There are authors unmentioned on purpose. Too few authors speak the whole truth; most prefer to ignore or skirt critical or sensitive areas for reasons earlier given. A stream of quite superficial, confusing and hackneyed bilge water flows—and it sells; it's small wonder so many have wrong ideas about flyfishing.

All videos are recent to flyfishing history. Videos fool. They're seldom real life experience, despite appearing so, and tend to make things look too easy. Instructional videos, as casting instruction, may be of help *if* instructors are qualified. What do you do, watch them then run outside and cast or do you take the TV outside? Videos are too often the lazy person's way and not as successful as industries' marketers thought. Desirable and traditional flyfishing has long standing and proven ways of doing and learning things. I'm not against change, but much modern is foolish, damaging or offensive. Proponents of too much modernism in flyfishing look and sound silly. They also scare the fish.

Danger always lies in accumulating insight. Obtaining *some,* owners often burst forth thinking what's needed is known. God's fish are great equalizers of men uncaring of what's thought known, amount of money accumulated or social position possessed. You can either catch them, usually, or you can't. Arrogant, upwardly mobile newcomers will regularly receive earned doses of flyfishing humility; many should then quit flyfishing. Kingsmill Moore believed:

> "Persons should fish for little trout in streams to become really competent; for they teach you much of what you need to know: striking, approach, rise forms, stealth—to fish like a cat."

Modern, "success now" thinking isn't often accommodated by flyfishing. Alaskan easiness or similar simplistic fishing with numerous imprudent fish accepted. While learning, and we're all learning, strive for broad understanding not technical specifics. The deck is stacked against a stereotyped approach to flyfishing.

Wrong Conclusions

Fish behavior can fail to conform to human notions of ideal conditions. As an example, fish may be slow to respond to changes in water conditions. I know from experience and reading that steelhead in many rivers respond best to surface flies in water near 51°F. But I've had fishless days, with fish known present, under ideal conditions, including water temperature only to have fine surface action a week later in "too-cold" 43°F water. I believe the difference was *when* water temperature changed. If water was in its first day of 50°F plus, having risen from lower temperatures, steelhead would not respond as they are supposed. Similarly, if water temperatures dropped, even significantly, only the previous night steelhead would readily rise to surface flies, but probably not the following day.

Fall storms, followed by clearing skies, bring colder air that decreases water temperatures quickly. Fish appear to adjust more slowly. In the described steelheads' case, it took about two days. Additionally, and importantly, water temperature eventually affects the type of water fish hold, most notably depth and speed. As water temperature drops oxygen content increases. Fish can obtain required oxygen for slowing metabolisms from slower water with less exertion. As able, select fishing times and methods giving thought to recent weather and its probable effects on water conditions and fish. Fishing several days in a row is preferable if possible. Time usually offers weather protection unless conditions are changing very rapidly.

If my limited observations are correct, they give partial explanation to goofy notions and conclusions about fish behavior we must endure regarding what *absolutely* will or won't work. Persons least knowledgeable and researched conclude wrongly most often, but that doesn't keep them from concluding, and often. A rank neophyte, however, unpolluted by too much knowledge and blissfully ignorant, can stumble into excellent fishing when others stay home or fish halfheartedly. It's wise to fish whenever possible, but if hoping to often blunder into ideal conditions, as many apparently do, know it's a very long shot. If you do so successfully and often, I suggest you start buying lottery tickets. Use your gift.

There are dangerous people in flyfishing. Dangerous to learning—theirs and ours—and flyfishing in general. Avoid them by study and digesting numerous opinions. Always be alert for what *might* work better. Use what works or makes sense and remember to "Cultivate your own garden." Syl MacDowell, another author worth reading, said of fishing writing: "A great deal is riddled with misinformation, fables, and half truths and lacks scientific study"—Amen. Flyfishing conversations are equally "riddled."

Shun weakly supported prejudice, yours and others. Haig-Brown again offers us timely wisdom. "The dividing line between the virtue of conviction and the vice of prejudice is often too fine to be measured by the owner of either one." He also believed too much "expertness" in a person's flyfishing stifles pleasure and imagination. Study and keep an open mind while learning, relying on self and having fun. Recoil from sales motivated distortion of the industries. It's most infrequent *new* things are so good as to be *needed* or will make you a better flyfisher. Yet countless flyfishers won't study, think, read or practice and fall for bunk—repeatedly. We all fall for some, but should strive to not. There is no quick or easy way to becoming a decent flyfisher. The effort required isn't extensive at any one time, and it's all fun.

Advice

A wise person takes and embraces sound advice. Nonetheless, decent advice is frequently unheeded. The knack is knowing to whom to listen. People are made leery and cynical by a preponderance of bad advice. So whom do you believe? The givers of the best advice were "born to the water," for lack of a better term, and have spent significantly long lives fishing, particularly from early boyhood. Some people are driven to fish by unexplained forces. They will often know and understand fish and fishing the best. There are many sophisticated, citified flyfishers, and many of those have come to flyfishing late in life. Be careful of what they say as a general rule.

Advice may be over the head of the recipient, for the time being, to be found useful later. I've sure had that happen. Suddenly, something told me or read long ago makes perfect sense. The advice lay dormant awaiting further study or most often fishing experience. Understand, as best you can at the time, any advice you deem worthy. Ask more questions and reread. Greatest help, however, comes from faith and respect, for some worthy reason, in an advice giver. Advice then adheres. Diverse "experts" and authors—speaking or writing because they want or have to, not because they have something worth saying—too often exhibit only questionable knowledge and information, not wisdom and understanding. They lead us astray if we let them. Of course those writing or speaking think they have something worth saying; it's up to us to discover if they do or don't. We'll get fooled some—learn and profit from mistakes.

A competent and willing teacher to take a beginner fishing is a tremendous find. Finding competency and willingness combined is difficult. The very willing probably lack competence and may have other undesirable qualities. Those competent are often loners. Some fish with only compatible friends. Quality fishing time is valuable to anyone; while top flyfishers are not uncaring, the opposite usually being the case, they are justifiably protective.

Traitors

Too many special and "secret" spots are divulged by people shown or told them in confidence. Such action ranks among fishing's, all time, disgusting acts. If you are told or shown where, exactly, to fish, *never* disclose it to another—outdoor writers, take special note. "Where-to-go" books and articles are the bread and butter of many. It's my opinion ethics, even self respect, are lacking or willingly sold for a few dollars. Jezebel writers couldn't write if there weren't publishers and readers for disgusting betrayals. Some "sportsmen" readily digest such writing trying to capitalize on what's not due them. Flyfishers competent and worthy will know where decent sport is to be found from their own experience or associations with others worthy who trust them. Crowd causing and detrimental dispensations ought not be published, wholesale, for someone's financial gain—but they are.

Persons availing themselves of prostituted advice are likely the type to also disclose information given them in confidence. They probably don't see the value and have small investment in and little feeling for valuable advice or special places. Be careful whom you speak to, read or trust. An old adage says, "how and when anytime—where—never." If a person can't solve flyfishing equations given two of three variables, he's probably not sincerely motivated, lazy or none too bright.

Under scrutiny, successful fishing boils down to knowing exactly where the fish are and fishing there correctly. People knowing exactly *where* probably learned over time and through effort. Learn your own places the same way. Go fishing alone all you can. People best learn alone without companion pressure (even innocent) and time to think and experiment as they wish.

Wading

Wading is important in lots of flyfishing. It needs doing safely, quietly and effectively. A well functioning sense of balance is important to most athletic endeavors, including wading. Keeping one's body fit and flexible facilitates balance. A dash of daring and boots with good traction are needed in current with rock, rubble or otherwise slick and treacherous bottoms. Knock on wood, but I haven't taken a bad spill in years. Perhaps my daring dash is waning or insufficient.

I've used about all commercial traction aids sold and made my own. Stream Cleats, made of aluminum and rubber galoshes and sold by Dan Bailey's of Livingston, Montana, work tolerably but are hard to walk long distances on when out of the water. They don't seem to last as well as they once did either. Felt soles alone don't work adequately for most of the fishing I do but may for yours. I have drilled holes, at correct places, in thick felt soles and taken them to a tire shop to have metal studs installed. That works quite well until the felt wears and the studs tear out. Traction aids can be put on over or added to wading shoes, boot foot waders or hip boots. I hope I've used my last wading shoes. They're heavy, time consuming, perpetual muddy mess makers. I much prefer faster boot foot wading gear.

Some people, because they have chest waders, feel they need use them to near-limit. It's often a mistake. Fish frequently lie and take in shallow water if fools are not constantly wading there. When I guided steelhead flyfishers I knew my water very well and kept my clients, invariably wearing chest waders, wading no more than knee deep unless a channel needed to be crossed. There are several good reasons.

In downstream fishing, debris dislodged by wading will drift downstream alerting fish if one wades too deeply or wades at all. Fish of any kind that come to the fly as it approaches or hangs downstream are difficult to hook solidly. If deeply wading anglers who are commonly unfamiliar with the water allow flies to terminate their swings in the "taking" water, fish often lose interest. Fish won't rise or their rise form causes the fly difficulty taking a firm hook hold. It's much better to wade more shallowly causing the fly to *swing over* the taking water. I wish more flyfishers understood more about wading correctly. Noisy, poor or too deep wading pushes fish from holds where they are easily hooked to deeper, heavier water where hooking them may be impossible or accomplished only by better flyfishers. Boat traffic does the same thing. It's fresh in my mind.

I've recently been doing some early steelheading in a large Western river before most think fish present. There aren't many fish, but there don't have to be if you know where to look and what are present aren't spooked by the damnable boats soon to come. I've lost two of the three fish I've hooked. Both were large (they jumped) and came free after short struggles, and both were poorly hooked because they took at the very bottom of the fly's swing. I know better, but got lazy. Actually, I'm a little hard on myself (we should be); the water is very large and difficult to wade or fish no matter your gear. It's tempting to wade deep when you may, to obtain more water coverage, and fun to fish long sweeping fly swings after long casts and mends. If I had fished a shorter line and moved downstream more often, *on* or more near the bank, my fly would have swung rather than hung over the fish. The two steelhead I hooked in a different river recently both came on the fly swing, and both were solidly hooked. Greater water coverage through incorrect wading and poor water knowledge or diagnosis is very often counterproductive.

I usually wear and prefer hip boots to waders even for "big" water. Chest waders are normally too hot, heavy, inhibit movement, expensive and short lived. Modernists, to look or maybe feel correctly dressed, always wear chest waders. Dave Hughes, in one of his books, opined that many such users haven't yet learned to relieve themselves before donning waders—another benefit of hip boots. Dependable, reasonably priced hip boots are hard to find. I often use three-quarter length irrigating boots sold at farm and ranch stores just as I did as a boy when a pair of them and a shovel were my tools and a big ditch full of water needing equitable distribution to crops my responsibility. My father, who wasn't much of a fisherman (but a fine man), said the only advantage hip boots—or for that matter waders—have over three-quarter boots is the ability to hold more water.

Wader materials come and go, new ones nearly every year. Neoprene may have outlived its usefulness. It's just too hot in summer or early fall and causes excess perspiration that results in waders smelling like locker rooms, heat rashes and general discomfort. If a person wishes neoprene's benefits, it almost forces ownership of a warm weather wader of nylon or one of the newer materials. I don't buy the idea of materials that allow perspiration to escape while sealing out water that's under pressure. Maybe such stuff works. But then how many "water-proof" leather boots have failed in the last 40 years or so? Why not use lighter waders or hip boots of cooler material then add modern clothing underneath if temperatures are cold? Let's take a look at fish themselves.

Fish And Behavior

Game fish are celebrated in written word and verbal tale telling. Many are very beautiful it's true; some, such as Atlantic salmon, have been placed on pedestals. Despite human awe, fish aren't very bright. They have small brains and notwithstanding untutored babble, or occasional slips of rationale, can't reason. The less highly evolved an animal, the more it's affected by its environment. Fish are not highly evolved and subject to what water causes or allows. Water clarity, volume, temperature and cleanliness, among other variables, hold life and death sway over fish. Fish fighting to survive hot, low summer flows or fighting pollutants are stressed. Feeding is not a high, or any, priority. But the wader clad sophisticate fishing away over them hasn't a clue.

Many flyfishers have small understanding of what transpires in a fish's world. They don't know what happens when or why and don't seem to care. None know completely, but better flyfishers are always trying to learn. Many experienced trout flyfishers don't know that within wild stocks of trout, brookies and browns spawn in the fall while cutthroats and rainbows are spring-spawning. Neither do such flyfishers know the ramifications of pre and post-spawning and its effects on fishing. Most steelhead fishers, for example, have a "food mentality" to their fishing.

Few steelhead are active feeders on spawning journeys (also other species) lasting as long as 11 months and culminating in death. (The steelhead I'm referring to do die.) Fish, being cold-blooded, don't *need* to feed regularly but live from stored energy for extended periods. Common sense would avail the food need believers the impossibility of all, save a very few, river systems capable of generating sufficient feed to sustain a great many, large, spawning bound, actively feeding and predatory fish without destruction, via cannibalistic predation, of their species' young rearing in the same water. Spawning bound anadromous (live in saltwater, spawn in fresh) fish have changed body functions diverting feeding and digestion to production of eggs or milt. Lots of steelheaders erroneously think an offering need represent food. Decent steelhead flies that work aren't taken as food and don't need to be so designed or fished, although the contrary can be effective.

Because fish don't feed doesn't mean they can't be caught on flies; we know that. Catch them by appealing to alternate sides of their psyches—meanness of spirit and territoriality being prime candidates. Another, and concerning anadromous fish, is dormant, but reachable, memory of pre-adult days of active freshwater feeding, according to some. The equivalent of boredom or curiosity in humans may result in fish taking flies. Fishing in acceptable ways learned through trial and error, or *known* and passed along only because of someone's earlier, perhaps extensive, trial and error experimentations is more important than worrying of reasons fish take flies or particular fly patterns. Appreciate the people discovering what now works for you.

Know yearly time tables of fish sought, habits and lifestyle. It's available in books, through competent advice and on stream. Read to magnify and clarify education given you stream-side. Find books avoiding maudlin mush, where to go, tackle goofiness and absurd technique. Many books are histories of personalities or flies and despite interesting reading, aren't much help. Books addressing truly useful subjects by qualified authors with adequate research and valid experience are not common. Of them, many are or were written and published in Great Britain. Books appearing useful, by title or cover, can turn out not to be and actually damage your flyfishing; books are "marketed" as much as any flyfishing item. Fisheries biologists may steer you to scholarly works capable of help. You might ferret some useful information about fish behavior from most flyfishing books, but it involves reading lots of unuseable stuff. Flyfishing information or that concerning fish might be inaccurate or out of date. Use books to capture basic, never changing (but often little known) truths about fish and their behavior. You'll know.

I reviewed a recent book by an author that covered a large stretch of river I raised my family on the banks of, fished and guided for some years. This author has roads and bridges where none exist and a US highway on the wrong side of the river. How does one do that? His recommended flies bear little connection to insects native and numerous. But he is a published "expert" and selling books. I feel sorry for the poor buggers buying them. The point, beware and always consult several sources.

You should know about a fish's food. What is preferred? What else does it eat? How does its food look, act, what size is it and when is it available? Flies most often suggest food, but we know other flies will undo fish as well or better. Very "different" flies often work, and matching the hatch is an absurdity when you are competing with very numerous naturals. If you disagree from a numbers standpoint, perhaps you've now had time to explain the presence of the hook in something that *matches* the hatch.

Fish are hatched spooky, some (the survivors) more than others. They fear and guard against something eating them, if not in adulthood certainly as juveniles. That danger often comes from overhead. Many are the flyfishers splitting hairs over inane leader diameters, rod actions, exact imitations or special techniques then sallying forth wearing fish spooking white hat, pale vest or something as absurd. They walk as drunk, wade without regard or bang boat sides forgetting or oblivious sound traveling five times faster through water as air. Light colored clothes may be acceptable on the bonefish flats with its washed out skylines but not contrasted against the rich greens and browns surrounding small lakes, rivers or streams. Sophisticated flyfishers are commonly negligent fish vision capabilities (it's available in good books), detrimental effect of noise and shadow, or wrong casting angle on spooky fish. Falkus believes, "Dressing like a hunter makes you feel like one." His comment causes wonder what stupidly dressed fly-fishers feel like? I know what they look like.

Common Mistakes

Poor casters slap or rip water with line, leader or fly when it's incorrect to do so. It's seldom correct. Fish are spooked in a dozen ways, and the angler thinks failure due not having the correct fly, rod, line or whatever. Flyfishers with inadequate understanding or skills defend foolish actions recounting fish caught. Once again, what of those they didn't catch? The larger, older, smarter ones. Ray Bergman considered splashy line work to be the worst of crimes in trout fishing. It's very damaging to self and others and all too common. Learn to cast and mend well. Use tackle that helps, doesn't hinder, your efforts.

Many flyfishers waste time at easy access, easy casting places. Others fish unsuitable water at wrong time of day or from wrong position. Fish don't have eyelids, and bright light probably bothers their eyes. It certainly hinders fish vision and can be an advantage to flyfishers if the fish are willing to respond under strong light. First you need know where in stream, river or body of water fish will respond under bright light then how to approach such places correctly. Fish seldom respond to surface presentations with bright light directly in their eyes (the rays of sun travel down your fished line). Strong light may be direct or reflected from clouds; it's often deceiving and should be on the minds of thinking flyfishers. Fish of the character we seek or large numbers of fish aren't found where access is easy or lighting wrong.

If new to flyfishing cover lots of water. Especially the mean access kind where others seldom go. If you aren't lazy or scared and have learned to roll cast you won't fear. Some souls seem petrified to leave sight of their vehicle or the campground. Maybe they don't want something from the little understood wilds to "get" them or risk break-in and damage to their fancy new sport-utility vehicle. Observe, learn, walk distances and investigate if your goal is to catch fish and learn, not something phony like looking right, being correct or sophisticated. See from a fish's viewpoint. Most beginners, and lots who aren't, fish too slowly, often fighting tackle problems or casting inefficiencies. They waste time in unproductive water. Fish are located in a relatively small portion of available water. Learn where. Available and productive fishing time is limited and valuable. Don't squander valuable time. However, if I had three days to fish unfamiliar water, I'd spend all or most of the first touring the water, asking questions, observing and devising strategy. Then I'd fish hard with confidence the remaining two days.

Productive water, once recognized, shouldn't be fished in a rush. Fish productive water thoroughly. Strive to approach fish closely without alerting them, for casting, mending and hooking is then always easier. Fish close first then gradually further away without missing or disturbing the water. Be cognizant of an observed fish's feeding rhythm. Be cautious, stealthy and unimposing in approach and motion. Be quiet. Do things as correctly as you can. Strive to improve. Remain earnest, but take a moment to enjoy pretty flowers, a colorful bird, vistas or a cloud configuration—but only a moment.

I've harped on reading and study. Don't, however, mistake academic astuteness for wisdom. People with heads full of disjointed facts fail miserably on the water. Light tippets are recommended a great deal. A neophyte about to fish for bass has been told to use a largish hair bug. He doesn't know his fine tippet won't cast his size-#1 hair mouse. Needed is a mix of study but more fishing time. There's flyfishing for something close to anyplace you may live. It doesn't have to be for glamour species. It's said you learn little while fishing, being too preoccupied with details. Learning comes later reflecting on things done combined with continuing book study and more fishing to test new ideas, knowledge and abilities. It's all very enjoyable with frustrating moments. Take time to think and reflect on your flyfishing.

Fishing Guides

Having the budget, decent guides can help a great deal not only with fish sense, but casting and tackle problems. Trouble is, too many considering themselves flyfishing guides are undergoing training, even basic, at your expense. Talk at length with guides considered for employment if you can. Tell them what you want or need. Ascertain, using straight forward questions and resultant findings, possibly intuitive, if guides are able or want to help you learn. Guides could be jaded, lacking flyfishing knowledge, poor teachers or too full of self esteem.

Ability to row a boat or rustle up a fine lunch doesn't extrapolate to flyfishing understanding or knowledge. Such abilities could be important if water to be boated is technical or if you value lunch over decent flyfishing help. Outfitting operations, however, often automatically cater to the wants of the spoiled and sophisticated in flyfishing. Employment decisions depend on a client's level of expertise and what you want to learn, if anything. Asking a guide to fish is a good idea. Tradition observing and ethical guides *will not* fish without being asked. Much can be learned by watching a true pro and asking questions or imitating them.

Fighting Fish

Surprisingly few people, I observe, know how to correctly and ethically fight a fish. Time needs to be minimized, for the fish's sake if you plan on release *or* if you wish to kill the fish. Flyfishers prolonging fights through ignorance *might* be excused. Those doing so for self gratification are despicable. Too light tackle—true 1-, 2- and 3-weights—are seldom the tools of conservationists or caring flyfishers but those of ignorance and haughtiness, often industries cultivated or aggravated. Likewise, 4- or 5-weights used for steelhead or Atlantic salmon class fish are ego motivated, not fish protecting. Balance tackle to fish, erring on the heavy side if at all.

Experience finds flyfishers enjoying the fights of a fish less and less, but never, ever, failing to enjoy fooling a fish, the strike, the hookup and certainly the initial power of larger fish. To fight fish, and stated in simplest terms: If the fish doesn't pull—you do. You need put pressure on fish with exuberance and *must* know the breaking strength of your tackle. Determine that strength by tying your leader to something solid and pulling, uniformly, with the rod. Caution: Don't damage your rod; most people are amazed at the amount of pressure you can exert with a rod before even light tippets break. Fight fish at all times with a high percentage of the predetermined, and reduced to intuitive, breaking strength of tackle.

Hook bite in fish jaw is often the weakest link in our chain. I prefer larger hooks than often recommended and assume a strong hook hold in fish unless known otherwise. It's most often the case. If it isn't, few lightly hooked fish will be landed using light pressure anyway. The hook will either wear a hole in the tissue or come free from a tenuous hold at some point in a prolonged and fish damaging fight. A majority of people use too little pressure. With decent weight rods, AFTMA 4-weights and up, a severe but safe bend in the rod is described when correctly fighting fish of decent size. That bend should be mostly in the middle and butt portion of the rod. The tip portion should be in line with, and form an extension of, the fly line—yet another most valid reason for softer rods. Maintaining a tight bend in a rod that equates to a high percentage of the breaking strength of the tippet used requires *instantaneous* release of pressure when a fish panics or vigorously shakes its head. The best method I know was illustrated and explained in Chapter Seven on reels, page 122.

Mistakes Made Fighting Fish

Fighting sizable fish at high pressure demands winding a reel with all the rapidity and efficiency possible. That's why knowing people, unless truly ambidextrous, set reels to be wound with master (strong) hand—the same hand used to cast. If you can throw a baseball as fast *and* as accurately with either hand you are truly ambidextrous. Few, perhaps none, are. Baseball has lots of switch hitters but *no* switch pitchers. Consider our tackle.

It's most popular for flyfishers to wind with their weak hand nowadays demonstrating modern, do as you like, thought reasonable but dangerous thinking. We aren't using spinning or bait-casting reels with high (3:1 or more) mechanical retrieve-ratio advantages. Those reels accommodate and encourage weak hand winding. Previous (or current) users of such reels ignorantly transfer weak hand winding to single action fly reels. Multiplying fly reels are problem laden, or at least less desirable, as earlier discussed. Every achievable revolution of a correctly filled single action reel is needed when a fish runs at you.

Weak hand winders, lacking maximum winding speed are too often forced to resort to stripping line when they can't keep up with a fish by winding—watch the TV programs or videos, you'll see what I mean. While you're at it, notice which hand *real* pros use and remember lots of people making videos aren't real pros as I define such. (If your chosen pro has an earring or a pony-tail, he [not she] will probably be using the wrong hand, a WF line and a stiff rod.) With stripping larger fish come many attendant problems culminating in more fish lost. Rapidly and efficiently retrieving line without wasting time during the myriad times required while fishing requires strong hand winding.

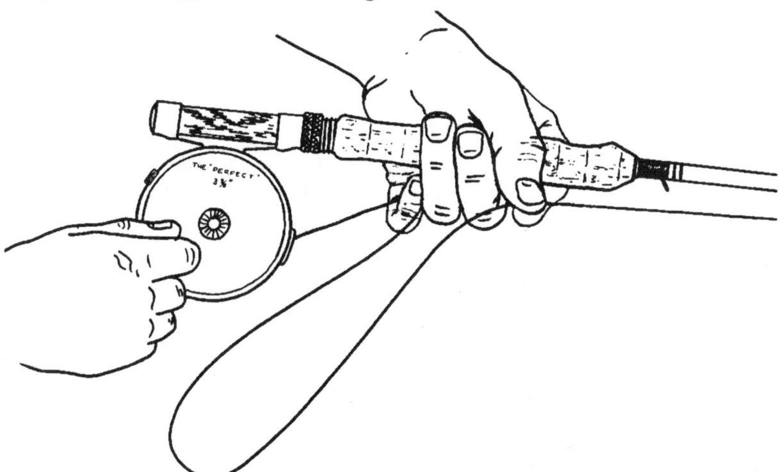

One common and most important time winding a reel with speed arises when a sizable fish is hooked with slack lying about between your stripping hand and the reel. You must get slack on the reel quickly, spooled correctly, under proper tension. Hold the line running up the rod to the hooked fish *lightly* with the thumb and forefinger of the rod hand. Allow the line to slip outward as needed if the fish requires line until you get the fish "on the reel." Pick a time when the fish isn't panicking and relax your pressure a little. To ensure correct spooling and tension grip the line or backing just outside the reel with the little finger. That's done by bending the end joint of the little finger tightly with line between (see illustration previous page).

Holding the line at the two points described, traps the loop or loops of slack between. Tension and even spooling is controlled by the little finger while the fish is controlled by thumb and index finger. Wind like mad, holding the rod with the remaining two, free fingers of the weak hand. It sounds scary but isn't too difficult and must be done. Fastest possible (strong hand) winding minimizes potential problems.

Many teaching flyfishing these days wrongly reason, then recommend and communicate, casting with dominant and reeling with weak hand. Many don't think it matters. Such people are new and ignorant (possibly forgivable), likely amassed most of their fishing experience using non-fly tackle (understandable), giving or withholding advice perhaps without sufficient experience (inexcusable, but common). If you take advice from someone reeling with his nonrod hand you are listening to someone "unserious" with more to learn, error to admit or a very, very rare ambidextrous person. Most will eventually learn the hard way (and still not change). You needn't. You might use a question about reeling hand to help ascertain a person's, expert's, or guide's depth of wisdom and valid experience.

Reeling and casting with the same hand naturally requires switching the rod holding hand. It's insignificant problem, easy to learn, and allows your casting arm to rest while fighting fish. The old saying, assigned to clever and smooth switching of rod from hand to hand, giving or taking line as required and deftly managing a fish, was called "hands." As in "so and so has hands." It's a compliment and testimony to the ability of a flyfisher. The rewards of proficient flyfishing continue to slip into oblivion under modernism's onslaught. Competence using tackle at maximum efficiency is critical fighting powerful or fleet fish. Anyone should prepare for the day the fish of dreams is hooked. Big fish do get away—many because anglers bungle in avoidable ways. Wrong hand winding is certainly one. Poor slack control is another.

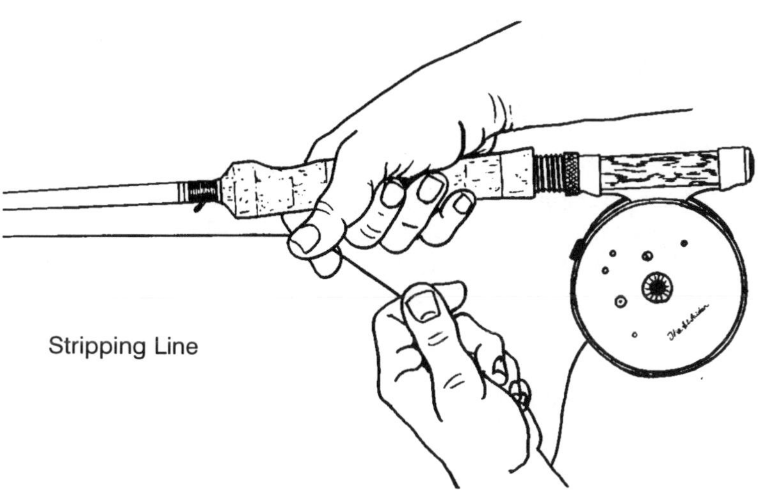

Stripping Line

Correct hand and finger movements ensure slack line will be under control at all times. When stripping line back as in recovering line for a next cast, recovering current-created slack, working a fly with a stripping retrieve or landing *small* fish, pin the line against the rod grip with the index finger or hold it lightly with thumb and index finger of rod hand. Either way, strip behind that point the line is pinned or held (see illustration above).

Similar control is needed when you reach for and release a fish. This hand-finger action and that required to quickly put slack back on a reel under tension must be learned. Such ability is deficient in many "experienced" flyfishers. Methods may vary slightly, but slack must always be controlled, to be in control.

The hand, arm and finger control involved in hooking and fighting fish varies a good deal. The type of fishing (upstream, downstream, lake, etc.), size of hook, tippet strength, the rise form or take of the fish are all variables. Sharp hooks, low barbs and slack control aid hooking in any circumstance. Being in control involves paying attention as well as learning and reducing certain necessary actions to habit. Such rod, line and hand actions are quite different from those of casting and scream the need for learning to cast before fishing so a person may concentrate on other vital flyfishing moves—moves such as fighting fish with correct rod angle.

Use a fly rod to exert pressure on a fish in any plane necessary from vertical to below horizontal. Keep fish constantly off balance. Sideways pressure causes fish in current to fight continuously to maintain preferred position. A rod held straight up, or nearly so, allows fish to react like a yo-yo on a string expending less energy than you need them to expend. But that's how most people fight fish. A high rod will hold the most line out of water and is useful when a strong fish runs. When it sulks use lower sideways angles to apply heavy pressure and defeat it quickly. "A minute per pound the world around," is not far from true, perhaps even excessive, in defeating correctly fought, healthy fish regardless of species. Fish in current need to be headed up-current to breathe; one running head downstream won't go far—usually. Fishing from a boat in deep water limits your rod angle possibilities when the hooked fish gets under or near the boat. Apply all the pressure you can and never relax it until you boat or are ready to release the fish.

A fly rod is a deadly thing properly used—overly so if the user isn't careful or uses joke-weight rods. The long slender shape of a fly rod is deceiving. Kept at maximum bend, a fish never has chance to escape unrelenting pressure. Light tackle proponents, if *honestly* concerned about making things more difficult for themselves, would use *heavier,* not lighter tackle. Do any of them? Fish would then be honestly harder to hook *but* easier to defeat, saving them wear and tear. Howard Blaisdell, writing in *The Philosophical Fisherman,* said: "The snobbish light tackle people are out to victimize as many fish as possible, just like the rest of us. They are nothing special; possibly quite the opposite."

Handling Tackle

Correct handling of a rod with a fish in hand, at side or feet seems clandestine. I frequently see pictures or videos of people handling fish with the rod held stupidly between their legs, reel dragging in the water or on the ground, even holding rods in their mouths. As often, the rod is casually thrown on bank or boat. Learn to tuck the rod grip high up into an armpit where it's easily held, safe, yet out of way by upper arm pressure against your body. That frees both hands to land, unhook or release fish, affix a fly, add tippet, rummage through pockets or whatever. The rod may be pointed forward or back as required.

While walking in brush, carry a fly rod with the tip pointing forward centered in front of you. The tip will naturally follow the best path selected by your eyes and the rest of the rod will follow with automatic hand adjustments. This method offers the rod the most protection from snagging, dragging against obstructions and general damage. Carrying the rod behind oneself subjects it to the most damage. Body pivots slam the rod into things. Humans think and react in forward mode mostly ignoring what trails behind.

Accessories

To accessories, there is no end. Discussing them could involve a small chapter. What a person uses is largely a matter of personal preference and perhaps fishing being done. *Many* accessories prey on angler ignorance, inability and failure to master basic flyfishing skills. I'll approach the matter by listing what I carry, then elaborating to clarify reasoning. Perhaps such treatment will provide you useful ideas.

I use a vest, several of them in fact. Vests should be comfortable and plenty large. Padded shoulder yokes contribute mightily to comfort. Adding tackle causes a vest to "balloon" rapidly, start with one large enough. I like lots of *large* pockets inside, outside and on the back of the vest. Zippers are OK, but Velcro closures clog with gunk and eventually pull off the vest. Columbia Sportswear makes fine, long-wearing vests. I always have a "shorty" model for deep wading and have been known to dye my vests to avoid fish spooking colors.

The tools and do-dads I carry in or on the vest have been selected and refined over many years for simplicity and usefulness. When I set out to fish flowing water I carry:

-A couple of boxes of basic, comprehensive and proven flies—insurance—my flies not to be without.

-Boxes of specialized flies as needed for species, conditions, hatches or other fish food I expect to encounter. Boxes of specialized flies of many sorts are carried in my duffel or vehicle to be transferred to vest or float tube as needed.

-Maxima Chameleon tippet material in 3-, 4-, 5-, 6- and 8-pound test with elastic spool tenders in place.

-Ten- and 12-pound test Chameleon for heavy tippet or leader repairs, also tended.

-Several basic, pre-tied leaders.

-A small tube for tying Nail knots.

-Hook file *and* hones.

-Quality, 4-inch, needle-nose pliers with cutter.

-Metal-cased stream thermometer.

-Fingernail clippers on a "zinger."

-A plush, wool-on-hide patch (from a saddle shop) pinned to my vest for drying used flies.

-Fly floatant—seventy percent Mucilin (plus or minus) mixed with thirty percent black-powder additive.

-Twist-Ons.

-Several mini lead-heads, 18 to 30 inches long with loops in each end.

-Extra floating DT line on an extra spool. Usually lighter but sometimes heavier (size) than the DT on the rod I'm carrying.

-Insect repellent and a couple of Band-Aids.

-Extra magnifying glasses.

-Often a raincoat, perhaps fingerless gloves and a flashlight.

-Since boyhood I carry a two-bladed pocketknife in my pants pocket—at all times.

-Polarized sunglasses in a shirt pocket.

-A hat that sheds rain and shades my eyes in a color that will least alarm fish.

If I were planning to fish slow water or lake:

-A reel or extra spool with a 6-inch loop (Bimini) tied into its backing end.

-A set of floating and sinking shooting heads. All to have loops whipped into both ends for easy mixing, adding or subtracting. I carry these coiled in the pockets of a leader wallet. They are various lengths and sink rates.

-A reel and extra spool with floating DTs, often 5- and 7-weights. I prefer full DTs but will use the floating heads I carry.

My float-tube always contains a separate set of tools as listed above. I won't rob my vest of tools and I seldom wear a vest when float-tubing. I do borrow boxes of flies from my vest to use in my tube. My tube also always contains: a cord fish stringer, red-flashing battery-operated bicycle light, a handy folding knife, extra glasses, a small flashlight and a small-hooped net with a 40-inch deep bag. I add cold weather or rain gear as might be needed.

I was once nearly run over by a large powerboat running full out just before dark. Once is enough; now the flashing red light protects me (I hope). I was concentrating on trying to fool one of several 20-pound class rainbows feeding on ants stranded in the lake's surface film. I hunt hard for situations as that, and now you know why I carry a net (seldom used) with a 40-inch bag. It's for *true* emergencies.

There are accessories I don't like. I started fishing before forceps became popular, or at least known to me, and learned to unhook fish with my fingers—anyone can. My needle-nose pliers perform many functions forceps can't and do so without pinching my fingers or twisting out of control. Landing nets are exponentially grief filled, seldom really needed and often hard on fish—you know my one exception. I don't care for anything hanging or flopping about on my vests. Such things snarl in the brush, rattle annoyingly, shine and occasionally tangle the fly line. My clipper zinger (a small spring-loaded retrieving reel) is pinned inside my vest front, handy yet hidden. My selection of gizmos works very well for me, and the idea was to get you thinking about what you *need* and can use. Maybe you need a 50-inch bag on your net; if so, please call.

Reality

Don't feel handicapped if you can't travel far and wide to flyfish. Datus Proper advises, wilderness fish have little to teach you. Fish extensively and often near home, if you can and if serious about becoming proficient. Be your own antagonist striving to learn and improve all the time. Ernest Hemingway said, and I paraphrase: believe the critics when they praise you and you have no choice but to believe them when they criticize you. Don't be overly influenced by opinion or anyone's comments about your flyfishing if it's ethical, pleases you and works. Take what you hear or read based on supported strength, foundation in natural law and horse sense.

Too many persons encountered will speak confidently from only hearsay knowledge and will lead you astray. That's paraphrasing Theodore Gordon. He also noted crowded conditions and poor angler manners were referenced in most books and was talking about the late 1800s and early 1900s. Become a better flyfisher than most, out-figure the competition and rise above the limiting, small minded and foolish in the sport. Learning to flyfish efficiently and effectively, therefore enjoyably, is a mildly complicated but delightful task. I sure haven't addressed everything; I couldn't. Learn well what's *needed* as you go and in your own way—avoid or eliminate the rest. In so going, perhaps ideas that follow, will give extra help.

It's hard to separate flyfishing from casting. Don't become overly concerned with casting. Attain competency and know how to mend line and control slack.

Flyfishing is a lifetime of separating wheat from chaff. Lots of people sincerely want to help, but their wheat bin is dreadfully full of chaff.

Haig-Brown said much fishing is mechanical in nature—trolling, spinning, etc. Many would push flyfishing that way with simple technology based methods. Technology has a dark side. What do you give up or miss that would make you a more accomplished flyfisher by substituting technology for skill? Technology seldom promotes ethical fishing or hunting and involves producer-planned obsolesence.

Possession of expensive tackle is thought (by many) to carry prestige; even though an owner doesn't know how to use it. Lots of too costly and damaging tackle is sold via prestige motivation—don't fall prey.

Haig-Brown believed people put too much pride at stake in fishing. They fish too hard, take all the blame and claim all success. There is luck. It's also true that the more you fish and the better you strive to be the luckier you get.

Lee Wulff noted that a wet-fly covers four times the water as a dry. Ted Trueblood and Charles Ritz believed newcomers should fish wet-flies for one full year concentrating on learning water, fish, casting and mending.

It's said flyfishers have "graduated" when they turn and face upstream to fish. That divulges ability to cast, mend *and* control slack, particularly when created by fast current.

You can't learn to cast when you're all keyed up trying to fish. People tend to forget things when excited or preoccupied. Slaymaker, Trueblood, Haig-Brown and many others caution beginners to practice casting *before* going fishing. You will short circuit some forgetfulness, feelings of self-consciousness, looking silly or inadequate.

Ray Bergman, writing in the 1920s, said:

> "We might create fancy names for different methods. We might invent fancy casts to overcome some problems, we might even make it appear that we have discovered a way to catch fish that transcends anything yet thought of, but when you really analyze all these things you find that all they do is arrive at fundamentals from different angles."

Remember that when you hear or read the next sophisticate babbling about something "new." You might read Bergman's *Trout* if you haven't.

When you read promotional matter or perhaps watch a video, remember all you are hearing or seeing is the success side of things. And all of that might not be true. You don't hear about or see failures, poor trips, mistakes made, fish lost, frustrations or time and money wasted. The tellers are just like you and me. Don't become discouraged or overwhelmed with the seeming weight of flyfishing's often superficial details. There is too much for one person to fully understand. Take things one step at a time, enjoy yourself and see mistakes as learning experiences. *Don't excuse yourself too lightly;* that's self deceit, the worst kind. Try to minimize needless mistakes by using your head, doing some research and becoming competent with correctly selected tackle.

Lots of people, *at all levels*, haven't fished enough particularly in tough circumstances. They engage in hearsay or "mind fishing," and believe delusions or writings that are warped by fear of truth or crony disapproval, even to the point of ignoring common flyfishing sense and reason. With a little thought and study, some practice and horse sense you can enjoy effective flyfishing, nearly eliminate wasted time and money and become your own flyfishing person. Have fun.

GEL

Chapter Thirteen: Flyfishing Survey

Several years ago I learned the North American Fly-Tackle Trade Association (NAFTA) wished to know the demographics and characteristics of flyfishers as there had been no comprehensive surveys conducted to determine such information. That, *but more* long suffering curiosity about the common comment that, "so and so is the *best* flyfisher I've ever seen or known" caused me to consider conducting a survey. Seldom are people who might be true experts known outside their local area. I know persons who qualify as you probably do, and they know things that might benefit many in flyfishing. Wouldn't it be interesting to talk to a whole lot of them?

What would a large number of experienced flyfishers, judged as something of experts, think and know? What is their commonality, or lack, in belief, practice and experience? I resolved to conduct a survey using, as pollees, only *experienced flyfishers who make very little, or no, money from flyfishing.* I didn't want profit-based biases from anyone in the flyfishing industries as the survey would be specific regarding tackle brands, writing, industry professionalism, accepted thinking and technique.

I wanted a large number of pollees. Statistical sampling theory says sample size is not as important as sample quality. It wasn't my desire or need to conduct a wholly scientific survey but rather to determine what many down-to-earth and competent flyfishers, free of monetary gain bias, thought about a great many pertinent things concerning flyfishing. If you want to learn something worth knowing, talk to lots of persons knowing something worth repeating and maybe learning. Despite my goals, the methodology used to select pollees and conduct the survey was most random and scientific.

I wrote a large number of persons and firms *in* the flyfishing industries and asked them to provide names and addresses of the three best and most knowledgeable, nonindustries involved, flyfishers known. A mediocre 18% complied. Deciding I could poll more persons than names obtained that way and thinking a large percentage of those requested to complete the questionnaire would not, I also asked the President of every Federation of Flyfishers Club (FFF) in the USA and Canada to provide a copy of the blank survey to three, top, nonindustry-involved, flyfishers in their club. A list of persons and firms providing names of potential pollees is found at the end of the chapter. They and the Federation clubs were very kind to help.

While assembling names of persons to poll I turned to devising questions. It took a whole winter and more. I have a friend who owns a substantial flyfishing library, 50,000 plus titles. I read or reread over 60 of the commonly judged best domestic and British flyfishing books to discover the origins, essence, and heart of flyfishing knowledge. I read a cross section of books addressing all types of flyfishing. Flyfishing is favorably tradition bound and the most written about of field sports. Most writing is British or North American in origin and concerns trout or salmon as does the bulk of modern flyfishing effort. Interest in other species and water types has grown recently. I tried to account for such growing interest.

After several rewrites, always striving for comprehensiveness, I devised a group of questions and had it reviewed by several knowledgeable flyfishers before final drafting. The completed questionnaire was eight pages long, with 124 questions requiring 175 pollee responses. It generated a great deal of demographic data concerning pollees in addition to their flyfishing knowledge and opinions.

Questionnaire devised, it was sent with a cover letter and a stamped return envelope to 816 prospective pollees. I was astounded to receive nearly a 32% return—unheard of in polling. Particularly for such a lengthy poll. I believe that shows common, but knowledgeable flyfishers want their largely ignored feelings and frustrations known and jumped at a chance to do so. Neither name providers or pollees were given anything to induce response other than promise to give them credit for their contribution by publishing their names when results were published and a copy of the raw data. Pollees' names are published later. I am very grateful to everyone who took the time and effort to help. My dear and hardworking wife was critical to the project.

As the completed surveys flooded back I collated them, separated by recommended and FFF pollee names among other criteria. There were over 50,000 responses to record. I did it longhand, in a big binder and don't plan to do something similar again. When NAFTA and FTD learned the results of such a comprehensive survey of flyfishers was available they became excited. Following review of sample data, both lost their fire. The survey results are heavily critical of the Elite and to some extent the Other industries. I believe results proved too embarrassing to industries' sophisticated officials despite tremendous potential usefulness.

The industries had no control over my questions or results as they always do with feeble surveys they occasionally facilitate. If discovered facts of surveys don't flatter, support agendas or say what's believed or wanted to be true they are probably not believed or used. (Remember all industries' members failing the FFF's simple casting competency test and the testing program's subsequent demise before a weakened, modified resurrection?)

The Elite is preoccupied with how many flyfishers exist. I don't fully understand why *(if* you could first define *what* a flyfisher is) but have some idea. Elite members want ability to calculate penetration, market share, brow-beat their competition and devise ever more strategy to sell. There is insignificant doubt the Elite operates under self-delusion with fear and more than adequate arrogance. Feeling there are large numbers of flyfishers (however inappropriately defined) eases Elite fear. To them it heralds continued ability to keep on fooling lots of people. Few in the industries apparently care what experienced flyfishers know and think or the tremendous benefits derivable from knowing, despite some earned criticism. Results of a diminutive telephone survey (150 pollees) the Elite recently conducted were based on defining a flyfisher as anyone who "flyfished" for at least *part of one day in an entire year*. No wonder the industries delude themselves and remain out of touch.

The first information asked for on the survey form and summarized is demographic data. Results were rounded to the nearest whole number and all replies were given equal weight for the entire survey. Percentage answers were calculated from the total number of persons answering a question. While tabulating results it became clear that the survey could have been written for better pollee understanding. I unwittingly confused pollees on occasion. I'm grateful for the understanding and decency of pollees. I had only one negative letter, and that, from a person I once guided for steelhead who was very pleased following the trip and in subsequent conversations. On the other hand 31% of pollees told me they enjoyed the survey.

Questions on the same topic were purposely scattered through the survey, and the same question is occasionally asked in two different ways, also on purpose. Such methods help reveal if pollees are indeed knowledgeable. There were passionate and interesting individual answers; I'll point some out and comment along the way. Any answer <u>underlined</u> shows pollees contributed answers asked for by blank line invitation—or not asked for, in some cases. A few questions generated very large numbers of asked for answers and they are not underlined to allow easier reading. Some answers will have an asterisk (*) appended denoting the "winning" or prevailing answer.

Combined pollee consensus differs from supported positions earlier presented in some cases. Most readers can be relied on to read a book from front to back taking chapters in order. Information builds on or amplifies itself. I wrote this book accordingly. But some readers invariably read chapters out of order or only parts of a book. A chapter entitled Flyfishing Survey will draw some readers directly there. It's my job to try and keep everyone informed without confusion while minimizing redundancy. As important, I must not cause readers to miss information useful to forming solid opinions, making judgments and then taking best action to improve their flyfishing effectiveness and enjoyment.

Earlier chapter reference is sometimes given concerning question results and done to expose potential danger to full understanding. Pitfalls lurk in believing pollee consensus or opinions that suggest they are "correct" but that are, nonetheless, incorrect. I recognize there is more than one way to skin a cat. Having been a bobcat trapper I sought out and learned the fastest, safest, most efficient and highest dollar yielding way to prepare a cat's pelt. One needs adopt similar methodology for flyfishing understanding, enjoyment and effectiveness. If less than absolute about something, consider different possibilities then decide for yourself based on what is proven correct, best supported or makes the most sense—it's your pelt. Remember there are few absolutes, and majority opinion concerning many things is often, even usually, wrong. Let's start with the demographic data.

The pollees have flyfished for a total of over 6,655 years and average 26 years flyfishing experience. They fish 14,500 days a year for an average of 57 days each (379,000 total days flyfished). Several flyfished as many as 200 days per year. Pollees were 96.5% male and 3.4% female (10 ladies). Remembering that I sought only knowledgeable and experienced flyfishers and that most women in flyfishing are quite new might account for the low percentage of females. Average age is 51 years with a range of 24 to 78 years. Data reveal substantial experience, but it's questionable if younger pollees could have amassed the adequate and sound experience I sought. Not that age is definitive. Diverse older flyfishers are unenlightened.

White collar flyfishers accounted for 41% of pollees, blue collar 25%, retired persons 18%, professionals 13%, with 3% unknown. Pollees hailed from: Northwest 38%, Northeast 21%, Southwest 15%, Southeast 13% and 13% were from Canada. Most Canadians were from British Columbia, and 37 of the United States were represented. It seems pollees live in numbers where and are made up of demographic types one might reasonably expect.

Questions are stated in bold type. Answers, mostly in percentages, are shown in regular type. The first question is the only one with two sets of answers. Explanation follows Question No. 2.

1.**Flyfishing experience, please check all appropriate:**

98% Trout/char **73%** — 27% Pike/musky **<1%**
22% Atlantic salmon **2%** — 44% Inshore saltwater species **7%**
43% Pacific steelhead **5%**
25% Great Lakes steelhead **2%** — 20% Offshore saltwater species **1%**
78% Freshwater bass/panfish **10%** — 7% Pacific salmon **2%**

2. **From the list above, please CIRCLE the one you feel you know the most about.**

The figures preceding fish categories are the answers to Question No. 1 revealing all fishing experience of pollees. Bold figures represent the circling requested in Question No. 2. The underlined category, Pacific salmon, was the only species with a significant number of write-in answers.

The following bold-faced note was displayed on the survey form. *It's important to remember pollee answers are often affected and justifiably variable solely due the type of fishing a pollee considers knowing the most about.*

NOTE: THERE WILL BE QUESTIONS ASKING FOR YOUR FAVORITES, OR WHERE TYPE OF FISHING COULD AFFECT YOUR ANSWER. PLEASE USE THE CATEGORY YOU JUST CIRCLED (bold figures in No. 2 above) AS THE BASIS FOR ANSWERS TO THESE QUESTIONS. THANK YOU.

3. **What type fishing in No. 1 above, and new to you, do you wish to experience?** Trout/char-8%, Atlantic salmon-28%, Pacific steelhead-20%, Great Lakes steelhead-7%, Bass/panfish-4%, Pike/musky-6%, Inshore-26%, Offshore-11% and Pacific salmon-2%.

4. **Do fish themselves sincerely interest you?** Yes 95%, No 5%.

5. **Please number in order of importance to effective fly casting and fishing. (1 is highest)**

Rod:	1st-71%*	2nd-13%	3rd-16%	4th-0
Reel:	1st-1%	2nd-5%	3rd-9%	4th-85%*
Line:	1st-22%	2nd-60%*	3rd-15%	4th-2%
Leader:	1st-12%	2nd-17%	3rd-59%*	4th-12%

Pollees have "roditis." It's natural enough; fly rods are the misunderstood icons, darlings and standard bearers of flyfishing. Answers contradict the supported findings of earlier chapters. I suspected rod worship was prevalent and worded this question to address ". . . *effective* fly casting and fishing." *Effective flyfishing*, even casting, nearly always requires decent and performing leaders and lines. Without those it's *impossible* to be effective even with the best of rods. It's encouraging to see 34% (22 plus 12) realize leader or line are most important.

6. **Will a person entering flyfishing find obtaining the right tackle for them?** Easy 18%, Difficult 7%, Confusing 75%.

Perhaps poor answer choices were given; Confusing likely means Difficult to most people. In any event it sure isn't Easy.

7. **Do you derive any income from anything associated with flyfishing?** Yes 24%, No 76%.

Results here distress as they represent possible breakdown of my criteria of limiting professionals and industries' persons. In the perfunctory demographic portion of the survey, I asked for pollees' "profession." I reexamined every survey with an affirmative answer to this question and discovered only ten listed a profession indicating full time flyfishing employment. Three of those were guides. Of the remaining 50 or so affirmative answers, another or no profession was listed. From survey comments: Pollees tie and sell a few flies, guide on a part-time basis or are writers. It's still disturbing; even part-timers might have a survey biasing attachment to the industries. What you see is what I got. In general, curiously and with redemption, pollees with connections to the industries were the *most* critical of the industries in their comments and answers.

8. **What knots do you consider necessary for freshwater fishing?**

82% Nail or variations	66% Surgeon's
38% Clinch	15% Improved End Loop
73% Improved Clinch	7% Duncan Loop
20% Turle	5% Uni
75% Blood	4% Perfection loop

Results cause wonder how 18% of pollees failing to select a Nail knot or variations connect backing or leader to fly lines. No alternatives were listed. Comments that the Improved Clinch works best in smaller leader were common. Why would pollees list both Blood and Surgeon's as almost equally *needed*? See Chapter Eight for why certain knots are used for certain applications.

9. **What fly rod action will best serve the beginner?**

4% Fast/stiff	35% Medium to slow
59% Medium to stiff	2% Soft/slow

10. **Many rods on the market are very stiff. Are the numerical (AFTMA) fly line weights recommended for them correct?** Yes 42%, No 57%.

Would these rods perform better with a fly line weight one or two sizes larger? Yes 79%, No 21%.

If fly rods are *correctly AFTMA* rated—42% say they are—then **why** will they perform better with a larger (heavier) line as 79% say? Pollees' answers contradict. Results reveal many experienced flyfishers are confused and fail to understand and appreciate AFTMA ratings. Several pollees comment that it "depends on the rod or line." Oh dear, by definition, *it most certainly does not.* Such comments bear sad witness to flyfisher unawareness and the effectiveness of industries' bogus and confusing marketing. See Chapter Six on rod-line balance for a full discussion. Fully one-third feel a beginner's rod (Question No. 9) should be on the slow side of medium, but that means two-thirds don't.

11. **Are the grips found on most factory rods functionally well designed?** Yes 74%, No 26%.

12. **Do you use custom built rods?** Yes 79%, No 21%.

Build fly rods? Yes 59%, No 41%.

13. **Do you prefer a reel seat that is:** Up-locking 63%, Down-locking 32%, Either 6%.

Pollees use or build custom rods to amazing degree. In collating, I noticed that people building rods do not like factory grips.

14. **Have you fished on other continents or foreign islands?** Yes 43%, No 57%.

15. **Please check those areas of the USA or corresponding coastal areas you have fished?**

41% Northeast	44% Central	40% Southwest
36% Southeast	71% Northwest	29% Alaska

16. **Do you have a basic or better understanding of freshwater entomology?** Yes 92%, No 8%.

17. **How important to success is being quiet in approach, casting and wading while flyfishing?** Very 80%, Moderately 20%, Minimally 0.

18. **Is flyfishing in danger of becoming too popular?** Yes 52%, No 48%.

19. **Do you consider the ability to control the fly line while it is on or in the water (mending) important, particularly in flowing water?**

10% Less important than adequate casting
68% Equally important
22% More important

90% (68 plus 22) consider mending as, or *more,* important than casting. So why does casting garner all the press and lip service?

20. **What is more important to success in your favorite type fishing?**

9% Distance in casting
91% Accuracy in casting

21. **You need to buy a light (trout/pan-fish) outfit with a floating line for an adult family member learning to fly fish. What would you choose?**

Rod length: 8 1/2 feet, 47%; 9 feet, 40%; 8 feet, 12%.
Line weight: #5, 43%; #6, 33%, #7, 4%.

5% Glass rod	1% Automatic reel	42% DT line
53% Softer graphite	98% Single action	57% WF line
41% Stiffer graphite	2% Multiplying	1% Level line

It's encouraging to see lots of beginners would receive a softer rod. Starting with a superior DT, even for practice, then turning it around for essentially a new line when fishing is undertaken makes good sense. Accuracy in casting was the near unanimous choice over distance. DTs are more accurate. Doing things to accommodate fishing success and save money is perhaps too simple for many people to believe.

22. **It's a year later and the family member now needs an 8-weight outfit for a variety of uses in flowing, still, fresh and saltwater. What would you buy?**

Rod length: 9 feet, 58%; 9 1/2 feet, 23%; 8 1/2 feet, 8%; 10 feet, 6%; 8 feet, 5%.

2% Glass rod	88% Single action reel
18% Softer graphite rod	12% Multiplying reel
80% Stiffer graphite rod	17% Pawl/click drag reel
0 Automatic reel	83% Disk drag

Why did a rank beginner stand a decent chance of receiving a superior, softer graphite rod and one year later (the person is *still* a beginner) a stiff rod only because the rod is an 8-weight? In collating, I noticed newer flyfishers and younger pollees favor stiff rods most—the persons who can least use them. Overwhelming selection of disk drag reels is puzzling.

23. **For the outfit just chosen, what line or lines would you choose for flowing water? (Choose at least one. Feel free to choose none or several from each category.)**

28% DT floating	30% Fast sink tip
71% WF floating	13% Slow full sinker
1% Level floating	49% Medium full sinker
30% Slow sink wet tip	38% Fast full sinker
39% Medium sink tip	

How much backing capacity? 100 yds., 34%; 200 yds., 33%.

Weight-forward disease is rampant—the question stipulated flowing water. See Chapter Four on lines. Pollees generated through the FFF were more WF prone and by their questionnaire answers in general, less experienced. There wasn't one comment that backing capacity should be whatever adequately fills a reel to make it function at top efficiency.

Now choose lines to be used in still water.

32% DT floating	32% Fast sink tip
68% WF floating	41% Slow full sinker
1% Level floating	48% Medium full sinker
37% Slow sink tip	30% Fast full sinker
31% Medium sink tip	

The relatively even split for all sinking type lines shows, I guess, that different folks do things differently and probably the effect of pollees answering questions according to their most known fishing, as requested. For both parts of the question most pollees selected one line from each class (floating, wet-tip, sinking) despite being told they did not need to.

24. **Do you use a system of shooting heads rather than full lines?** Yes 32%, No 68%. **Would you recommend a head system for beginners?** Yes 9%, No 92%.

25. **Your favorite fly line manufacturer is:**

38% Cortland 2% Air-flow 8% Wulff
46% SA 4% Teeny

Scientific Anglers (SA) makes lines for other sellers listed. Desirable characteristics of SA's own lines carry over into that process and add to SA's winning edge. Some pollees checked two line brands. Orvis and Sunset lines received a couple of votes each.

26. **Do you mostly: Tie your own leaders?** 48%, **Use commercial leaders?** 44%, Both 8%.

27. **If you tie your own leaders, what is your favorite material for butt and mid-section?**

12% Mason 12% Orvis 4% Climax
59% Maxima 7% Umpqua 1% Dai-Riki

One pollee said he uses Maxima to "fix" commercial leaders. Bass fishers were less fussy about leaders.

28. **What is your favorite brand of tippet material?**

21% each Maxima, Orvis and Umpqua 15% Dai-Riki
9% Climax 4% Cortland 2% Mason

Maxima is heavily used by steelheaders and saltwater flyfishers. Seventeen brands of tippet material were listed. For Question No. 29, following, ten brands of commercial leaders were listed. I'd guess Maxima ranks low because of difficulty in obtaining their commercial tapered leaders.

29. **If you buy leaders, what is your favorite brand?**

27% Orvis 19% Umpqua 15% Climax
10% Dai-Riki 6% Maxima 5% SA and Cortland

30. **Consider tippet material. What is most important to you?**

17% Low fish visibility 11% Abrason resistance
6% Stretch 18% Suppleness
*29% Knot strength 19% Diameter

What is second most important? Diameter. **Third most?** Suppleness.

The winning selection, "Knot strength," still remains *most* dependent on correct knot tying procedure, then material's abrasion resistance to defeat heat and damage created as knots tighten. Diameter worship seems incurably entrenched. There is much to consider; see Chapter Three concerning leaders for detail.

31. **Many new reels continue to come to the market. Do these reels:**

20% Offer substantial new features that are needed.
80% Offer few new features over older, proven reels.

32. **Do you think these new reels are:**

16% Fairly priced for what they offer
83% Overpriced
0 Underpriced

There was considerable wonderment why prices of reels (and other tackle) are so high and have not come down given heavy competition. There are lower priced new reels deemed to be fairly priced by pollees. Chapter Two discusses prices and Chapter Seven reels.

33. **Do you recommend <u>right-handed</u> casters set their reels to be wound with their:**

32% Right hand
64% Left hand
4% Either

There is misunderstanding here. Please see Chapter Seven concerning reels and Chapter Twelve on flyfishing to see why a certain hand is used.

34. **What percent of the fish you catch do you release?**

100%, 30% of pollees 95-99%, 51% 90-94%, 11%
75%, 3% 30% or less, 3%

Bass fishers often keep panfish and Canadians often keep Atlantic salmon.

35. **Some industries are characterized by "new" models, colors and styles of product every year, even if little changed from previous years. Do you see flyfishing moving this way?** Yes 71%, No 29%.

36. **Please list three fly patterns you would not want to be without.**

Overall and Trout	First: Gold-Ribbed Hare's Ear Nymph (GRHE) 34%
	Second: Woolly Bugger 32%
	Third: Adams 30%
	Fourth: Elk Hair Caddis 24%
Bass and Panfish	First: Woolly Bugger
	Second: GRHE
	Third: Dahlberg Diver
Steelhead (Pacific)	First: Muddler
	Second: Green Butt Skunk
	Third: General Practitioner

Steelhead	First: Egg patterns
(Great Lakes)	Second: Stonefly, probably the nymph
	Third: Hexagenia, probably the nymph
Atlantic	First: Bomber
salmon	Second: Buck Bug
	Third: Butterfly
Inshore	First: Clouser Minnow
	Second: Deceiver
	Third: Woolly Bugger
Canadian	First: Tom Thumb
	Second: Leech, specific patterns unlisted
	Third: Chironomid, no specific pattern

There was no survey request for patterns by species as shown. It was derived. Seventy-eight different patterns were listed. There were no specific or readily recognizable patterns for offshore or pike/musky categories. Other large vote receivers in the overall class (listed in order of placement) were: Muddler, Pheasant Tail Nymph, Royal Wulff/Trude, and Soft Hackles. Interestingly, two of three Atlantic salmon flies are dry flies. The third might be classified a damp fly.

37. **Do you tie flies?** Yes 95%, No 5%.

Fly tying, as rod building is more practiced than might be anticipated. *Fly Fisherman* magazine says only 67% of flyfishers tie flies. I'd guess it depends on how "flyfisher" is defined. We have real flyfishers here.

38. **Do you prefer:** Weighted flies 58%, Weighting your leader 34%, Both 4%, Neither 4%.

39. **Do you sharpen the hooks of flies before using them?** Always 29%, Usually 36%, Seldom 36%.

40. **Do you use barbless hooks?** Always 44%, Usually 45%, Seldom 11%.

41. **Do you care if a fly you purchase is foreign or domestically tied?** Yes 42%, No 51%, Don't buy flies or pay attention 7%.

42. **What portion of your success, in a day's fishing, would you attribute to having confidence in the flies you fished?**

Less than 50%-	51%
50%-	30%
More than 50%-	19%

In your ability to present the fly?

Less than 50%-	20%
50%-	30%
More than 50%-	50%

Confused? Pollees believe presentation is much more important than flies fished to a day's fishing success.

43. **Please rate numerically for importance to success of a fly.**

Size:	First 65%*	Second 22%	Third 6%
Color:	First 11%	Second 20%	Third 69%*
Shape:	First 24%	Second 54%*	Third 23%

Rating in order is Size, Shape and Color, but not overwhelmingly. You might see Chapter 8 on flies for reasons to select flies. Northeastern pollees tend to be more cognizant of fly size rather than shape.

44. **Do you generally prefer flies that are:**

Imitative of something as possible	43%
Suggestive and provocative	57%

45. **Do you think most people giving casting instruction are able to teach newcomers without confusing them?** Yes 48%, No 52%.

FFF pollees said Yes more often than others. FFF clubs sometimes use amateur instructors at club functions. A pollee comment: "Many giving instruction should be taking it."

46. **What <u>two</u> faults will casters have the most trouble correcting?**

65%	Radically bending the wrist on the back cast.
38%	Failure to use adequate power or line to load the rod.
71%	Failure to pause on the rearward stroke.
19%	Failure to control slack line with the left hand (RH caster).
2%	<u>Timing too fast and failure to move tip in straight line.</u>

One insightful comment revealed, "Beginners can't feel the rod's power or flex." That's due inadequate line length being used, or commonly a too light line on a too stiff rod.

47. **Please indicate the maximum range of fly line you can consistently cast under ideal fishing conditions:** 20-40 feet 6%, 40-60 feet 56%, 80-100 feet 33%, over 100 feet 5%.

There was no category for 60-80 feet. My mistake of the

missing category would affect results as some, perhaps many, pollees would have selected: 60-80 feet.

48. **Do you prefer:** Thumb-on-top of grip 72%, Thumb alongside grip 24%, Index finger on top of grip 4%.

Do you use them all? Yes 26%, No 74%.

49. **Do DT lines hang in the air on casts over 40 feet better than WF lines?** Yes 53%, No 37%, Don't know 10%.

Do DTs mend more effectively than WFs at the same long distances? Yes 70%, No 30%.

DTs and WFs are (or have been) nearly identical over the first 45 feet or so. The question should have asked over 50, not 40 feet. One pollee has it nailed: "WFs are a waste of money." Many pollees said they "didn't know" the attributes of DTs. See Chapter Four on fly lines to find out.

50. **What are your favorite makes of: Fly rod? Fly reel?**

Rods, in order of place: Sage, Loomis, Winston, Scott, Orvis, Fenwick.

Reels, in order of place: Hardy, Orvis, SA, Lamson, Ross, Able, Pflueger.

Seventeen makes of rods and 27 of reels were listed. Many pollees listed custom rods as their favorites. Hardy made some of Sage's and many of SA's reels (perhaps others). The Hardy made SAs are favorites of lots of flyfishers, thus Hardy's ranking would be an even stronger first place.

51. **Should newcomers be certain of having practiced enough to have casting proficiency before going fishing?** Yes 47%, No 52%.

Despite the advice of knowledgeable writers and flyfishers, many pollees don't grasp the advantages of learning to cast before going fishing. One said his son has more fun on stream than in the back yard—hard to argue with—but having the type fun available a competent caster is the goal.

52. **How important is the line handling hand in casting?**

Very 64%, Moderately 33%, Minimally 4%.

Despite saying the line hand is very important, only 19% of pollees see it as a major problem to learning casting in Question No. 46. It is important but puzzling for many to learn. One pollee classed line hand use as the "forgotten element in fly casting."

53. **We all meet people saying they would like to learn to flyfish. Why have they not? (Check all appropriate.)**

80% Perceive it to be too difficult for them
45% Believe it will be too expensive
68% Do not know how to get started
8% Apathetic, lack motivation, lazy
5% Had no success after trying

54. **Do you often use strike indicators?** Yes 45%, No 55%.

A dry fly on a dropper can serve as a strike indicator as might a bright mark on a fly line. I want to think pollees were referencing such methods and not little bobbers.

55. **Can you retrieve line, by reeling, faster with your:**

43% Dominant (rod) hand
54% Weak hand
3% Either

57% of pollees (54 plus 3) say they have the ability to wind a reel as fast or even *faster* with their *weak* hand. Nothing surprised me more in the survey. Most have likely never compared hand-winding speed. There was a strong correlation between individual weak-hand winders and strike indicator use, whatever that means. Weak-hand spinning reel winding, with mechanical advantage, no doubt accounts for some weak-hand winding. See next question.

56. **Do you fish with other than fly tackle?** Yes 55%, No 45%.

Results show more "flyfishers" using other gear than might be expected from persons with 26 years each flyfishing experience.

57. **Are you quite relaxed when fly casting well?** Yes 99%, No 1%.

Would a new caster, being instructed, likely be? Yes 5%. No 95%.

58. **In your opinion, what percentage of fish caught by fly methods and released die within a short period of time?** None, 5%; 1-5%, 47%; 6-10%, 24%; 11-15%, 12%; 16-20%, 10%; over 20%, 3%.

59. **What is you favorite magazine? (Any type)**

Tie: *American Angler* and *Fly Fisherman* 16% each.

Fishing type?

First: *Fly Fisherman* 35%
Second: *American Angler* 22%
Third: *Fly Rod & Reel* 14%

Despite asking for "Any type" magazine, flyfishing titles were most listed. Nonflyfishing type magazines listed were: News/business 13%, hunting type 7%, and *National Geographic* 7%. Eleven fishing magazines were listed.

60. **Do you have mixed feelings about helping people into flyfishing considering much fishing is crowded?** Yes 26%, No 74%.

61. **Please number in order of importance to you.**

Landing and killing or releasing the fish:
1st- 4% 2nd-12% 3rd- 85%*

Fooling and hooking fish:
1st- 89%* 2nd- 6% 3rd- 3%

Fighting the fish:
1st- 7% 2nd- 82%* 3rd- 12%

Answers clearly show what is important and movement away from the 1940s attitude of fish fight supremacy or sportsman versus noble hard-fighting fish nonsense.

A recent book I read states: "A really good fight is, when it's all said and done, what I want most." That's entitled opinion, but this author, an "experienced" flyfisher, misses the mark concerning the heart and soul of flyfishing. The pollees don't.

62. **Do you often buy tackle or accessories by mail order?** Yes 69%, No 31%.

What percent of your total purchases, dollar wise, are mail order?

60-100% 23%
50-59% 29%
0-49% 48%

63. **Are most of your mail order purchases, if any, from:**

63% Flyfishing specialty shops that offer mail order
25% General outdoor catalogs that offer fly tackle and accessories
12% Manufacturers

Mail order purchases avoid shop problems and sales personnel. Some pollees were quite isolated, and mail order is about their only way to buy.

64. **Flyfishermen, as a group, are sometimes perceived as snobbish or elitist. Are they?** Yes 40%, No 60%.

Does this perception need to be combated? Yes 54%, No 46%.

Considering all answering are flyfishers, 40% Yes answers are worthy of examination. Many pollees said some flyfishers are elitist and some not. Bass flyfishers see flyfishers as less snobbish. Some pollees say personalities are unimportant and others that flyfishing requires more knowledge, athletic ability and perseverance. One quote is perhaps indicative of competent and serious flyfisher attitudes: "I worked long and hard to perfect skills. If the quick-fixers see that as elitism tough-shit." "Take the mystery out of fly fishing was the industries' cry in the 1960s" and the pollee stating such also says, "flyfishing has come full circle with many wanting to make it not only more difficult but also more expensive."

65. **Why did you start flyfishing?**

26% A family member inspired

11% Challenge and reward

7% Friends' influence

As would be expected and shown by a lack of overwhelming consensus there were many answers. A natural progression from "other tackle" and "fun" were common answers. A surprising number came to flyfishing from fly tying. Added together, there were large numbers of artistic, beauty and nature enjoyment answers. Nature enjoyment is a fine thing, but arty reasons often align with shallow, poor and potentially damaging understanding of flyfishing. Some said it was less crowded or the only legal way to fish.

66. **What do you like or dislike about fly shops?**

71% Negative answers

29% Positive

This question is the only one given coverage earlier. First the negative:

> "Too high priced, snooty, snobbish, elitist, cliquish, bad advice, lack knowledge, poor attitude, in-bred, full of bull-shit, useless inventory, pushy clerks, poor quality, hard sell, degrade certain brands, poorly stocked, push only high-priced brands, arrogant know-it-alls, all the same, make me feel inadequate, treat women poorly, treat beginners poorly, only go to the good ones and don't use them."

Regarding the "positive," pollees stated the following things they like, but do not necessarily find, in fly shops. Answers often had the qualifiers "usually," "some," "most" and "generally" in apposition. Those modifiers minimize positive connotations. Answers are in order of frequency listed:

> "Atmosphere, friendliness and to talk, information particularly local, browse, see and try equipment, variety, service and helpfulness."

One pollee said he had seen beginners "turned away at fly shops over and over." I believe he means turned away from flyfishing.

67. **Do you belong to a national fishing organization?** Yes 85%, No 15%. **Have you belonged in the past?** Yes 90%, No 10%. **Do you belong to a local club?** Yes 78%, No 22%. **Belonged in the past?** Yes 84%, No 15%.

A large number of pollees came from FFF membership, so results are skewed toward membership

Note: Using the results of this question and those of No. 59 (pollee preferred magazines) with known magazine circulations and total FFF and TU membership, it is possible to calculate, via simple math, the total number of *noncasual* flyfishers. Results may be as, or more, accurate than methods used by the industries or pollsters. At least we would also know we're talking about flyfishers and not someone who, one afternoon on vacation, used his uncle's fly rod to punish the water, scare the fish and now considers himself a flyfisher—as does the Elite. I did such calculations. Results show there are *far fewer* flyfishers (at least *real* ones) than what the industries want to believe.

68. **Do you make an effort to dress in a manner that will blend with your surroundings when flyfishing?** Yes 75%, No 25%.

69. **Are you aware of kickbacks from manufacturers to retail people selling their products?** Yes 40%, No 60%.

Cortland pays $1 to anyone selling their fly lines. There must be other salesperson incentives I'm unaware; I wish I had asked for them.

70. **If a person interested in learning to flyfish read several issues of *Fly Fisherman, Fly Rod & Reel, Flyfishing* or any other flyfishing magazine, what would their reaction most likely be?**

77% Negative comments: "Confusion, overwhelmed, bewildered, expensive, complicated, loss of interest, need go to exotic places."

23% Positive comments: "Interested, better understanding, look for more information, nice pictures."

71. **If encouraged by such reading would they see how to get started flyfishing?** Yes 43%, No 52%, <u>Unsure</u> 5%.

"Advice would cater to the elitist fly tying and fly casting schools of the industry manufacturers and distributors," so said one pollee. Another, regarding magazine articles: ". . . many provide excellent information, but mixed with large doses of self-praise by authors." I've read magazine management emphatically stating it isn't their place to start beginners. Is it then their place to alienate them?

72. **It has been said of much recent flyfishing writing: Knots and knits and how to pick them, tremendous knowledge but negligible wisdom." Do you:** Agree 65%, Disagree 34%, Unsure 1%.

73. **Do you often view flyfishing videos?** Yes 43%, No 57%. **Learn much from them?** Yes 42%, No 58%.

One pollee inquired: ". . . to watch Teeny throw rocks?"

74. **What two pieces of advice would you give a prospective or new flyfisher?**

1. Get a patient, experienced, knowledgeable mentor
2. Enthusiasm, patience, practice, go fishing—for easy fish
3. Get balanced, not necessarily expensive equipment
4. Take a course from a good instructor

As expected there were lots of suggestions. Those above list the most common in order. Others of note: "Buy used equipment, learn basics well including knots, read good beginning books, avoid trends, learn fish and habits, flyfishing is not competition against man or fish." Decent, balanced equipment yields confidence. Don't pick the wrong expert.

75. **Do you most prefer to catch? (choose one)**

16% Lots of fish
39% Big fish
45% Difficult fish

This answer suggests less than half of the pollees have entered Edward Hewitt's second to last stage of flyfishing maturation (Chapter Twelve). One might expect a larger representation from experienced pollee flyfishers. There are circumstantial considerations; some fishing is naturally for "big" fish (Atlantic salmon, steelhead, etc.); big can be either difficult or not.

76. **Do you condone fishing tournaments and contests for prizes or notoriety?** Yes 23%, No 77%.

77. **Do you enjoy fishing of a competitive nature? (biggest, most, etc.)** Yes 16%, No 84%.

Quite a few pollees said competition is enjoyed with close friends.

78. **Is access to your favorite public water:** Increasing 29%, Decreasing 42%, Constant 30%. **Are there:** More fish 10%, Fewer fish 55%, Stable numbers 35%. **Is the quality of the fish there:** Increasing 12%, Decreasing 60%, Constant 27%.

Results here are sad and prophetic. The industries could certainly learn and take positive actions concerning these discouraging results, *as may we all.*

79. **Have you ever been polled or surveyed concerning flyfishing before?** Yes 30%, No 70%.

80. **Are you confused by the many colors, lengths, types, densities, stiffnesses, and designs of fly lines available?** Yes 32%, No 68%. **Are they all needed?** Yes 21%, No 76%, Unsure 3%.

Since pollees are not very confused they understand the new lines and clearly see all are not needed.

81. **"The principles of fly casting are quite obvious." In the final analysis, everyone must teach themselves. Given balanced tackle, fly casting "feel" will come with practice. Confidence in this eventuality is all that is needed to learn.** Agree 54%, Disagree 46%.

Here pollees told me people fear looking stupid but also that flyfishing is no different from other disciplines—people teach themselves. I was told confidence, while being important, was not all one needs as some of the worst flyfishers have ego and confidence galore. Amen, but that comment doesn't address "confidence" (reliance) as used in the question.

82. **Large fish can be landed on very light rods; yet prolonged battles with large fish on too light tackle can kill them even if they are released. Do you see any need for 1- or 2-weight systems?** Yes 36% No 64%. **Three-weights?** Yes 62%, No 38%. Comments: (regarding 1- and 2-weight systems) "Ego motivated, toys, industry contrived to sell more tackle, 4- and 5-weights will do it all, permissible for small fish."

Did the comments ever flow. Those listed above are again the most common. Others follow:

> "Best suited for small vulnerable fish, so why use them?, use longer lighter leader on 4- or 5-weight, few people know how to land fish, negate spirit of catch-and-release, industry would sell you a 1/4-weight if they could, only need for light-weight systems is heavy ego, only if you follow the hatchery truck, symbolic of

what is wrong with the flyfishing industry, trendy, unnecessary, harmful, impractical and silly."

Defensive remarks:

"Some places have only small fish, fish aren't killed by fight, proper people can use them properly, OK for bluegill and crappie, small fish give good fight."

It's nice to know fish aren't killed by fight. What is a "proper" person?

83. **Does the flyfishing industry (now industries) conduct its business differently from other businesses you are familiar?** Yes 30%, No 64%. **How so?** "Hype and image not function, little discounting, protected dealers, elite marketing, some lack sophistication, concerned with conservation. A mom and pop attitude is presented, however false it may be."

84. **Numerous TV fishing shows air on a regional and national basis. Do you watch them?** Yes 62%, No 38%. **What is good or bad about them?** The good:

"Show interesting areas, some on flyfishing are good, show technique, mild cure for cabin fever."

The bad:

"Poor respect for fish (handling, releasing, etc.), fishing appears too easy, simplistic and idiotic view of fishing, contrived and phony, boring, dull, redundant, not all anglers like country music. Peter Barrett's flowery prose is sickening."

85. **How can a beginner gain self-confidence in flyfishing?**

64% Acquire adequate casting skills
38% Learn all can about quarry
62% Gain broad understanding of flyfishing
8% Adequate desire and practice
11% Get with it
10% Learn as you go

86. **Strong winds are common and deter many fly casters from trying to fish. What advice do you have?** Most common answers:

Correct position, casting (ducks fly low to water) and tackle, persevere, learn to cast, quit or use other tackle, get closer to target.

Quitting or using other tackle were *common* comments.

87. **Is obtaining a strike from fish more dependent on:**

13% Mood of the fish
32% Skill of the fisherman
55% They are equal

Those believing the criteria are equal (55%), separately added to each of the other answers give a decided edge to fly-fisher skill being most important.

88. **Have you changed your methods, opinions, theories and ideas a great deal over your years of flyfishing?** Yes 82%, No 18%.

Perhaps the best way to excel at flyfishing is to be the one in five born or starting flyfishing with perfect knowledge. Charles Brooks believed the willingness to change (after due consideration) was the only mark of an advanced fisherman, it having nothing to do with years fished or fishing travels which often yield only a "patina of sophistication."

89. **Are numbers of female flyfishers growing?**
Yes 78%, No 2%, Uncertain 19%.

Despite having only ten female pollees their comments were very interesting. One said the men she met flyfishing were better educated, polite and well groomed.

90. **When buying or tying flies are you most usually concerned with:**

6% Color
63% Specific pattern
38% Style

A poor question, specific pattern encompasses style and perhaps color. The 38% willing to select style show scholarship in escaping specific pattern thinking.

91. **What <u>two</u> stimuli, other than hunger, listed below do you believe responsible for fish striking flies?**

14% Anger	16% Close competition	0 Playfulness
20% Curiosity	53% Reflexive reaction	
35% Territoriality	61% Instinct	

This type of speculation requires putting words for human reactions on unknown or misunderstood fish motivations (anthropomorphism); that's dangerous, difficult and perhaps impossible. Reflexive reaction and instinct *may* be words for nearly the same fish reactions and are important.

92. **Do you use a stomach pump on live fish to ascertain their diet?** Yes 17%, No 83%. **A small net to sample air or water for fish food items?** Yes 54%, No 45%.

93. **Have you donated your time to conservation or resource renewal projects?** Yes 83%, No 17%.

94. **Some anti-hunting groups have said: "Fishing is next." Do you believe?** Yes 59%, No 41%. **Should we be doing something about it?** 80% think so including: "Education, education does little to fanatics, catch-and-release, catch-and-release is seen as cruel, join with hunting groups, and wait for it to pass."

95. **What spells success to you in an average day's fishing?**

"A fish or two, being outdoors on the water, good friends, uncrowded conditions, learning something."

Catching fine or big fish or at least having the chance received more than a few votes. Flyfishers as experienced as pollees might have said more about learning things or catching difficult fish. It seems even experienced fishers do so just to get away. That might give insight into why some pollees fail to understand basic flyfishing truths. One pollee said success meant not breaking a fingernail.

96. **Do you attend general interest consumer sport shows?** Yes 62% No 38%. **Flyfishing specialty shows?** Yes 76%, No 23%. **If flyfishing was adequately represented would you rather attend:** Fly specialty show 81%, General interest show 19%.

97. **Would you rather attend a show in:** Downtown area of a major city 21%, Suburbs of the city 70%, Either 9%.

98. **Are flies that wobble or dive by mechanical aid within the realm of what you consider flyfishing?** Yes 24%, No 76%. **Scenting of flies?** Yes 13%, No 87%.

Flyfishing suffers from lack of a full, respected definition. I'm not sure what constitutes mechanical wobbling, but it, or scent, doesn't belong in flyfishing in the pollees' opinion.

99. **Should a guide hired by you fish only if you ask him?** Yes 80%, No 20%. **Have your guided experiences been mostly:** Satisfactory 75%, Unsatisfactory 9%, Never been guided 9%.

Younger pollees in particular seem unaware of the age old rule that guides don't fish unless asked. The guides who slipped into the poll were adamant in its observance. Younger, newer flyfishers revealed need for help and guidance here and with other topics.

100. **How may a beginner learn to find correct water and catchable fish?**

50% Cover lots of water on their own, observing carefully
70% Hire guides, observe and ask lots of questions
71% Ask information of friends, tackle shops, etc.
10% Read

101. **Do you recommend beginners play all but small fish from the reel?** Yes 65%, No 34%.

Pollees know there is no better way to attain comfort using a reel on fish than to fight *all* fish that way until competence is acquired. Fishers of warm water species often do not and skew the answers some.

102. **Do you know ways, short of experience, to learn to fight fish with correct pressure?** Yes 17%, No 83%. **If yes comment:**

Considering few Yes answers, there were few comments. Several suggested that if you can't hold the rod vertical (fish is pulling) then give line. That's poor advice (see Chapter Twelve). Most said to test tackle strength by tying the leader to something and pulling or have the "something" pull. Examples given were: pulling on scales, a retrieving dog told to fetch a stick or perhaps tying to the *neighbor's* cat.

103. **Do you consider yourself well read concerning fly-fishing?** Yes 81%, No 19%. **Do you have a favorite book you would recommend newer flyfishers read?** Yes 50% No 47%. **Its title and author:**

Trout Bum, John Gierach
The River Why, David Duncan
A River Never Sleeps, Roderick Haig-Brown

Only two votes separated first and third places. There were numerous suggested titles and authors. Lefty Kreh's books placed high with saltwater flyfishers and Alfred Davy's with Canadians. The three winners are strangely "mood" rather than more useful "instructional" books that represent the large *bulk* of the many titles listed. Haig-Brown (for his other titles), Ray Bergman, Swisher and Richards, Dave Hughes and Dave Whitlock were often recommended authors. Older books were noted as possibly being outdated concerning some tackle but still capable of tremendous help. Some said there are too many books to recommend one.

104. **Do you regularly use DT lines?** Yes 49% No 51%. **Level lines?** Yes 3%, No 97%.

105. **Do you have criticisms of current factory rods?** Yes 50%, No 50%. In order of listing:

> "Too expensive, too stiff, fragile, line ratings wrong, overrated and hyped, frustrate beginners, lack feel, arm wrenching and poor fittings."

Nearly all comments were negative, even more so considering *numerous* pollees admitted not using newer rods. It was noted: "Moderate priced rods were not advertised or available, too much emphasis was placed on up-locking seats and grips were poor or too large." Only 6% of pollees said new rods were fine.

106. **Have you had reel screws come loose or fall out?** Yes 48%, No 52%.

107. **Do you use reels smaller than 3 inches in diameter?** Yes 36%, No 64%.

108. **Given same capacity and weight would you rather have a reel with a:** Wider spool 41%, Narrower spool 59%.

Many have experienced loose reel screws. The percentage would be higher but pollees' favorite reels were Hardy's and those made by Hardy. Hardy reels are of riveted and dovetailed construction to avoid screws. Pollees see the fallacy of dinky reels. But *why* would 41% prefer a wide, therefore inefficient and slow, over a narrow spooled, efficient reel? Please see Chapter Seven on reels for more information.

109. **Do you have complaints about current production fly reels?** Yes 40%, No 59%.

Comments received were mostly negative: "Priced too high, supposed quality is not, too heavy, inaccurate or missing backing capacities, parts of even newer reels unavailable."

Pollees frequently commented that they do not use "modern" reels. Several pollees said that what you need is "out there." *Many* commented and questioned why more complicated and highly engineered bait casting reels cost much less than many fly reels. Overrating of "palming rims" and lack of decent multiplying fly reels were shared comments.

110. **Why do you choose a particular fly line color?**

41% Angler visibility
24% Color unimportant
12% Prefer dull colors

111. **Do you believe stainless steel hooks should be used in freshwater?** Yes 12%, No 82%. **Saltwater?** Yes 64%, No 36%.

112. **Should a brand new entrant, who cannot cast:**

17% Try various tackle and choose what seems right

83% Follow competent advice from shop or individual

113. **How will newcomers know if advice given them is competent?** Comments: "They won't, seek more than one opinion, try something to see if it works." Only 2% of comments suggested a newcomer go to an established fly shop. If you haven't already, see Chapters Four, Five, and Six. There is much to consider concerning tackle selection.

114. **A relatively few fly tackle manufacturers, editors, authors and fishing organizations wield considerable influence over flyfishing.** Agree 77%, Disagree 23%. **Are their actions in your best interest?** Always 2%, Usually 77%, Seldom 21%.

Profit dominated selling and thinking with short term focus are seen by pollees as primary goals of the industries and are understood to be necessary evils, or worse. Many referenced the questionable "new breed" of flyfishers: "Great men, McClain, Brooks, Wulff, are all dead so yuppies and their thoughts prevail." "Always tell a yuppie, can't tell them much." Flyfishers are cautioned by pollees to avoid the industries, not to listen to them or fall for their tricks. Pollees believe *knowledgeable* fishers can sort things out remembering basics are what's important. It was noted that too few personalities, forming a arrogant clique, control flyfishing and flyfishing writing, and that there are many talented but unknown flyfishers.

115. **Would you wear bright white, yellow or orange clothing while flyfishing shallow clear water?** Yes 10%, No 90%.

116. **Which, if any, of these shortcomings do you find in currently manufactured fishing vests?**

35% Too small pockets	10% Too few pockets
11% Wear poorly	28% Uncomfortable
14% Wrong colors	9% They are OK
4% Velcro closures	

Pollees had a variety of annoyances, those above most common. Bass and saltwater flyfishers seldom use vests, and women have trouble finding acceptable vests. Wrong color was frequently mentioned as was foreign manufacture. Pockets are habitually seen as too small.

117. **Can you cast and fish decently with your weak hand?** Yes 50%, No 50%.

These results speak to a high degree of pollee ability and maybe an abnormal percentage of near ambidexterity. If that's the case, I may have been overly critical of weak hand reel winders. Remain skeptical and see the next question.

118. **Please check all the casts you use in your fishing:**

97% Roll and variations	83% Slack line or "S"
49% Hooks (curves)	77% Backhand
12% Reach	10% Hauls

This question assumed everyone uses overhand casts. The added answers, Reach and Hauls, are not true casts only arm extensions or line hand motions. There was a smattering of foolish casts listed: Parachute, Belgian, Slam, Pile, Puddle, etc. It's interesting that 77% use Backhand casts considering 50% of pollees claim decent casting ability with either hand in Question No. 117.

119. **Do you often use a float-tube?** Yes 46%, No 54%. **Boat under 16 ft?** Yes 54%, No 46%. **Over 16 ft?** Yes 29%, No 71%.

Quite a few pollees didn't answer this question. Maybe they are wading or stalking trout and salmon fishers.

120. **Do you believe findings of product reviews or product comparisons:**

67% **Are** influenced by companies large advertisers in the publication

33% **Are not** influenced

121. **Certain manufacturers spend more on advertising and promotion than others. Do you believe these companies have:**

36% Prices comparable to competitive goods
63% Higher prices
0 Lower prices

Do they have:

82% Same quality equipment as the competition
15% Better quality
3% Lesser quality

The pollees know that advertising only adds to product costs and does nothing for product quality or fishability. A full third believe publications disregard their advertisers when advertisers' products are reviewed and perhaps green cheese being the moon's composition.

122. **Which of the following items do you usually have on your person, or very close, when flyfishing?**

90% Line clippers
84% Floatant
42% Ldr. "straightener"
56% Insect repellent
48% Thermometer
30% Magnifying device
66% Extra reel-spools
35% Camera
26% First aid kit
76% Hook hone
45% Landing net
51% Sinkers
58% Pliers
28% Fly drying material
35% Leader sink
91% Extra leader
87% Polarized glasses
57% Rain jacket
6% Creel
46% Scissors
76% Forceps
9% Extra flies
7% Suntan lotion

I'm sure more than 9% carry extra flies; it wasn't listed as one of the options, and 9% volunteered that answer. Other write-ins were a sharp knife, binoculars and toilet paper. One soul suggested a .44 magnum, but no mention was made of planned use (bears, boats, self-defense, suicide?). We may only speculate.

123. **Please list the two elements of flyfishing ethics everyone should observe:**

61% Do not crowd-in or hog the water and keep your distance
30% Catch and release—properly done
25% Improve and protect habitat

124. **Please comment on problems or positives you see with the industry and sport or anything else you wish.**

31% Enjoyed survey, provocative, comprehensive
18% Overpriced tackle limits new entrants
12% Fishing is too crowded
7% Poor ethics and manners encountered on water
3%ea. More flyfishing only water needed, more political clout needed, leave fish in water when handling, too many hucksters in industry, useless tackle and accessories pushed and promoted.

Questions No. 123 and 124 elicited a great deal of comment. The overwhelming spirit was sincere concern for fish, flyfishing and frustration over slob or modern fishers as well as the industries' neglect of what's important about flyfishing. Industries' apathy and greed are well known to pollees. So are the actions of persons, many new to the sport, masquerading as flyfishers, but devoid understanding or caring for what flyfishing means. As perceived by pollees, lack of adequate flyfishing education and crowding are primary stimuli for things wrong with flyfishing—the latter result of the former. "Few newcomers realize how much better things were only 15 years ago," per one pollee—he's right.

Observance of Aldo Leopold's land ethic, the Golden Rule and Haig-Brown's passing on of resources to future generations with "unimpaired potentiality" were often mentioned. Being quiet astream and obeying all laws received numerous votes. Despite that, laws were seen as often contrary to flyfishing's best interests. "Too many wildlife agencies are too political, into meat fishing, plant fish amid native populations and condone the killing of too many fish in general." Fishing is brimming with *law abiding* persons damaging resources through ignorance or greed.

Too many flyfishers are seen as bringing wrong attitudes to the water including stress, aggression and competitiveness resulting in crowding, "combat fishing," "safari mentalities," poaching, pollution and the use of any, loosely defined, flyfishing method. Lack of regard is viewed as universal and flyfishing etiquette unheeded. Problems could be avoided, even eliminated, if everyone considered, *in order:* fish and resources, other fishers, then self.

Flyfisher actions are seen as overly influenced by "experts" who aren't and all the phonies in the sport. Specific abhorred actions included: "Hole sitting, low skill technology based methods, fishing through without permission, literally throwing fish back, moving in upstream from a dry fly fisher (or downstream from one fishing wet [sic]), taking five minutes to mishandle and take pictures of a fish before its release, use of fish damaging hard nets and tearing hooks free." Too many are seen as having a sparkly bass-boat, contest, mentality.

From an old timer, and former user of gut leader, silk lines and cheap cane rods, came chastisement and refreshing wisdom: "Remember to credit Jim Green of Fenwick for developing excellent rods, Myron Gregory of Sunset Line Co. for developing and selling the industries on the AFTMA rod-line balance system and SA for developing plastic line coatings." (Don Green may have been more responsible for rod development, but the idea holds.) Those truly super developments brought sensible, effective and affordable flyfishing to the masses. *No recent "discovery" approaches the importance of such advancements.* It was noted the essence of the sport can be enjoyed with only a modest investment.

Where is flyfishing now? This pollee has an idea: "The average person does not have time to fish properly. Advertising causes too many to come out, kill fish through ignorance and eventually trespass trying to find good fishing." People disparaging ethical flyfishers could be guilty of this pollee's observation: "It's easier for those who abuse and overkill to call us snobs, perhaps out of their own guilt. Name calling follows lack of reasonable argument."

Respondents dislike "shows" seeing them dominated by fly tiers. One said, "Anyone can tie a fly that will catch fish." Some people were noted as being dominated by flies, specific patterns and tying; they need to fish more to gain proper perspective. Fly tying is fun and rewarding. Too many flyfishers use fly tying as a surrogate, however, for flyfishing or place unimportant emphasis on flies. It was noted shows overpromote and foster feelings that the more flyfishing stuff you own, particularly what some "paid expert" uses, the more successful you will be. *Repeated reference to damaging, indifferent and profit dominated industries, by the pollees, cannot be overstated or ignored.*

Decent landowner relations and respect for landowner rights were mentioned by some pollees but not as often as you might think considering importance of landowner relations. It was sadly noted lots of good water is going private or being leased by the wealthy.

There were positives, including finding the most relaxing, enjoyable and remembered of times in flyfishing and meeting courteous, intelligent and genuine persons. Some think the "yuppification" of flyfishing will pass as those with shallow or incorrect motivation drift to the next "correct" thing. I wonder; permissive and simple technology based methods and sundry industries' baloney have polluted the minds and "flyfishing" methods of lots of "flyfishers." And the industries themselves are overflowing with yuppies. There was much comment to join and support what flyfishing clubs stand for and do.

As was earlier mentioned, all pollee replies were given equal weight in calculating percentage results. Collating surveys from so many pollees took a lot of time, both causing and allowing me (or any competent flyfisher), understanding of the level of common sense, cognizance of flyfishing reality and expertise displayed by each pollee. Despite control parameters of knowledge and expertise on the part of pollees, 20-25% of pollees exhibited obvious lack of understanding primary flyfishing truths.

Flyfishing fact and common sense can't be ignored because a portion of pollees lack basic understanding affecting poll consensus. Readers shouldn't be further and trustingly misled to the ranks of the unknowing, by the unknowing. That's commonplace today but still wrong. Pollee opinion largely supports common sense and nature's laws, particularly when the effect of the 25% unknowing, new or perhaps overly industries-influenced are discounted.

Some pollees were rank neophytes and stated such. Whoever gave them the survey (FFF presidents) or recommended them (industries' people) failed to recognize the importance of deep and wide flyfishing knowledge I desired. All in all, it wasn't a bad group of pollees considering the preponderance of flyfishers with shallow understanding and what might have been. Pollees, to a person, seemed to be trying to answer questions their best, and I'm proud of and indebted to them all.

Following are lists of the persons and firms supplying potential pollee names. Requests for names of three knowledgeable flyfishers, unconnected to flyfishing by income, were sent to almost 200 persons and firms in the flyfishing industries. About 35 (18%) responded, some sending more than three names, a few none. Considering responding persons cared enough to take valuable time and provide names to help an unknown, suggests they are decent people or at least interested in the survey results. I *did not* send requests to every flyfishing manufacturer, but be assured the major and common ones were asked. As you read this listing you might note who is *conspicuous through absence.* Some could care less (a follow-up request was made), and perhaps some didn't have the time to spare. Others did. They deserve consideration if flyfishing purchases or recommendations are considered.

Immediately following the list of name providers are lists of contributing pollees. I again thank each and every person for the time and consideration shown me in this project. Pollee knowledge is capable of saving flyfishers extensive grief. Comments and advice, if followed, offer tremendous benefit to flyfishing and flyfishers.

Name Providers

Al Caucci Al Caucci Fly Fishing Tannersville, PA	Brooks Bouldin Angler's Edge, Inc. Houston, TX	Kurt N. Brekke Angler's Covey Colorado Springs, CO
Brian Ward Cortland Line Co. Cortland, NY	Al Frens and Scott Forristall Tycoon Fin-Nor Hallendale, FL	Howard S. Cox Select-a-Fly West Boulder, CO
Ken High Dr. Slick™ Dillon, MT	John McBride & Sons Blackledge River Co. East Lyme, CT	Joe Gablick Custom Flies Lower Burrell, PA
Tim Tollet Frontier Anglers Dillon, MT	Rusty Gates Gates AuSable Lodge Grayling, MI	Robert Borden Hareline Dubbin, Inc. Monroe, OR
Rick Hinton Jorgensen Inc. Fort Wayne, IN	Chuck Voss Lamiglas Woodland, WA	Phil Camera Larva Lace Products Woodland Park, CO
Ferris McMullin Loon Outdoors Boise, ID	Joe McFadden McFadden's Fly Shop Cochecton, NY	Donald H. MacLean Lacloon Fly Fishing LaGrange, KY
Dale Williams McKenzie Fly Tackle Co. Eugene, OR	Tom Travis Montana's Master Angler Livingston, MT	Jeff Hahner Mystic Bay Flies Greens Farm, CT
Rod Tochihara Pacific Crest Flyfishing Thousand Oaks, CA	Skip Halterman White River Fly Fishing Eureka Springs, AR	Mike Wikerson Pott Fly Co. Missoula, MT
Larry Kenney Scott PowR-Ply Co. Berkley, CA	Bill Grake Sportsmen's Outfitters Avon, OH	Joe Martinez Superior Fly Products Englewood, CO
Jim Teeney Teeny Nymph Co. Gresham, OR	Pat Ehlers The Fly Fishers West Allis, WI	E.J. Schaefers Terminal Tactics, Inc. Sauk Rapids, MN
Doug Tucker-Eccher The Bass Pond Littleton, CO	Kemp Harr Shakespeare Fishing Columbia, SC	Mark E. Transue Transue's Tackle Box Kittitanning, PA

Hank Evers
Valley Tackle
Summit, NJ

John V. Underwood
John's Guns & Fly Fishing
Tallahasse, FL

Kim Vletas
Westbank Anglers
Teton, WY

Mike Harding
Harding & Sons
Idleyld Park, OR

Tony Gehman
Tulpehocken Outftrs.
West Lawn, PA

FFF Pollees

Clifford E. Adams, Eugene, OR
Travis Adlington, Incline Village, NV
Dick Allebach, Phoenixville, PA
Bill Alspach, Lewiston, ID
Jere Anderson, Plano, TX
Mike Arnold, Highland Hts., KY
Don Avondozio, E. Northpoint, NY

Paul J. Bach, Missoula, MT
W. L. Beach, Atlanta, GA
Paul Bedharz, Cordova, AK
Dorothy Bergman, Lansing, MI
J. Kevin Berry, Spring Grove, IL
John Berry, Memphis, TN
Jim Bishop, Burlington, WA
Harry M. Blessing, Lombard, IL
Zane Boyd, Dayton, OH
Boo Boyers, Alex, KY
Bob Brazell, Albuquerque, NM
John D. Brown, Airway Heights, WA
Stan Brown, Moreno Valley, CA
Peter Burton, Middlebury, VT

Del Carraway, Twin Falls, ID
James G. Cave, Bend, OR
Dr. E. T. Ceder, Fairfield, CA
Phil Chase, Port Vervis, NY
Daniel Conlon, Andover, MA
John Crocker, Reedsport, OR
Frederick Cummings, Andover, MA

Frank Diamond, Colorado Springs, CO
Richard Dickerson, Reno, NV
Leon K. Doar, Jr., Boise, ID
Paul Dremann, Salt Lake City, UT
John Dyer, Bend, OR

William S. Emmerick, Fairfield, CA

Doug Fagerness, Coeur d'Alene, ID
Daniel Ferrow, Green Bay, WI
William & Pat Fortier, Buffalo, MO
Bob Franson, Springfield, MO
Thomas A. Fulk, Anacortes, WA

Ron Graupmann, Bakersfield, CA
Dana Griffith, III, Gainesville, FL
Elliot W. Gritton, Reno, NV

Bob Haglund, Green Bay, WI
Norm Hall, Racine, WI
William A. Halls, Flushing, MO
Jeffrey Hamme, Lake Elmo, MN
Marie Hammond, Venice, CA
John Harasta, Johnson City, NY
John Hardin, Redlands, CA
David Hendersen, Bristol, VT
Foster S. Hickett, Colorado Springs, CO
Robert Huddleston, La Conner, WA

Frederick E. Jackson, Burlington, VT
Curtis Jacobs, Bothell, WA
Jennifer Jenkins, Memphis, TN
Rod Johnson, Eugene, OR

Edward A. Kluck, Hamden, CT
Kevin Kompolt, Salem, OR

Bill Lambing, Lufkin, TX
Robert Larsen, Tahoe City, CA
Robert Laviano, Saddle River, NJ
Ronald Lewis, Brandon, VT
Ted Long, Tahoe City, CA
Curtis R. Longanecker, Pismo Beach, CA
Vance Luff, Longview, WA
Craig T. Lynch, Ridgefield, WA

Gregory B. Lyons, Denver, CO

Joe F. Madden, Sanpedro, CA
Joseph V. Marto, Jr., Indiklawtic, FL
Irvine McConaghy, Bellflower, CA
Billy T. Mead, Texarkana, AR
Bill Meir, Salem, OR
Jaun N. Menchaca, Bliss, ID
Greg Miheve, Ft. Walton Beach, FL
Henty Miller, Lafayette, LA
Bill Moore, Hooks, TX
Pete Morris, Portland, OR
Joseph F. Mulson, Maitland, FL

Jeff Nissle, Phoenixville, PA
Isla Nolan, Kirkland, WA

Frank Pankiewicz, Cumberland, IN
Jeff Passante, Clinton, CT
Bill Paulsen, Kelso, WA
Steve Payseur, Iron Station, NC
Ted Pearson, Seattle, WA
John E. Peterkin, Puyallup, WA
Steve Petit, La Canada, PA
J. Pfeifer, Issaquah, WA
Jack R. Porter, Bakersfield, CO

Skip Quade, Coeur d'Alene, ID
Tom Quill, Indianapolis, IN

John D. Randolph, Racine, WI
Fred Reimhear, Salt Lake City, UT
Kim J. Reineking, Missoula, MT
Julian Renken, Lufkin, TX
Robert R. Reynolds, Bristol, VT
Rod Robert, Yakima, WA
John Rueff, Concord, CA

Lee Sager, San Luis Abispo, CA
E.B. Scholes, Jr., Jerome, ID
Doug Schonewald, Moses Lake, WA
Eric J. Schubert, Hayden Lake, ID
Bob Slaughter, Brackney, PA
Don Spatz, Albuquerque, NM
Richard Steinhorst, Jr., Lafayette, LA
Connie Stelter, Seattle, WA
Eugene Sunday, Flushing, MI

Michael Tansey, Los Angeles, CA
Dan Trachsel, Keizer, OR

Dennis Verdine, Lafayette, LA

Jon Williams, Pensacola, FL
Nathan Williams, Manistee, MI
Raven Wing, Bend, OR
Ron Winn, Indian Harbor Beach, FL
Maukeen Wise, Berkley, CA
Robert A. Wisecarver, Walnut Creek, CA
Ernie Worster, Indianapolis, IN

Manfred Zanger, Sparrow Rock, NY

Recommended Pollees

John Africano, Oakland, NJ
Dr. J. Galt Allee, Tallahassee, FL
Frank Ambrose, Sussex, NJ
Paul Anderson, Mayer, MN
Phil Anderson, Boise, ID
James Asselstine, New York, NY

Henry Babson, Morris, IL
Lee Baker, Coral Gables, FL
John Begovich, Lower Burrell, PA
Rod Beland, Livingston, MT
Stan Benton, Woodland Park, CO
Ed Bielejec, Barneveld, NY
Mike Bilyew, Littleton, CO
Jack Bock, Tallahassee, FL
Shirl C. Boyce, Boise, ID
Don Allen Boyd, Wayland, MI
Phil Braun, Bozeman, MT
David A. Burdine, Fairfield, CT

Brent Campbell, Renton, WA
Del Canty, Leadville, CO
Ken Carlisle, Tigard, OR
Ken Harmon, Hialeah, FL
Rudy Chavira, Salt Lake City, UT
Nick Chiovitti, DDS, Thornton, CA
John Clark, Fort Wayne, IN
Jim Cloniger, Antioch, CA

Edward C. Craft, Jr., Lancaster, PA
Karl Crapse, Rantoul, IL

Martin T. Daack, Colorado Springs, CO
Alice Deaver, Rathdrum, ID
Paul P. Dickes, Jim Thorpe, PA
Chuck Digby, Northglenn, CO

Jack Ellis, Woodville, TX
Ken Erb, Grayling, MI
Howard Eskin, Stoney Brook, NY
Craig Estell, Boise, ID
Robert J. Estlund, Wauwatosa, WI

M. Fadum, Harvard, IL
Glenn Flutie, Plantation, FL
Ken Folwell, Boise, ID
Jonah Freedman, Reedsport, OR
Allen Frens, West Palm Beach, FL

Vern Gallup, Spokane, WA
Anthony Gargulio, Califon, NJ
Phil Genova, Ithaca, NY
Jeffrey Giansanti, Superior, WI
Leon Gusiewicz, Philadelphia, PA

Chris Hadley, St. Louis, MO
John Halterman, Festus, MO
Kurt Hargett, Keizer, OR
Gordon Harrop, Rexburg, ID
Dave Hickson, Castro Valley, CA
William Hutchison, Bristol, TN

Anthony Jansic, Yorktown Heights, NY
E. D. Johnson, Cape Girardeau, MO
Anthony Jordon, River Grove, IL
William T. Jordon, Boulder, CO

John B. Kline, Boulder, CO

Barry Leeds, New York, NY
Verne Lehmberg, Dayton, TX
Robert Lin, High Bridge, NJ
Bruce Lowder, Houston, TX
William L. Luch, Portland, OR
Frank Lukac, Mountain Home, AR
John Luscz, Butler, NJ
Philip A. Lutin, Chattanooga, TN
Alex MacGrath, Portola Valley, CA

Denny Mailey, Billings, MT
David Mann, Portland, OR
Donald S. Mayo, Sr., Norwalk, CA
John McCall, New York, NY
Bob Mead, Scotia, NY
Carole D. Miller, Delphane, VA
Jerome Moiso, Carmel Valley, CA
B. Morrison, Nyssa, OR
Rob Musser, Lakewood, CO

Richard Nashel, Ridgewood, NJ
Charles Nelson, Lakewood, CO
Stan Nicholas, Longmont, CO

Dr. Deems Okamoto, Seattle, WA

Dr. Eric Pettine, Fort Collins, CO
Joe Petrella, Jr., Downingtown, PA
Andy Pickens, DDS, Billings, MT
Bruce Pierce, Lessburg, IN
Stephen Pinowsky, Cedarburg, WI
Arthur B. Post, Jr., Louisville, KY
Dennis Potter, Grand Rapids, MI

Bart Queary, Bend, OR

Dave Rabe, Milford, OR
Ron Rick, San Rafael, CA
Dr. Loren Rogers, Missoula, MT

Jim Sabin, Otis, OR
Rick Sadleir, Laguna Beach, CA
Bernard C. Scott, Sayre, PA
Pete Serene, Kittanning, PA
James W. Sines, Fort Wayne, IN
Dave Skoraszewski, Reading, PA
Shawn Smith, Frisco, CA
Allen Sporich, Green Mountain Falls, CO
Richard K. Stoll, Poulsbo, WA
Alan Stone, Honeoye, NY
Bob Sullivan, New York, NY

Kelly P. Towers, Eugene, OR
David Townsend, Cazenovia, NY
Honorable Neil Travis, Livingston, MT
Tom Twyman, Medfield, MA

George P. Vlassis, Phoenix, AZ
Jack Wadlin, Tulsa, OK

Troy Waite, Madras, OR
Robert C. Walsh, Flemimgton, NJ
John L. Warner, Newark, OH
Bob Whalen, Jr., DDS, Missoula, MT
Gary White, Winsted, CT
Jim Whitehead, Boise, ID
Dan Will, Colorado Springs, CO
James Williams, Wakeman, OH
Jerry Wolland, New York, NY
Jim Woodhull, Livingston, MT

Rob L. Yobp, Kittanning, PA
Robin Yount, Boca Raton, FL

Foreign Pollee Contributors

Greg Boone, Langley, BC

Tom Dellamater, Penticton, BC
Shawn Dery, Kelowna, BC

Paul Fling, Harrowsmith, Ont.

Mark Hopley, Penticton, BC
Steven Hum, Ottawa, Ont.

Bob Lafort, Pitt Meadows, BC
Allen Ledgerwood, Charlottetown, PEI

Gary McLaughlin, Kelowna, BC

Patrick Orpen, Jonquierc, PQ

Doug Porter, Alexis Creek, BC

Ronald Ripley, Clearwater, BC

Harry Shaw, Penticton, BC
Doug Stewart, Ottawa, Ont.
Oskar P. Sveinsson, Gardebaer, Iceland

Gerald Woloshyn, Regina, Sask.

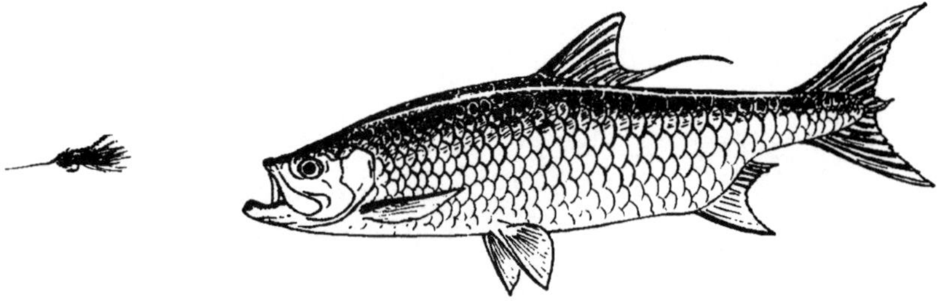

GEL

Chapter Fourteen: Rules

"Any preoccupation with ideas of what is right or wrong in conduct shows an arrested intellectual development." Oscar Wilde.

Why should I care how somebody else fishes and where do I obtain authority to tell anyone how to fish? I wouldn't care how others fish if some people and practices were not such an assault on flyfishing's good name and traditions, even common decency unrelated to flyfishing. I grasp authority since what you will see written has been proven workable or is based on fairness and common sense. The actions of growing numbers of people show little concern for fish, fisheries or fellow fishers; the latter often includes me, and likely you. Problems aren't exclusively the fault of growing numbers of fishers and others on limited and decreasing water but selfishness, ignorance and stupidity.

Crowded fisheries existed well back into history. Methods and manners, now largely ignored, evolved to accommodate crowded conditions. Mannerly solutions were rooted in fairness and equal chance for all with maximum consideration for fish and habitat. Participants in crowded conditions knew, understood and complied with usually unwritten rules or were straightforwardly informed of their transgressions. Newcomers learned by asking, observing or being scolded. We live in a disgusting new age of permissiveness. Arrogance and brashness prevail. Maybe I'm guilty of living in older, better (but not irretrievable) times—times respectable flyfishers would prefer to what we now have.

Many of today's fishing participants respect little. They have their rights and will exercise them despite costs and frustrations to others or themselves. Some are doubtless only unenlightened or oblivious and might be changed. But ignorance is often poignantly accompanied by impudence, lack of decency or brains. What else are we to expect? Individual-oriented, secular humanism seems unstoppable. With crowding and "get yours now" thinking, flyfishing continues to suffer.

Codes of behavior are easier to state than uphold. Ethics and morals are variable according to intellect, depth of thought, background training, situation, presence of other people, willingness to take or restrain action, knowledge and humility to name some more salient variables, noted by others. For some, ethics consideration ends with the chance of being observed, chastised or caught. When all's said and done we have ourselves and our God-given conscience to serve. Some people, however, have poorly developed or desensitized consciences. What of them? I don't know, except to hope that we may effect change by decency and example. There is no ethics exam before fishing license issuance.

I also excuse writing these rules because they might help, and I've perhaps lived, fished and studied enough to know what works in many fishing situations. You may recognize some from previous chapters, but I put them here in list form.

1. Consider what is virtuous and correct for the fish and fishery, other anglers and oneself. If we always do so and *only in the order given,* we are ethical flyfishers.

2. Public water belongs to everyone. Individual runs, riffles, parts or pieces of fishable waters belong to whoever was

there first. Do not start fishing near the "owner" without first asking and receiving permission. What's near? It's hard to say and variable per water and fishing type. It should be far enough away to not infringe the owner's immediate fishing or what he will logically do in the next while. That's further than most I've observed think. If you wonder what the next while is, your not into the spirit of this. Always err on the side of extra distance and time. Recognize an apparent nonfishing owner could be resting the water or the fish. Speak up and protect your rights, in a spirit of educating, when someone encroaches or plans to encroach on your water.

3. Despite "owning" water you were on first, do not occupy a piece of water too long. Where fishing and moving is the accepted or reasonable method—nearly all should be—moving allows everyone a chance at better water. It's up to each of us to both know and exercise ethical behavior. Behavior varies and because "camping" is done on some water doesn't make it right. Hogging water encourages others to do the same.

4. If you use a boat of any kind on small- to medium-sized water, heavily fished by wading or bank anglers, quit. No matter what you do you will offend and damage the fishing and enjoyment of some, often many. Is your right to fish the way you want, no matter the cost to others, worth it? One person in a power boat can destroy the enjoyment of 100 people in 15 minutes. It only takes longer to do the same damage if a raft, drift or row boat is used. Speak reasonably and calmly to intruding drift-boaters, canoeists, white-water floaters, jet-skiers, or power boaters who haven't a clue about flyfishing or claim not.

5. Learn to cast and wade or stay away from popular water. If you join a chain of anglers, sloppy or too slow casting and noisy wading will damage not only your chances, but those of others near and particularly following you. Fish elsewhere, on uncrowded water, until you develop skills needed to join serious flyfishers.

6. Keep quiet near all fishing places. Don't yell or play music, roll rocks or even talk too loudly, and that includes controlling the kids or nonfishing persons with you. Most fishing environs are naturally quiet, and sound carries long distances. Noise pollution is *most* offensive. Wear subdued clothing. Let the tournament bass and flats fishers wear the snappy light or

bright colored clothes. *Everyone* doesn't wear light colored tee-shirts in the summer, not if they flyfish.

7. Keep your dog under control and out of the water. Old Ranger may be a best friend and a great joy to you, but to me he's a fish scaring and unwanted nuisance if anything but impeccably mannered. Few are.

8. Stay out of the water unless there is a remarkably sound, benefit exceeding harm, reason to be in the water. Way too many people wade where they shouldn't—often where they should be fishing—destroying sport for themselves and others. The tendency to wade excessively is accentuated by inability to cast competently, particularly inability to use roll casts and mends to avoid obstacles behind the caster or in the water. WF lines and stiff rods accentuate such problems.

9. Don't mishandle fish. Release fish without touching them or taking them from the water. Forget senseless picture-taking. Why use a net if it isn't needed? They seldom are. Constant use of a net is a bad habit made popular by sophisticates. Nets, even soft-bagged ones, damage fish. Defeat fish quickly, reach down, twist the fly out and the fish is gone, immediately, with little damage. If you need revive an occasional fish, do so quickly. If reviving them often you need to learn to fight fish correctly or use heavier tackle.

10. Leave no garbage or trash in water or waterside including pieces of leader material.

11. Know the strength of your tackle and use real tackle, not toy stuff. Fight fish at near full tackle strength. Land fish quickly; release or kill them without delay. Don't cause any fish to suffer. If you kill fish take care of them.

12. Know your fisheries. Kill planted, stunted or overpopulated fish to help or at least not damage a fishery. Feel no guilt in doing so. Killing a valuable, large, possibly rare, native, or sexually mature fish that may eventually spawn requires thought and *strong* excuse. Bragging rights and ego are no excuse—only ignoble and loathsome.

13. Help other fishers as you may. Set the best example possible when impressionable persons or newcomers are present.

14. Summon up courage, if needed, to politely inform others of transgressions. Odds are high these days people are only ignorant and will later appreciate well meaning comments.

How else will the ignorant learn? Or you could curse under your breath and stomp off agitated. What good is done by that—for either party?

15. Support, with time or money, those firms and organizations that actually, with substantial time and money, protect and enhance all our fishing. That does not include many, perhaps most in the flyfishing industries. Too many "industryites" think words are deeds or dollars. Force them to change as you may. The industries' advice or rhetoric aren't needed, some of their profits are.

16. Doing something because it's legal does not make it moral. Fish and Game regulations are recurrently contrary to true sportsmanship and sometimes common sense—they're too political. Use your own power of reason and fairness, but obey laws. If they're incorrect work to change them.

17. Flyfishing is sport. Sport implies competition, but competition has *no place* in flyfishing. Etiquette and ethics problems often stem from competition, formal or casual. "Out-fishing" is a term to avoid.

18. Keep an open mind, have fun and learn. Welcome the challenges and joys of flyfishing.

19. The Golden Rule is a dandy. But it's subject to appalling ignorance of too many about what is good for or damages flyfishing for others *or* themselves.

GEL

Appendix I

Polar Bear Hair Information

All hair, dubbing and flies sold by the Serious Fisherman come from bears killed prior the Marine Mammal Protection Act. They are legal to sell or use anywhere in the USA. Polar bear products may be exported with proper documentation including, but certainly not limited to, an export permit. The Serious Fisherman owns such a permit—U.S. F&W #764657.

Colors: Hair and dubbing are dyed nearly all colors and many shades of those. Chances are the color you need is on hand. If not, it may be custom dyed. Dyeing shrinks the hide up to 60%, by several tests. Hair then becomes denser on the hide. Square inch measurements are of the hide *before* dyeing or washing.

Grades and Lengths: Several grades and many different lengths of hair, dyed and natural are available. All hair is sold on the hide *by the square inch.* A 2 inch by 3 inch piece equals 6 square inches, *before dyeing*. Grade descriptions and comments on length follow:

- **Premium:** For fishing flies. Few broken ends, all lengths and colors. See Premium hair packaging below.
- **Super Premium:** For display flies or those wanting the best available. Minimal broken ends, uniform and dense, usually under 2 inches long, most colors. Mask hair (from the bear's head and face area) usually fits this grade.
- **Jig Quality:** Stiffer, sparkling hair but with lots of broken hair ends. Mostly under 3 inches long. A good buy that ties decent flies with a little work. Some colors, lots of supply.
- **Long Hair:** Long hair is anything *over* 3 inches and up to 8 inches long. Available natural and in all colors. Price increments: 3-4 inches, 4-5 inches, 5-6 inches, 6-7 inches, 7-8 inches. Polar bear is a tremendous streamer material for fresh or saltwater flies. Price goes up with length. Most bear hides have very little hair over 4 inches long.

Premium Hair Packaging: Three square inches on the tanned hide. This hair is ideal for Atlantic salmon, bonefish, steelhead, fresh or saltwater streamers, any fly *under* 3 inches in length. I will select the length you need between 1-1/2 and 3 inches. Larger patches may be ordered as well. If you need hair over 3 inches long, order long hair by the number of square inches needed.

Dubbing: Sold in 3 inch by 3 inch packages, in all colors. Quantity is slightly less than in most packages of other types of dubbing. Polar bear yields sparkling, spiky and translucent bodies. Floatant dressed, it floats well with lots of ends to catch the surface film. Colors may be easily hand blended to achieve *any* color desired. Polar bear is probably the best seal fur substitute available. Note: After extensive research, I see no way to legally deal in seal.

Special offers (bulk-packs, selections, etc.) are sometimes made and available to retail buyers—inquire. Dealer and commercial tier discounts are available on hair under 3 inches in length. Orders must be in commercial quantities. ***Orders Only:*** 1-800-347-4654. Visa and Matercard accepted. For ***Information*** call 1-509-922-5832 or Fax 1-509-922-7585.

I custom tie flies of *any type*, for any fish, from polar bear. A sample is always best to work from.

Tips On Tying With Polar Bear

Correct fly presentation remains more important than any fly or what it's tied from. If you can present correctly, polar bear flies should give you an edge. The recommendations of so many old timers and continuing testimonials I receive keep me convinced. Polar bear isn't magic, only a very good material with unique characteristics.

Polar bear usage suffers from ongoing, incorrect information regarding legality (see Chapter 10). Ignorance of writers, editors and people who sell or have sold poor quality hair at premium prices continues to damage a fine material's reputation. I don't sell less than premium hair at premium prices; that's why I have lots of jig-quality hair for sale.

Legal polar bear is rare and consequently might be considered expensive. It also has properties and abilities missing in commonly substituted materials. Those qualities are tapering hair ends, stiffness (body), durability, natural sparkle, shine and translucency. Legal hides are old by necessity and most have suffered some age-born damage. Finding top quality hides is difficult and they are expensive. I often suggest newer tiers avoid its use until skills develop. No sense wasting money.

Polar bear is *no more* difficult to use than any hair and easier than some, slick squirrel tail for instance. Device stacked wings look phony to my eye. I even tips by hand only, suit yourself. Polar bear dubbing is wiry and that's part of what makes it great. Wax the thread or use prewaxed, use only a little dubbing and twist hard. Forget dubbing loops. While you're building your loop and starting to scatter dubbing along it you could be finishing the fly. Pick the body out if it isn't scraggly enough. Laying cement under dubbing, wing or throat hackle yields durable flies.

Polar bear's supposed substitutes, natural or synthetic, are always too limp and floppy to duplicate the real thing. Limp materials collapse in the water under pressure of current or retrieve. Polar bear might be too stiff for very small flies. I have a limited supply of soft hair for small flies. Synthetics don't have tapered hair ends and people tend to use way too much in my opinion. Sometimes it doesn't matter to the fish—sometimes it might. Phony metallic flash is not like that of a baitfish, but some fish are very gullible. If you enjoy beautiful natural materials; you'll like polar bear.

Dyeing polar bear is either difficult or not. I haven't decided. One time things go well and the next I have to dye, re-dye and re-dye ruining more hair with each process. Different bears dye differently probably due care, past cleaning or lack and certainly due tanning and bleaching processes. Some bears are nearly impossible to dye. I've had the supposed best "experts," try to dye them. If they succeed, they invariably ruin the hair—by using too much heat. Polar bear is not like dyeing a pile of chicken's feathers.

Pure white polar bear has been bleached. I bleach hair sometimes but don't like to for it damages the hair. Most people prefer the natural-ivory hair and it has many subtle shades. Washing with mild shampoo, in warm water, almost always brightens hair. Rinse well, shake the hair dry, lay it on a newspaper and comb straight several times as it dries. You may easily take kinks from hair by this method.

Polar bear has many textures (stiff, coarse, fine, etc.) according to the part of the hide it comes, bear age, sex and on and on. Stiff hair always sparkles most and dyes best but doesn't have much movement in water. Lower leg and foot hair is the stiffest but has the most broken ends. Bears break the stiff hair rambling in their frozen environment. Individual, longer hairs have a double tapered shape. They're fatter in the middle than base or tip. Very long hair comes from the front leg "elbow" area and often has lots of broken tips. Uniform, dense, shorter hair comes from the bear's head near the face. Back and flank hair is less dense but longer.

Many broken tips in a three- to eight-inch streamer wing do little to looks or effectiveness. Broken tips in the wing of a size-4 steelhead fly look dreadful but may not affect the fish catching ability of the fly. I often use broken hair in my own smaller flies.

Polar bear is not hollow. Dressed it will float, but the fact it sinks when undressed is desirable for wets and streamers. It won't rapidly dry out in false casting to then float as does bucktail and to a lesser extent, calf tail.

If you use polar bear hair save the shorter, stripped out underfur for dubbing. It blends well and can be added to other dubbing or used "straight."

"Standard pattern" thinking and tying limits so many fly-fishers. I often receive orders from people wanting to tie some specific pattern they've stumbled across that calls for polar bear. Nearly any fly can be tied and probably improved by using polar bear. I'd guess the Black-Nose Dace streamer calls for only a belly of white polar bear because Mr. Flick didn't have red, black and brown polar bear for the remainder of the fly, maybe not. The ones I tie completely from polar bear sure work well. Most old innovators used what was cheap or available, particularly if a fly goes "commercial." Some well-known tiers use polar bear in their own flies but publish calf tail, bucktail or synthetic trash in lieu of polar bear, perhaps due misunderstanding of laws. I use polar bear in *all* steelhead fly wings, tails, tags, tips, for throat hackle and to dub all bodies, as an example. Same goes for Atlantic salmon or bonefish flies to mention a couple more possibilities. I often rib fly bodies with three twisted polar bear hairs. A few added strands of polar bear cause an otherwise hair- or feather-winged fly to "light up." Nymphs and wet flies calling for other materials but dubbed of polar bear are most suggestive of insects. Don't be limited by specific pattern or material thinking.

Sparse flies usually work best and a little polar bear goes a long way. Don't buy polar bear longer than you need. Long hair (over 3 inches) is rarest and more expensive. The thought of people cutting the butts of polar bear hair markedly shorter makes me cringe, but I know it happens.

Despite best efforts in photography and printing the color fly plates of this book still do not do full justice to the attributes of polar bear. I'm quite proud of the plates, but the hair sparkles even more than is shown.

If you know of polar bear rugs for sale I'm always interested. If you have need of polar bear claws please contact me—they must have some use.

Appendix II

Dressings of Flies Shown on Plates

The "Flies Not To Be Without" list of pages 178-80 and the text of Chapter Ten discusses alternative sizes, materials, good and useable variations of many of these flies. The following listing gives the dressings and the hook exactly as they are shown in the plates.

Hook style and needed characteristics are listed rather than a make or hook model as there are often several hooks that might work. Exceptions are noted. Short-shanked hooks (1XS) for standard dry flies result in small flies with large bites. Short-shanked streamer hooks minimize wing fouling under the hook bend in casting.

Thread used is normally UNI-Thread in 8/0 for smaller and 6/0 for larger flies. I often use white UNI-Thread, then color the fly's head with felt pens before final head-finishing. Black thread will work for most smaller patterns, Use "matching" colors if you prefer. Leave space for knots to set behind the eye of TUE and TDE hooks.

Thinned rubber cement ensures bodies and wings of larger flies will stay put. Use a final, clear head cement that will not cause felt pen coloring to run. I use Gloss Coat.

I don't believe in "magic" or "standard" dressings, mine or anyone else's. Feel free to substitute materials or hooks. Just know darn well what you are doing and why.

Dressings are given in order the flies appear on the plates.

First Plate

GRAY WULFF
Hook: *Standard length and weight dry fly, size 8*
Thread: *Black*
Wings: *Dark elk, tied in and divided first, two times gape*
Tail: *Dark elk hair, shank length*
Body: *Dubbed of medium gray polar bear fur*
Hackle: *One dark, one light dun neck*

GOOFUS BUG (HUMPY)
Hook: *Short, standard wire dry fly, size 10*
Thread: *Yellow*
Wings: *Pale elk, upright and divided, 1-3/4 times gape*
Tail: *Pale elk, slightly longer than shank*
Body Cap: *Pale elk, tied in at rear by tips*
Body: *Built up of tying thread*
Hackle: *Two pale ginger neck*

HAIR CADDIS (STONEFLY)
Hook: *Long-shanked (2XL), York bend, standard wire, size 4*
Thread: *Brown*
Ribbing: *Tag end of tying thread, counter wrapped*
Body: *Blended yellow, orange and brown polar bear fur, picked out*
Wing: *Medium colored elk, heavy, well cemented*

Hackle: *None*
Head: *Flared, of wing butts*

ADAMS
Hook: *Short, standard wire dry fly, size 10*
Thread: *Black*
Wings: *Grizzly hackle tips, tied in and divided first, 1-3/4 times gape*
Tail: *Moose body hair, slightly longer than shank*
Body: *Dubbed of dark gray polar bear fur*
Hackle: *One brown, one grizzly neck*

LIGHT CAHILL
Hook: *Standard length and wire dry fly, size 10*
Thread: *Tan*
Wings: *Dyed lemon mallard breast, upright and divided, 1-3/4 times gape*
Tail: *Pale elk, shank length*
Hackle: *Two ginger neck*

MIDGES
Hooks: *Both short, standard wire dry fly, size 14*
Thread: *Black*
Wing (of first fly): *Grizzly hackle tips, angled back*
Ribbings: *Yellow thread, counter wrapped*
Bodies: *Black mole*
Hackle: *Grizzly neck, ahead of wings on first fly, fore and aft on second*

HAIR CADDIS
Hook: *Regular length and weight, silver dry fly, size 12*
Thread: *Black*
Ribbing: *Tag end of tying thread, counter-wrapped*
Body: *Medium olive polar bear fur, picked out*
Wing: *Gray deer, cemented*
Hackle: *None*
Head: *Flared, of wing butts*

ROYAL TRUDE
Hook: *Short, standard weight dry fly, size 10*
Thread: *Black*
Ribbing: *Tying thread tag end*
Tail: *Short, of dark moose body*
Body: *By thirds, peacock herl, red polar bear fur, peacock herl, all reinforced with tying thread tag end*
Wing: *White polar bear, angled back, near length of tail*
Hackle: *Ahead of wing, two Coachman brown neck hackles*

JOHN'S HOPPER
Hook: *Standard weight, 2XL, size 6*
Thread: *Brown*
Ribbing: *Tying thread tag end*
Tail: *Red polar bear, trimmed blunt and short*
Body: *Dubbed pale yellow polar bear fur, counter-ribbed*
Wing: *Stacked, pale elk, tail length*
Collar: *Gray deer hair, 1/3 wing length, spun and trimmed from bottom*
Head: *From collar butts, trimmed "square" all around, blunt face*

POLAR ANT
Hook: *Black, standard or fine wire, size 8*
Thread: *Black, red for body division*
Body/Abdomen: *Black polar bear fur, large at rear tapering forward,*
Wing: *Gray polar bear, "veined" with black felt-tip pen, tied in with red thread*
Head: *Black polar bear fur, large and bulbous*

SOFT HACKLE
Hook: *Standard dry, size 10 (wet-fly hooks work well)*
Thread: *Tan*
Ribbing: *Thread tag end*
Body: *Thin, dubbed of orange polar bear fur, counter-ribbed*
Hackle: *Brown-cast partridge, two or three wraps*

WET COACHMAN
Hook: *Standard or 1XL wet-fly, size 8*
Thread: *Brown*
Ribbing: *Fine copper wire*
Body: *Peacock herl, counter-ribbed*
Wing: *White, soft polar bear*
Hackle: *Beard style, Coachman brown hackle fibers*

GOLD-RIBBED HARE'S EAR
Hook: *1XL standard wire, heavy wet-fly or nymph, size 8*
Thread: *Gold*
Ribbing: *Thread tag end*
Tail: *Short tan polar bear*
Body: *Golden-tan (blended) polar bear fur, counter-ribbed*
Wing Case: *Dark brown polar bear hair*
Thorax: *Same dubbing as body, well picked-out*

POLAR DRAGON
Hook: *Partridge Draper, size 6*
Thread: *Brown*
Ribbing: *None*
Tail: *Soft partridge fibers*
Body: *Dark olive-brown (blended) polar bear fur*
Hackle: *Soft partridge, trimmed off top and bottom*
Eyes: *Plastic, painted shiny brownish-red with felt pens*

DAMSEL
Hook: *5XS bait, offset removed, size 10*
Thread: *Brown*
Ribbing: *None*
Tail: *Three times shank length, mink hair on hide, dyed olive (or colored with felt pen)*
Thorax: *Olive-brown (blended) polar bear fur*
Hackle: *Partridge, sparse, trimmed top and bottom*

TRUEBLOOD'S SHRIMP
Hook: *Standard or heavy wet-fly or nymph, size 8*
Thread: *White*
Ribbing: *Thread tag end*
Tail: *Gray-cast partridge*
Body: *Natural polar bear fur, counter-ribbed*
Hackle: *Beard style same material as tail*

Second Plate

POLAR BITCH CREEK
Hook: *2XL standard wire, heavy nymph or streamer, size 2*
Thread: *Black*
Ribbing: *Thread tag end*
Tails: *Black rubber, shank length*
Body: *Orange polar bear fur, counter-ribbed then colored black on top*
Wing Case: *Black polar bear*
Thorax: *Same dubbing as body*
Hackle: *Dark dun neck through thorax*
Head: *Black with black rubber feelers ahead*

GOLDEN STONE
Hook: *1XL standard nymph or wet-fly, size 6*
Thread: *Brown*
Ribbing: *Thread tag end*
Tails: *Brown rubber, shank length*
Body: *Blended yellow and orange polar bear fur, counter-ribbed*
Wing Case: *Dark brown polar bear (can be eliminated)*
Thorax: *Same dubbing as body but larger*
Hackle: *Brown-cast partridge forward of thorax*
Head: *Brown with brown rubber feelers ahead*

BOMBER
Hook: *1XL, standard or light wire, bronze, size 2*
Thread: *Heavy, color unimportant*
Wings: *White polar bear, divided for balance*
Tail: *Stacked black polar bear, shank length*
Body: *Spun then trimmed to shape, salt and pepper color of Dall sheep*

BLOCK-HEADED MUDDLER
Hook: *Mustad 9671, size 2 (important)*
Thread: *Strong*
Rib: *None*
Tail: *Medium color elk, short, heavy bunch*
Body: *Gold braided tinsel*
Wing: *Sparse white polar bear under, elk over*
Collar: *Gray deer hair, heavy, 1/3 wing length, trimmed on bottom*

Head: *Additional gray spun deer hair, trimmed to be blunt on the face and squared everywhere else*

CLARET AND BLACK
Hook: *Black, heavy wire, size 1/0*
Thread: *Black*
Ribbing: *Three twisted, white polar bear hairs*
Tail: *Claret polar bear*
Body: *Dubbed black polar bear, counter-ribbed*
Wing: *White polar bear, black polar bear over, 2/3 length of white*
Hackle: *Beard style of claret polar bear*
Cheeks: *Jungle cock*

THOR
Hook: *Heavy, standard length TDE bronze, size 2*
Thread: *Brown*
Rib: *None*
Tail: *Hot orange polar bear*
Body: *Dubbed red polar bear fur*
Wing: *White polar bear*
Hackle: *Beard style of brown polar bear*

POLAR LEECH (MINK)
Hook: *2XL standard, heavy nymph or streamer, size 8*
Thread: *Red*
Weighting: *Fine lead wire, slight in head area only*
Rib: *None*
Tail: *Long natural brown mink on hide*
Body: *Of blended red, gray, brown and black polar bear fur, picked-out*
Head: *Red*

POLAR BI-BUCK
Hook: *Standard or short, bronze, size 4*
Thread: *White*
Rib: *Tail, none*
Body: *None or white thread*
Wing: *2/3 white, 1/3 light brown polar bear over, half of white hair tied under hook shank*
Throat: *Red polar bear*
Head: *Felt pen color top brown, yellow eye iris and black pupil*

POLAR LEECH
Hook: *2XL, black, heavy or standard, size 2*
Thread: *Red*
Rib: *None*
Tail: *Long soft black polar bear*
Body: *Blended purple, claret and black polar bear well picked-out at sides*
Head: *Red*

MARABOU MUDDLER
Hook: *2XL bronze, size 1*
Thread: *Strong, orange*
Rib: *None*
Tail: *Red polar bear, short*
Body: *Gold braided tinsel*
Wing: *Dark over light olive marabou*
Throat: *Long white polar bear*
Collar: *Dark elk, spun*
Head: *Additional spun dark elk, trimmed tapering up, front to rear*

Third Plate

Note: *The next five flies are tied in trolling style. Shorter hooks shown may be cast but are quite heavy.*

FALL FAVORITE
Hook: *Short Limerick size 2/0 (a custom hook is shown)*
Thread: *Red*
Rib: *None*
Tip: *Red thread holding down body*
Tail: *None*
Body: *Gold mylar tubing*
Wing: *Red over shorter orange polar bear*
Throat: *Long white polar bear. (I view this as part of the wing tied under the hook's shank.)*
Cheeks: *Imitation jungle cock*
Head: Red

RAINBOW FRY TANDEM
Hooks: *Front black, short and heavy (3/0), rear black (2/0), looped onto wire cable and tied down on front hook's shank nearly to eye, cable is bent back and tied down. Cement several times.*
Thread: *White*

Rib, Tail: *None*
Body: *Silver and white rod-wrapping thread, front hook only*
Wing: *Light blue over bright green over sparse hot pink over white polar bear hair; parr marks and spots made with felt pens.*
Cheeks: *Hot pink polar bear*
Throat: *Red polar bear*
Head: *Colored blue-green on top, yellow sides with black pupil*

JACOB'S COAT
Hook: *6XL custom stainless, size 2/0*
Thread: White
Rib, Tail, Body: *None*
Wing: *Dark gray over equal parts blended red, blue, green and yellow polar bear; four bands colored onto wing with black felt pen.*
Throat (part of wing): *Sparse, long white polar bear*
Short Throat: *Red polar bear*
Cheeks: *Jungle cock*
Head: *Colored black on top*

BLACK GHOST
Hook: *8XL custom, black, size 2/0*
Thread: *Black*
Rib: *Flat silver tinsel*
Tail: *Bright yellow polar bear*
Body: *Black polar bear fur, ribbed with tinsel*
Wing: *White polar bear*
Throat: *Long white polar bear under short yellow polar bear*
Cheeks: *Jungle cock*
Head: *Black*

KAM KILLER SUPREME
Hook: *Custom black 3Xshort, size 2/0*
Thread: *White*
Rib, Tail: *None*
Body: *White thread, lacquered*
Wing: *Sparse black over sparse purple over blend of pink, hot pink, orange and hot orange polar bear*
Throat: *Long white polar bear under short red polar bear*
Cheeks: *Jungle cock, short*
Head: *Colored black on top*

Fourth Plate

POLAR ROUND BOY
Hook: *Points up, short, black, stout (size 2/0) on cable tied to a regular shank length front hook as noted in Rainbow Fry Tandem above; front hook cut off at bend after fly is tied.*
Thread: *Black and red*
Rib, Tail, Body: *None*
Wing: *Sparse black over purple polar bear (should be blended)*
First Collar: *Blended orange and pink polar bear spun evenly around hook's shank*
Second Collar: *Short black polar bear evenly spun*
Head: *Black with red band at middle to avoid any horizontal reference in the fly.*
Note: *Don't make the front portion of this fly too bulky.*

JACOB'S COAT BLONDE
Hook: *Short and heavy could be silver or bronze, size 2/0*
Thread: *White*
Ribbing: *Oval silver tinsel*
Tail: *Long white polar bear*
Body: *Flat silver counter-ribbed with oval*
Wing: *Blend of polar bear as described in Jacob's Coat, then barred with black felt pen; two-thirds length of tail.*
Throat: *Red polar bear*
Head: *Colored black on top, yellow on sides with black pupil*

POLAR/MARABOU ROUND BOY
Note: *This fly uses a hook (size 2/0) and methods the same as the Polar Round Boy above. Substitute gray marabou for wing and use sparse gray polar bear hair along sides. Head band is orange.*

ADJUST-O-LEECH
Hook: *Short, black with final fly section tied on it, size 4*
Thread: *Black, red*
Ribbing: *Clear mono-thread*
Tail: *None*
Bodies: *Tied on varying length hollow plastic tubes, dubbed mixture of heavy gray, claret and black polar bear fur, picked-out*

Wings: *Tied down on body sections front and back, then ribbed; black rabbit shown—mink works well.*
Head: *Is the front section used, may be tied with red thread or to denote weighting*
Note: *Tie and fish as many sections as needed.*

DORADO
Hooks: *Tandem rust-resistant, front larger, cable connection as described in Rainbow Fry Tandem above. Main size 4/0, trailer size 3/0.*
Thread: *White*
Rib, Tail, Body: *None*
Wing: *Blue-green over bright yellow over pale yellow polar bear. Spots applied with sharp felt marker*
Throat: *Sparse, long, white polar bear*
Head: *Top colored blue-green, sides have yellow lacquer eye, black pupil*

BILLFISH
Hooks: *Tandem rust resistant connected with cable per Rainbow Fry Tandem above. Main size 5/0, trailer size 4/0.*
Thread: *White*
Rib, Tail, Body: *None*
Wing: *Natural polar bear (partially tied on trailing hook). Remainder tied on main hook, selected so length blends evenly with the hair tied on the trailing hook. One-third of white portion of wing tied beneath main hook's shank. Topping 1/3 of total, of blended orange, hot orange, pink and hot pink polar bear*
Cheeks: *Yellow, colored with felt pen*
Throat: *Red polar bear*
Head: *Colored top to match wing, sides yellow, black pupil, silver center*

BONEFISH
Hook: *Short, strong, rust resistant, size 2*
Thread: *Brown*
Ribbing: *Tag end of thread*
Tail: *Hot orange polar bear*
Body: *Dubbed of tan polar bear fur, counter-ribbed and picked-out*
Wing: *Dark brown polar bear, barred with black felt pen*
Eyes: *Gold barbell, black pupil*

COCKROACH
Hook: *Saltwater, round-bend, size 2/0*
Thread: *Orange*
Tail/Wing: *Silver-gray polar bear, vertically barred with black felt pen*
Collar: *Dark gray polar bear spun evenly around shank, flared*
Head: *Long and tapered to cover last half of hook shank, painted yellow iris, black pupil*

DECEIVER
Hook: *2XL rust-resistant, size 2/0*
Thread: *White*
Ribbing: *None*
Tail: *White polar bear*
Body: *White thread*
Wing: *Equal bunches of white polar bear, one tied on either side of fly and 2/3 length of fly. Top, blend of blue and green polar bear shorter than tail*
Throat: *Red polar bear*
Cheeks: *Imitation jungle cock*
Head: *Colored on top to match wing*

CLOUSER MINNOW
Hook: *Short, strong, saltwater, size 1/0*
Thread: *White*
Ribbing: *None*
Tail: *White polar bear*
Body: *White thread*
Wing: *Gray over olive polar bear, slightly longer than tail*
Eyes: *Gold barbells, painted black pupil, tied 1/3 of shank's length back from eye to leave room for head*
Head: *Colored to match wing, with colored red throat*

Index

Entries for the title are used as this book generates uncommon flyfishing terms (economics, industries, etc.). Chapter Thirteen (Flyfishing Survey), being detailed and brand specific, is completely indexed by broad terms only (e.g. rods, not Fenwick or Winston rods).

continued

continued

continued